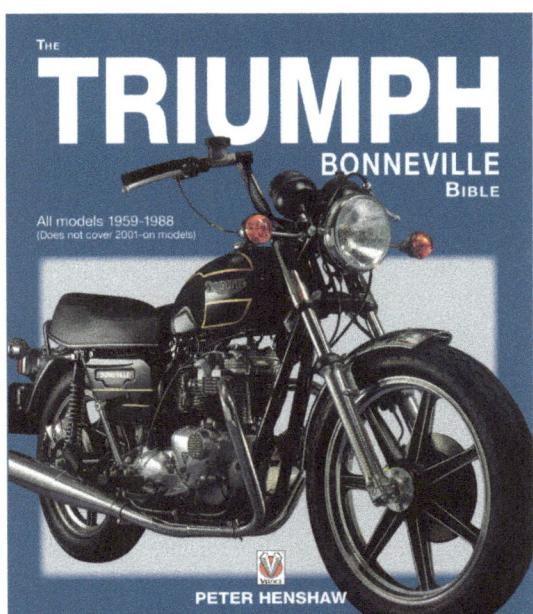

Dedication

This book is dedicated to the men and women who worked at the Meriden co-operative, who tried to find a new way of working to save their jobs and keep the Bonneville alive. Against all the odds, they did just that for eight years.

www.veloce.co.uk

First published in August 2013. this paperback edition published February 2023, reprinted 2025 by Veloce, an imprint of David and Charles Limited. Tel +44 (0)1305 260068 / e-mail info@veloce.co.uk / web www.veloce.co.uk.

ISBN:978-1-787119-29-1

© Peter Henshaw and David and Charles 2013, 2023 & 2025. All rights reserved. With the exception of quoting brief passages for the purpose of review, no part of this publication may be recorded, reproduced or transmitted by any means, including photocopying, without the written permission of David and Charles Limited.
Throughout this book logos, model names and designations, etc, have been used for the purposes of identification, illustration and decoration. Such names are the property of the trademark holder as this is not an official publication. Readers with ideas for automotive books, or books on other transport or related hobby subjects, are invited to write to the editorial director of Veloce at the above email address. British Library Cataloguing in Publication Data – A catalogue record for this book is available from the British Library. Design and DTP by Veloce.

The TRIUMPH BONNEVILLE Bible

All models 1959-1988
(Does not cover 2001-on models)

Veloce

PETER HENSHAW

Contents

Introduction and Acknowledgements 6

1 Origins 9
   The Thunderbird 9
   Tiger 110 & TR6 11
   Speed records 13

2 1959-62: Pre-unit 14
   1959 17
   1960 20
   1961 23
   1962 24

3 1963-70: Prime time 28
   1963 28
   1964 32
   1965 35
   TT Special 37
   The Thruxton Bonneville 38
   1966 39

   Thruxton & TT 41
   1967 42
   1968 46
   1969 49
   1970 53
   The first 750 55

4 1971-74: Fall from grace 60
   1971 60
   1972 66
   1973 69
   1974 74

5 1975-78: Yes, we can 80
   1975 80
   1976 83
   1977 86
   1978 92

6 1979-83: On the slide 98
   1979 98

1980	102
1981	105
1982	110
1983	115

7 1985-88: Final fling 119
1985-88 119

8 Living with a Bonneville 122
Choosing • Buying • Owning
  • Restoring 122
Is it for me? 122
Upsides 123
Practicalities 124
Where to find your Bonnie 126
Auctioneers 126
Ready-to-ride or restore? 127

Which model?	128
Points to look for	131
Registration	138
MoT	139
The 21st century Bonneville	140

Appendix 1 Model profiles 141
Appendix 2 Engine and
  frame numbers 147
Appendix 3 Major changes,
  year-by-year 149
Appendix 4 Road tests 152
Appendix 5 Clubs, contacts
  and suppliers 154

Index 159

Introduction and Acknowledgements

Introduction

More than 50 years after its introduction, the Triumph Bonneville remains one of the most iconic motorcycles of all time. Many bikes encapsulate a particular era or national industry – a Harley FLH for the USA; BMW flat-twin for Germany, and Ducati V-twin for Italy – and the flagship British twin (though Norton Commando owners might not agree) has to be the Bonneville.

For most of the 1960s, the Bonnie was one of the fastest standard production bikes money could buy, and from the middle of the decade it set a standard for handling that few could match. Even in the late '70s, left far behind in the performance stakes, the Bonneville still went round bends better than most bikes.

It was this red-blooded image, combined with beautifully balanced styling, that made the Bonneville such a rip-roaring success: it's thought that over 300,000 were built between 1959 and 1988, making this the best-selling British twin of all. It was also the British bike that conquered America, carving a niche in road riding and desert racing that endured for nearly 20 years. For a generation or two of riders, a Bonnie was their first big bike, one forever linked with memories of youth and freedom. Maybe that's why the name has enjoyed a renaissance: in 2001, the reborn Triumph company launched a brand new Bonneville, which turned out to be a best-seller.

There were bad times as well as good, however, and the Bonneville's story is inextricably linked with that of the industry which built it, from world dominance in the 1950s, to a short-sighted pursuit of short-term profit in the '60s, then collapse and a struggle for survival in the '70s. The old British motorcycle industry *did* die, but the Bonneville was its sole survivor into the 1980s. Today, thousands of these bikes are up and running, cared for by a legion of committed owners. Despite a roller coaster ride, the Triumph Bonneville lives on.

The slogan said it all. The Bonneville became a legend in its own lifetime.

Introduction & Acknowledgements

Acknowledgements

This book would not have been possible without the help of many people. Roger Fogg took many of the pictures, and was a great help generally, while Peter Old provided some of the brochure illustrations. Annice Collett and staff at the VMCC library were generous with their time – many of the brochure illustrations and period adverts come from the library's large collection. Mortons Media gave kind permission for quotes from *The Motor Cycle* and *Motorcycling*.

Another stalwart slogan for the faithful.

Then there are the Bonneville owners who allowed me to photograph their bikes: Richard Marsh, Mark Venton, Adrian Salisbury, Adam Mason, David Smith, Gerald Sedgemore, Richard Crook, Peter Nichols and Howard Stevens. Thanks also to Alan Bennallick for the picture of his Bonneville racer.

If anyone has been left out, this is by accident, as your help is also appreciated. Finally, thanks to my wife, Anna, for her patience whilst I 'wrote another book.'

Note: Years referred to are model years, usually running from August to July (ie 1968 model year was August '67 to July '68). Bonnevilles were generally built in two specifications – 'USA' and 'UK and General Export' – for brevity, the latter are simply referred to as 'UK.'

Origins

The Bonneville did not spring into life fully formed from nothing: it was evolution, not revolution – the logical progression from other twin-cylinder Triumphs, with fewer ccs or fewer carburettors – a line that kicked off back in 1937 with the Speed Twin.

The original Speed Twin was much more of a new idea than the Bonnie ever was. There had been vertical twins before – Triumph had itself offered one a few years earlier – but nothing like this. At the time, a typical 500cc sporting single was a lusty, lumpy thing that needed some commitment from the rider. The Speed Twin was just as fast – able to break the 90mph barrier – but also able to run at 12mph in top gear. It was smoother and easier to live with than any contemporary single.

Edward Turner was the man behind the model; someone who will be forever associated with all Triumph twins, and not just the Bonneville. An effervescent character who knew his own mind, Turner had joined Triumph as chief designer just the year before the Speed Twin was launched. Although he designed complete bikes, his real genuis was in styling, and his first job at Triumph was to transform the company's dull-looking range of singles into the Tiger 70, 80 and 90. Finished in blue and silver with chrome-plated tanks and high-rise pipes, the bikes looked fantastic, and sales boomed.

The Speed Twin was out of the same mould, carrying the Triumph twin lines that would continue for over 40 years. Then, as now, the motorcycle market was a conservative one, and a secret of the Speed Twin's success was that, despite its twin-cylinder sophistication, it was as light and compact as the more familiar single. It was actually narrower across the crankcase than a 500cc Tiger 90 single, and the complete bike weighed only 5lb more. It even *looked* like a single (albeit a twin-port) and, to keep down costs, used several existing Tiger 90 components.

Smooth (short of its 6000rpm rev limit, at least), fast and good-looking, the Speed Twin caused a sensation, and sold very well. And its success triggered a whole generation of British

That nacelle, that badge: very 1950s Triumph.

Origins

A 360 degree crankshaft was the heart of every single Triumph twin.

According to one brochure Triumphs could do anything – and they did!

twins: a new type of motorcycle had been born.

In typical Turner style, the bike wasn't left on its own for long. The Speed Twin was an elegant piece of work in Triumph's Aramanth Red, but it wasn't sporting and flashy in the way that the Tiger singles were. This was remedied in 1939 with the Tiger 100. Higher compression and polished internals brought more power, and the bike came with detachable end caps on the silencers – unbolt these, and the latest Tiger could break the 100mph mark promised by its name.

And of course, it followed the cosmetic formula of the Tiger singles, with a silver and chrome tank, plus matching mudguards and wheel rims. It was a great follow up, and Edward Turner planned a 350cc Tiger 85 next, but World War II put an end to all that.

The Thunderbird

If the Speed Twin was the Bonneville's grandfather, then dad was the Thunderbird. The story of the Triumph twin is one of a constant search for more power, and the engine certainly had potential.

But the real sea change was an increase in capacity and, in this, the United States was the spur.

The USA is indelibly associated with postwar Triumph twins in general, and the Bonneville in particular – without strong demand

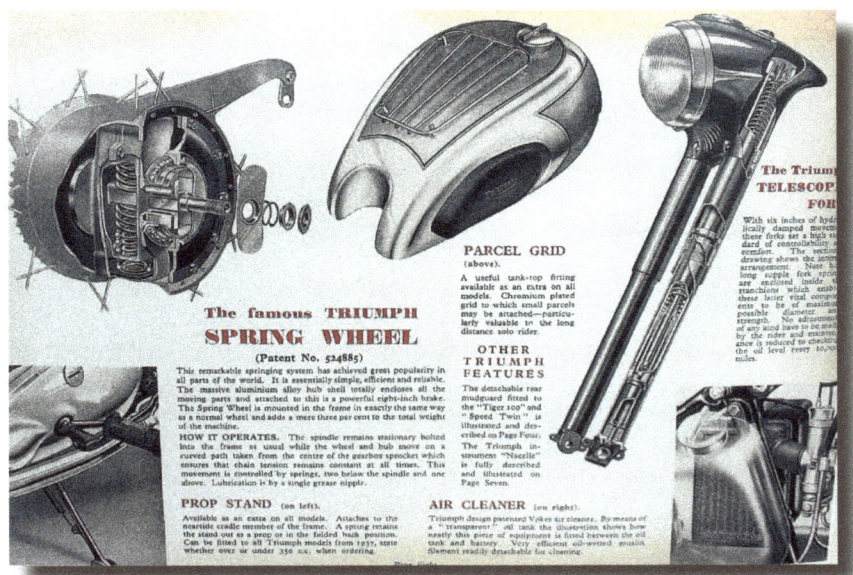

Triumph features circa 1950, though only the sprung hub was unique to Meriden.

The Triumph Bonneville Bible

Tiger 100, quick and tuneable though it was, was a baby bike, and American riders and dealers had long wanted a bigger version with more power and long-distance stamina. Launched in 1949, the Thunderbird gave them just that. The engine was on exactly the same lines as the original, but bored and stroked to 649cc.

Fitted in the 500's running gear, it gave an extra 7bhp and a much improved power-to-weight ratio. Or it would have if Triumph hadn't restricted it by fitting the same one inch Amal carburettor as the Tiger 100. West Coast importer Bill Johnson was most disappointed; dubbed the T-bird the 'cast iron snail,' and petitioned Triumph to fit a bigger carb.

This it quickly did, and once done the Thunderbird proved itself to be a torquey and well-mannered bike with scorching acceleration, capable of travelling long-distance, two-up. Triumph decided to capitalise on the bike's high-speed stamina by sending three T'birds to Montlhéry, the 1.6-mile, high-speed bowl circuit south of Paris. Standard apart from racing tyres, sparkplugs and rearset footrests, the bikes were lapped continuously for 500 miles at an average 90mph, with a final flying lap at just over 100mph. With all three riders in matching white overalls, it was a great publicity event, which Triumph topped off by having all three bikes ridden back to the factory, then to appear at the Earls Court Motorcycle Show.

The Thunderbird certainly had the desired affect on Triumph's US fortunes, with sales nearly tripling in 1951. So successful was Triumph (and the other British twins) that Harley-Davidson petitioned for increased import duties on foreign bikes: the request was thrown out.

Top: Happiness is your very own Thunderbird, according to this Cornish couple.

Above: The Thunderbird was the first 650 Triumph.

Right: Typical Triumph owners meet in the 1950s – the company was building a strong following that would continue for 20 years.

from this lucrative market, we may never have seen the Bonnie at all. Exports were Triumph's big success and, as early as 1948, when a night shift was introduced to keep up with demand, two-thirds of production was going overseas. Before the war, small numbers of Triumphs had been shipped to the States, but sales only really took off once Triumph established its own East Coast sales organisation, and launched a new bike designed expressly for the American market – the Thunderbird.

In a land where the smallest Harley-Davidson was the 750cc W-series, the 500cc

Origins

Tiger 110 & TR6

But Triumph couldn't rest on its laurels in the USA, where buyers were constantly requesting more power, a trend that would lead straight to the Bonneville. The first stepping stone from the Thunderbird was the Tiger 110. Just like the Tiger 100, this used some mild tuning to great effect. The touring T'bird was hopped-up with bigger inlet valves, higher 8.5:1 compression and sports cam, adding up to 42bhp, a 20 per cent increase. This was backed-up by an 8-inch front brake and Triumph's new swingarm frame, which was more comfy than the old sprung hub or rigid predecessors. The frame didn't have the handling precision of Norton's

Left: Art Deco artwork helped convey the image of speed and glamour.

Below, left: Averaging 90mph around Montlhéry was something to shout about in 1950.

Below: 3 x 90 x 500 = a big impact launch for the Thunderbird.

The Triumph Bonneville Bible

Above: One of the last T'birds, now very much the tourer of the range.

Above, right: Heavily accessorised Tiger 110 – the fake leopardskin seat cover is a real period piece.

Right: The Tiger 110 was a stepping stone in the evolution from T'bird to Bonneville.

Right: The Tiger 100 and 110 were Meriden's sporting flagships until the Bonnie arrived.

legendary featherbed, and added a whopping 45lb to the weight, but the Tiger 110's extra oomph was more than compensation enough. At 105mph in standard form (110mph if you unbolted the silencers), this was the fastest road bike available in Britain and the States, bar a Vincent. And in polychromatic blue, it looked a million dollars.

If the Tiger 110 was a direct response to the American road rider, then the TR6 did exactly the same for desert racers. Desert racing, and off-road riding in general, was a big deal in the western half of the US, and Triumph already had a fine reputation there, thanks to the 500cc Trophy TR5. A 650cc TR6 was the obvious next step, and this arrived in 1956.

Origins

A cooler-running aluminium head (soon adopted by the T110) topped the changes, which included a bigger, 20-inch front wheel, waterproof magneto and quickly-detachable headlight. For the East Coast, which lacked the desert racing culture of the west, it was turned into a road-going street scrambler with high pipes. Either way, the Americans loved the TR6 – it was Triumph's most popular Stateside seller until the Bonneville came along – and it sealed the deal by taking the first three places in 1956's Big Bear Run. Triumph would dominate US desert racing for the next decade.

Speed records

"Triumphs," ran a 1978 brochure, "have been setting records on the Bonneville salt longer than most motorcycle companies have been in business." Back then, this was true: Triumph had been out on the salt flats from the first invitation speed event there in 1948, and between 1955 and 1970, except for a 33-day hiatus, held the 'World's Fastest Motorcycle' title. The FIM may not have always agreed, however …

A modified Thunderbird achieved 132.26mph at Bonneville in 1951. Four years later, 27-year-old short track rider Johnny Allen rode a Triumph-engined streamliner to 192.3mph, cracking the World Speed Record for motorcycles. That record, in turn, was pipped at 210.77mph by a factory NSU team with a supercharged 500cc streamliner in the summer of 1956, but the team didn't hold it for long because the Triumph was back at Bonneville a few weeks later, with a reworked version of the tuned Thunderbird motor, which raised the record to 214.7mph. Once again, the FIM refused to ratify, but that didn't matter, because the record brought huge publicity for Triumph and underscored its strong performance image in the USA.

That Triumph streamliner, unlike any production 650cc Triumph, had twin Amal carburettors. For a few years, Triumph Corporation in the US had been offering a twin-carb cylinder head for the 500cc twins, but never for the 650s. Not for much longer, however, as a factory twin-carb 650 was just around the corner. And given its achievements at the Salt Flats, Triumph saw fit to name it Bonneville, after the location.

Valanced mudguards and nacelle – but no bathtub for the T110.

Even before the Bonneville was launched, Triumph made much of that Salt Flats speed record.

2
1959-62: Pre-unit

If it had been left to Edward Turner – and if he hadn't been so aware of the potentially vast North American market – the Bonneville might never have happened. Turner's vision for the twin-cylinder Triumph was for a smooth, well-mannered mount: fast, certainly, but far easier to start, ride and live with than the fussy, lumpy, high-compression singles that many enthusiasts loved. According to this vision, the touring Thunderbird and slightly quicker (but still single-carb) T110 were as far as his beloved twins would go. Instead of immediately following up the T110 with a super-sports Triumph, Turner designed the infamous 'bathtub' enclosure, aimed at riders who wanted a clean and convenient motorcycle, and the 'Slickshift' automatic clutch for those who wanted one that was easier to ride. With hindsight, both of these were simply out of step with the way the market was developing.

In Britain, as more of the middle-aged bought cars, motorcycles became an increasingly teenage obsession: day-to-day practicality was of less interest to the leatherboys than speed, power and noise; for them, twin carburettors were an almost iconic item, preferably with two large bellmouths splayed out from the head in a display of boy racer intent. By 1958 there was increasing pressure at home for Triumph to give them what they wanted. Norton and Royal Enfield were offering twin carbs, while BSA had just launched its quick (albeit single-carb) Road Rocket. Twin carbs helped

Pre-unit Bonneville immortalised in watercolours.

1959-62: Pre-unit

Left: Pre-unit timing gears, showing oil pump.

bring Triumph ISDT success in the '50s, and Production Racing was on the up: increasingly popular, these events pitted production road bikes against each other on the track, and race wins carried a huge amount of kudos. The T110 acquitted itself well enough, but the competition was heating up, and Triumph would soon need something faster to keep pace.

On the other side of the Atlantic, North America was undergoing a similar transformation which, arguably, had begun earlier, with the added impetus of longer distances and punishing desert enduros such as the Big Bear Run. It certainly hadn't come from Harley-Davidson. Back in 1951, Harley had lobbied for higher import duties on foreign bikes. The following year, its answer to the Triumphs and Nortons was announced as the KH, a heavy, 750cc side-valve V-twin that was out-dragged by a 500cc Triumph. It was hardly a serious threat, and not many were sold.

But things changed in 1957 with the arrival of the overhead valve XL Sportster, shortly followed by the high compression XLH and stripped-down XLCH. Harley had finally got serious about keeping up with the British, and even if it hadn't, Triumph's American customers had long been crying out for twin carburettors. The factory did offer a dealer-fitted twin-carb head for the 500s, which sold well, but it still wasn't the same as something straight from the crate.

So in 1958, Triumph's two US distributors – Johnson Motors (West Coast) and Triumph Corporation (or TriCor, in the east) – lobbied hard for a twin-carb Triumph.

By then, the way in which these two quasi-competing organisations would influence new model decisions was well-established. Denis McCormack, boss of TriCor, would write out a report on what he wanted from Meriden, send a copy to his opposite number at Johnson, then incorporate comments from both sides in a final written submission to Meriden. The factory would (hopefully) take all this into account when planning the next year's models. In 1958, McCormack had reason to push Triumph harder than usual. The bathtub enclosure and Slickshift gearchange hadn't gone down well with American buyers – Triumph had a fine reputation in the States for making fast, rugged bikes that many people wanted to own, but it wouldn't take too many gaffs like those to lose it. "At the top of both distributors' shopping lists," wrote Lindsay Brooke in *Triumph Motorcycles in America*, "was a twin-carb 650 model. Dealers across the country were screaming for such a bike …"

Denis McCormack wrote to Johnson Motors about that 1959 wish list in May 1958. It probably would have been good for his blood pressure to learn that a twin-carb 650 was already under development.

Love your Triumph? Give it a polish. Screen sticker reads 'Bonneville Squadron.'

The Triumph Bonneville Bible

Above: Interesting US spec Bonnie with high-pipes, but pictured (and registered) in Britain.

Above, right: Waistcoats, winkle-pickers ... and look at the clip-ons!

In fact, one of the Bonnie's most fundamental features was being tested back in March, by which time, it was clear that the three-piece flywheel, as introduced with the original Speed Twin, was nearing its limits as the 650cc twin kept gaining more power, and with a twin-carb 650 on the horizon, this became a real cause for concern.

Johnny Allen had faced the same problem with his Triumph-powered record breaker, and he had solved it with a far stronger one-piece forged crankshaft, using Cadillac main bearings. Meriden didn't go quite that far, but did design a new one-piece crank, to which a cast-iron flywheel was fixed via three radial bolts threading into the central mounting web. It made for a substantial heart to the engine, and one that the Bonneville would stick with throughout its life. But it wasn't right first time, and the balance factor would be changed three times before Triumph hit on the right figure of 85 per cent in 1963.

With the engine's heart sorted, Triumph could concentrate on increasing power. Each piece of R&D at Meriden was documented with an Experimental Instruction Sheet, which recorded what modifications had been made and how well they worked in practice. Sheet No 419 is a key one in Bonneville history, detailing bench test results of a T110 engine with a splayed port cylinder head, twin type 6 Amal carburettors, high-lift E3134 inlet camshaft and E3325 exhaust plus 8.5:1 compression ratio. There was nothing radical about any of this – the E3134 inlet cam, which acquired a mystique all its own, had been around since 1952 – but adding these together made up what would be the first Bonneville power unit. And it delivered. On 19 March 1958, according to that Instruction Sheet, best power of the day was an impressive 48.8bhp.

After those full power tests, the motor was stripped and no problems were found, while Edward Turner apparently 'expressed satisfaction' with the results: a lukewarm endorsement, perhaps, from the man whose natural inclination was to leave the 650 in single-carb form. Regardless, the prototype was promising enough for experimental manager Frank Baker to get the order to install the engine in a T110 frame for a high-speed test at MIRA, the Motor Industry Research Association test track.

The tests went well, with legendary Triumph tester Percy Tait hitting 128mph on the MIRA straight, though he then had difficulty stopping before running out of road! Hughie Hancox, a fitter in the experimental department who would be at Meriden for much of his working life, later recalled that Tait hit 132mph on the MIRA banking while racing a Jaguar driver who was testing the prototype E-type.

Hughie and his mates nicknamed the Bonneville prototype 'The Monster,' and a typical day would involve Percy Tait setting off from the factory in the morning, riding up to the end of the newly-opened M1 motorway, then turning round and coming back for lunch. While he ate, Hughie and fellow fitter Alan Gillingham would check over the bike. Lunch over and bike ready, Percy did the same run in the afternoon, fitting 400 high-speed miles into a day. Eventually, he was caught by the police and prosecuted for dangerous driving, but was let off when his lawyer pointed out that this highly-skilled ex-racer was as safe at high speeds as most folk were when driving far more slowly!

Inevitably, the extra power and speed revealed some T110 components to be marginal

1959-62: Pre-unit

for their new role, notably (as Percy would attest!) the single leading shoe front brake. Ditto the six-plate clutch, and during May memos within the experimental department were noting that the standard T110 produced 850lb/in of torque, the twin-carb prototype (it wasn't called a Bonneville yet) 964lb/in, and the clutch's limit was 1005lb/in … It was too close a margin for comfort on a production bike and had to be changed. But as various prototype machines racked up miles both on the Midlands roads and at MIRA, no major problems emerged. Surely Edward Turner would agree to its production?

The trouble was, time was running out for the announcement of a major new model for 1959. It's not known exactly when Turner decided that the 'twin-carburettor T110' (as it was still known in some circles) would go ahead, but the first announcement came in a meeting at the Experimental Department in late August, as recalled by John Nelson in his book *Bonnie*: "On this day there was anticipation in the air. Inside the shop stood Edward, one foot resting on a nearby motorcycle workbench, wearing a light blue American lightweight suit, saying in a stage whisper to Frank Baker (which we were all intended to hear), 'This, my boy, will lead us straight into Carey Street.' The object of his apparent derision was a very smart dark blue and grey two-tone finished twin-carburettor T110 (what else could it be called?) with short racing-style handlebars protruding from under a shiny black instrument nacelle unit."

Crucially, Denis McCormack from TriCor and Bill Johnson from Johnson Motors were at that meeting to witness what amounted to an unofficial unveiling. In answer to their, no doubt, breathless questions, Frank Baker confirmed that the bike weighed 404lb, had hit 128mph at MIRA, and had been fully costed as a production item, but no, retail prices weren't worked out yet. Priced or not, this was just what the Americans had been asking for, and they must have been delighted – even more so when the name was agreed as the Bonneville, in honour of Johnny Allen's 214mph speed record at the eponymous Salt Flats, and something that meant a great deal to American riders.

This was all very well, but it left very little time to squeeze the new bike into the 1959 production schedules. These had already been written up, and had to be completely revamped to take account of the Bonnie. In the meantime, it was hastily decided to add it to the '59 brochure (initially listed as a 500, so maybe someone was in too much of a hurry), and squeezed into the line-up for the 1959 Motorcycle Show at Earls Court. As the '59 US brochure had already been printed, an extra sheet about the Bonnie had to be printed and loose inserted. At the last minute, and very much by the skin of its teeth, the Bonneville had arrived.

1959

Model:	T120 Bonneville
UK price:	£294.8s.3d
From engine number:	020076
Tank colour:	Pearl Grey/Tangerine; later Pearl Grey/Royal Blue

Officially, the Bonnie's launch was low-key. Unlike the introduction of the Thunderbird, with its sensational 100mph lapping of Montlhéry, or, for that matter, the more recent launches of the little Terrier and 350cc Twenty One, there was no big publicity splash. It was almost as if Meriden had given birth to the Bonnie only in a grudging sort of way.

Happily, none of this really made any

Below, left: Bonneville engine/Norton frame equalled a typical Triton.

Below: Early American advertising preferred its models clear-complexioned and clean-cut.

The Triumph Bonneville Bible

America soon convinced Triumph that this touring-style Bonnie wasn't right.

Top: Twin-carburettors, high-compression and E3134 transformed the 650 Triumph.

Above: Lovingly restored '59 Bonneville in two-tone Pearl Grey and Royal Blue.

difference, as the twin-carburettor 650 was so longed-for on both sides of the Atlantic that the public needed no artificially induced incitement. The new sports twin was, according to *Motorcycling*, the "latest – and fiercest – specimen of the genus tiger, the T120 'Bonneville 120' is a road-going machine with a maximum speed nearly 20mph over 'the ton'."

Production kicked off with a specification surprisingly close to that of the prototypes that Percy Tait and his colleagues had mercilessly caned around the West Midlands. The engine retained the 8.5:1 compression, E3134 intake camshaft and one-piece crank (this adopted by all of the 650s for 1959) as the prototype. The twin Amals were 1 1/16in Monoblocs, unusually sharing a single float chamber which was suspended from the seat post by a rubber block and supplied by two fuel taps. This would lead to trouble … There was no air filter, just a chrome bellmouth for each carb, which didn't do much to filter out impurities but did look superb. Otherwise, much of the spec was the same as that of the T110, except that Slickshift wasn't fitted, for the very good reason that muffed high-speed clutchless gear shifts could have resulted in over-revving. The gearbox, frame, forks, wheels and brakes were carried over from the T110 largely unchanged.

In fact, sharing of components with the other 650cc Triumphs was to lead to one of the most puzzling aspects of the Bonneville's first year – its styling. The Bonnie, everyone agreed, was the super-sports roadster of the Triumph range, and styling had long been a Meriden strongpoint. So it would have been reasonable to expect it to follow the style of the slimline TR6, with separate chrome headlight, slim fuel tank, skimpy mudguards and gaitered forks.

Except it didn't. The first Bonnevilles off the production line looked just like the single-carb T110, complete with the smooth headlamp nacelle, sensible, full-valanced mudguards and touring seat, large fuel tank and high-rise bars. UK buyers had lower bars and the slimmer TR6 seat, but this wasn't much use to the Americans. The Yanks, of course, didn't like Edward Turner's smooth touring look, and

1959-62: Pre-unit

At first, the sporty Bonneville retained Triumph's nacelle, but not for long.

The Bonneville trademark – twin splayed Amal carbs; here with the single remote float chamber.

1959 Bonnies are rare, especially in Britain.

had found his bathtub enclosures a real turn-off – the first thing some US dealers did with this tinwork (now a collector's item, of course) was to unbolt it and throw it into the backyard. The Bonneville's tank did have its own colour – Tangerine and Pearl Grey two-tone – but even that sat uneasily with the sobersides styling (later in the year, the Tangerine was changed to Royal Blue). There wasn't even provision for a tachometer. (History repeated itself in 2001, when the reborn Triumph company launched its 21st century Bonneville without a tachometer; something that it took a while to rectify.)

In the USA, dealers soon found that the Bonnie's styling was a real barrier to sales, even though most knowledgeable customers knew that it was the fastest road-going Triumph ever, and thus probably the fastest bike on the market. So much so, that in late February 1959 TriCor released the following memo to dealers: "If you feel that you will lose the sale of a T120 because of its style with nacelled forks, and that there is a definite demand for the TR6/A-style T120 (sports headlight, tachometer etc), there is a simple method of conversion by fitting a splayed-port cylinder head and extra carburettor to a TR6/A to give the rider what he wants: a TR6 Super Sports Bonneville. It is recommended that this conversion be made in extreme cases only, where a sale might be lost. Otherwise, sell the T120 as is."

It says a lot about the pent-up demand for a twin-carb Triumph that some buyers forked out the extra $100 for this conversion, but it didn't stop the US importers having a glut of unsold standard Bonnies in their warehouses, which had to be sold off the following season. Subsequently, many of these original '59 Bonnies were stripped of their touring parts, which makes a fully-equipped '59, as it left the factory, a real collector's piece.

Compared to all of this furore over the styling, the Bonneville's early mechanical problems weren't too bad. The most serious issue was occasional failure of the flywheel bolts: soon cured by increasing the interference fit between the flywheel and the crankshaft. This tighter fit meant that the flywheel had to be heated to 95 degrees C before assembly: still

The Triumph Bonneville Bible

"... the highest performance available today from a standard production motorcycle."

Slimline symmetry was part of the appeal of every Triumph twin.

done by hand but now with the aid of protective gloves! Pistons could also fail if the bike was ridden hard for long periods in high ambient temperatures. In this case the piston crown could collapse and the skirt distort; the cure was a thicker crown achieved in two stages: one increase made early on and another when the piston die was changed.

Other more minor changes were made during that first year of production. The front mudguard could crack at its centre mounting point, and spot-welding the guard cured that. To beef up the transmission, longer screws were used to secure the outer primary cover to the inner, and an extra gearbox adjuster was added. The gearbox camplate was induction-hardened (it had been wearing quickly in American racing events), and a more robust voltage regulator replaced the original.

So the Bonneville's first year wasn't completely trouble-free, and trying to sell it as a stodgy-looking twin-carb tourer had gone down like a lead balloon. The point was, though, that the Bonnie existed.

1960

Model:	T120 Bonneville
UK price:	£284.13s.6d
From engine number:	029424 and D101
Tank colour:	Pearl Grey/Azure Blue

Triumph might have got a few things wrong with the very first Bonnevilles, but no one could accuse the company of failing to listen to criticism. First off, styling of the 1960 Bonnie was very different to the first one: gone were Edward Turner's beloved headlamp nacelle, deeply valanced mudguards and shrouded forks, replaced by a separate, chrome-plated headlight, slimmer mudguards and gaitered forks. There was a slimmer TR6-style seat as well, while USA Bonnies had high-rise handlebars and a smaller 3-gallon tank. These few items transformed the Bonneville's appearance, making it the rugged-looking sports bike it should have been from the beginning.

American importers decided to mark the change with a new designation. They still listed the old big-fender bike as a 1960 model, but these were just leftovers from the previous year. New for 1960 were the sports-styled TR7/A Road Sports and TR7/B Street Scrambler. The only difference between them was low-level exhaust pipes on the A, and high-level pipes on the B.

The Street Scrambler highlighted a significant difference between the USA and European markets. In Europe at the time, off-road competition was dominated by lightweight single-cylinder bikes, and big twins were mostly only thought of as pure road burners. In the States, by contrast, long-distance desert racing – in which power and strength were great attributes – allowed big bikes to compete off-road. Some road riders liked to have a road bike that reflected some of that glamour, even if a gravel car park was as close as it got to the dirt. A decade later, the street scrambler look acquired its own following in Europe as well, but back then, it was a peculiarly American style. And in a way, it lives on into the 21st century with the adventure tourer style pioneered by BMW's R80GS.

Both TR7 designations were only ever used in North America for 1960, and in fact the crankcases were still stamped 'T120' and the decal on the toolbox read 'Bonneville 120.' For restorers, it's worth noting that any engine stamped as a 'TR7' is therefore fake. After 1960, the TR7 designation didn't reappear until 1973 (as the single-carburettor Tiger 750).

Just as significant as the new styling for 1960 was a brand-new frame. The T110 frame had revealed a weakness in the Bonneville with a high-speed weave and wobble, which was disconcerting to say the least. So Meriden came up with a brand-new duplex frame (fitted to all 650s that year), immediately recognisable with its twin front downtubes which cradled the engine

1959-62: Pre-unit

1960, and in comes a separate chrome headlight and briefer mudguards.

and swept back to meet the vertical seat post. The bracing rail, which had mounted the fuel tank and steadied the top of the motor, was gone. This main frame was bolted to a new welded subframe that was far stronger than the old one, and the forks were now at a steeper angle (67 degrees), which made for quicker steering and a shorter 54.5inch wheelbase.

The end result was a stronger, shorter frame that handled better at high speed, and was also easier to assemble at the factory, although it had severe problems of its own. Deleting the lower bracing rail was a real mistake, and there were several cases of the frame cracking or even breaking below the steering head, often in US desert racing (a tough environment for any frame). After a rider was killed while racing, the factory ran two bikes around the pave at MIRA until the frames broke, and with the information that this provided reintroduced a lower rail (from engine number D1563). It also offered a retrofit to bolt a bracing rail to an existing frame. The potentially lethal breakages ceased.

The downside of the bracing rail was that it delivered more vibration! The higher-revving, harsher nature of the Bonneville engine compared to its single-carb cousins brought this into focus, not helped by the engine mounting system which kept the fore-aft shakes in check, but failed to control the up-and-down movement.

There were other changes, too, and in fact, the 1960 Bonneville was far more of a new bike than the '59 had been. New forks were similar to those of the 350/500 twins, with two-way damping and a manual steering damper. Wheels and tyres were now the same as those of the Trophy, with a 19inch front, 18inch rear wheel (though some markets had a 19inch rear) with a ribbed front tyre and universal tread rear – scrambler Bonnies had a trials block tread. Doing away with the headlamp nacelle meant there was room to fit a matching tachometer alongside the speedo.

Keen types poring over a 1960 Bonneville in their local showroom would also notice that the ignition advance lever had disappeared from the handlebars, because the Lucas magneto now sported auto-advance. Looking more closely, they might notice that the front-mounted dynamo had gone, too, replaced by a Lucas RM15 alternator as already fitted to the Thunderbird and Speed Twin, and hidden inside a slightly bulkier primary chaincase.

The engine itself was very little changed

The Triumph Bonneville Bible

A Bonnie on the beach, or a remake of Alfred Hitchcock's The Birds?

from the previous year, although, as noted, there had been some mid-season mods to prevent failed pistons and crankshaft bolts. The single float chamber's habit of allowing fuel surge on sudden stops and starts (which could cause the engine to falter or die), was a headache, and it was moved to a new position slightly closer to the carbs in an attempt to combat this. Vibration made the fuel froth inside the chamber, playing havoc with the mixture at idling and low speed. In an attempt to tame the frothing, the chamber was suspended from the engine torque stay by a threaded rod, but this didn't really work. Finally, from engine number D5975, the single float chamber was ditched in favour of conventional Amal Monoblocs, each with their own chamber,

Enter the Japanese

In 1960, as the Bonneville entered its second year, Honda set up an importer in Los Angeles, attracting a number of ex-Johnson Motors personnel to come and work at establishing Japanese lightweights in the States. That was bad enough, but when one high-level Triumph dealer broke ranks and began selling Hondas, Johnson Motors took steps to prevent others doing the same.

Wanting to find out more, Johnson Motors set up a meeting with Hirobumi Nakamura of American Honda. Nakamura was happy to oblige; keen to meet up with what was acknowledged to be a very efficient Triumph operation on the West Coast. At the meeting, Bill Johnson asked how many Honda lightweights American Honda expected to sell – 5000, came the reply. Well, said Johnson, that should just be possible by the end of the year. "Oh no," replied Nakamura (or words to that effect), "We are planning to sell 5000 motorcycles a month!"

This was a staggering number, far more than any other manufacturer could contemplate, but Honda was able to do it by reaching out to new customers who hadn't considered buying a small motorcycle before. The Americans prepared a report on all of this for Edward Turner, and arranged for him to ride a selection of Japanese bikes when he next came over. This he did, and pronounced them "too good be true," prompting him to fly to Japan to discover how all this was happening.

The visit was an eye opener; Turner found a highly efficient, vibrant industry that was building over 500,000 bikes a year, when Britain built just 140,000: any one of the major Japanese manufacturers out-produced the entire British industry. Turner was astonished by the ability of Honda, Yamaha, et al to produce such high quality bikes at low cost, which wasn't, as was sometimes assumed, based on low wages and shoddy materials, but on efficient manufacturing and good design. Turner was astonished by how the Japanese devoted so much attention to research and development and quality control.

He came home chastened by the threat from Japan, though, oddly, didn't seem inclined to do much about it. By now sixty years of age and suffering from diabetes, it could be that he didn't relish the thought of the wholesale change that was needed at Triumph in order to compete, which would have been a struggle; going against the inclinations of the BSA parent company as well as Meriden. The conventional view at home was that BSAs and Triumphs were in high demand and making good profits – why upset the applecart?

Nor was there any urgency for change in America, where importers seemed convinced that Honda wasn't (at least for the time being) a direct threat. Indeed, Honda's success was regarded by many as good news, attracting new people into motorcycling, who after a couple of years with a small bike might be ready for a bigger one ... maybe a Triumph? So Triumph's dealers got an official blessing to take on Hondas if they wished, and many did. By 1965, nearly one in ten Triumph sales were against a traded-in Honda.

1959-62: Pre-unit

which did much to cure the fuelling problems. A balance tube between the inlet manifolds (another mid-year change) also helped.

But not all of the changes worked. As noted, reintroduction of the lower frame rail actually increased vibration levels, and could cause the fuel tank to split. The tank was now held on by an aluminium strap, with a rubber strip between it and the metal tank, which ran over the top of the tank and was tensioned at the front. These snapped on a regular basis. The new alternator electrics brought their own problems as well, down to control of the charging rate and vibration affecting the battery, as related by Detroit Triumph dealer Bob Leppan, quoted in *Triumph in America* by Lindsay Brooke and David Gaylin: "The 1960 generator electrics were beyond bad. The Lucas AC generator system lacked proper voltage regulation; a fast ride would cause the battery to boil over. Some batteries were so badly damaged the plates would warp! The extra vibration from the duplex frame split battery cases, which then leaked acid on the frame and exhaust pipes. Needless to say, we dealt with a lot of angry 650 owners that year."

There were other quality issues, too, with the Lucas dipswitch, the wiring harness, clutch plates and petrol taps. All of these were delivered to Meriden from outside suppliers, so one suggestion was to have a full-time quality control person to inspect the stuff as it came in: Edward Turner said 'no.' Of course, for Lucas, Smiths and other suppliers the motorcycle contracts were small beer, and made small profits, compared to their mass production car industry deals, so they had little incentive to improve quality.

1961

Model:	T120 Bonneville
UK price:	£288.5s.11d
From engine number:	D7727
Tank colour:	Sky Blue/Silver Sheen

If 1960 had been a year of major changes, then '61 was one of consolidation, with few modifications to the Bonneville. Triumph still wasn't happy with its handling, and steepened the steering head angle by another two degrees to 65 degrees in an attempt to sharpen it up. To tackle splitting fuel tanks, the tank was strengthened at the nose bridge, and its retaining strap was now of stainless steel, which remedied the epidemic of snapped straps. New anti-vibration mountings for the toolbox also sought to dampen the evil vibes.

The brakes were updated, with fully floating shoes and a new backing plate, while the Smiths speedometer now read to 140mph instead of 120. The speedo change was odd, because the Bonnie certainly hadn't gained another 20mph, though it would have looked good to showroom cowboys. Home market and T120C Bonnevilles still made do without a tachometer and the associated timing cover which included its drive. The engine and gearbox were almost untouched, though the alloy head now had cast-in spacers to reduce buzzing of the fins, and

New colours for 1961: tank top half in Sky Blue; lower half in Silver.

Engine and gearbox were barely changed for '61.

The Triumph Bonneville Bible

A complete set of instruments, but UK buyers had to pay extra for the tachometer.

Beautiful T120 at Dorset Steam Fair, September 2012.

thus curtail noise. There was a larger layshaft thrust washer, a smaller engine sprocket (down to 21 teeth from 22), and a folding kickstart was fitted for the first time.

Overcharging at high revs, plus vibration, had blighted the 1960 Bonneville's electrics, blowing headlight and taillight bulbs as well as ruining batteries. Triumph reduced alternator output, which helped, although, with hindsight, would seem to be more like treating the symptoms rather than the cause of the problem.

American market Bonnevilles were renamed, losing the short-lived TR7 tag and gaining T120C for the high-pipe variant; T120R for the road-going, low-pipe bike. The C (for 'Competition') wasn't just a cosmetic street scrambler, having a competition magneto as well as Trials Universal tyres and bashplate for the crankcase. US bikes also had Silver Sheen oil tank and toolbox – those on UK bikes were black, though as ever there was some 'leakage' of black-detailed bikes across the Atlantic.

The *Motor Cycle* tested a 1961 Bonneville in December 1960, a few months after its announcement. In the way of road tests of that era, the magazine was unfailingly polite, delicately referring to the vibration as a "high frequency tremor at the handlebar," criticising the wet weather capabilities of the skimpy mudguards and the siting of the light switch, although the writer, David Dixon, added that "idling was not always reliable." In those deferential days, that was about as fierce as criticism got.

Dixon was in much happier mood when it came to performance, because even allowing for softly-softly journalism, the Bonneville was clearly an exciting bike to ride: "In bottom gear in an almost alarmingly short time, the Bonneville will reach 50mph," he wrote. "A quick upward flick on the gear pedal and 70mph shows. As third is snicked home there comes another beefy surge, 88-90mph comes up and things begin to get exciting …" Top speed, he reckoned, was an indicated 105mph on a wet road with a rider in wet weather gear in a semi-crouch. Given a dry road and a two-piece suit, he thought 110-115mph would be nearer the mark. "Very, very fast," Dixon concluded, "and with its excellent handling and superb brakes, safe to ride almost irrespective of the conditions … this latest Bonneville is an absolute honey, with no vices – and attributes by the score."

A quarter-century later, Mike Nicks rode a '61 Bonneville for *Classic Bike*, loving the handling and performance, but not liking the brakes, forks and vibration – how standards change.

1962

Model:	T120 Bonneville
UK price:	£295.1s.4d
From engine number:	D15789
Tank colour:	UK – Sky Blue/Silver. USA – Flamboyant Flame/Silver

This was the final year of the pre-unit construction Bonneville, and many still believe it was the best

1959-62: Pre-unit

Far left: 1962, and the Bonnie still got the spotlight amongst a 'package of power.'

Left: Right through the '60s, copywriters seemed convinced that only men rode Triumphs.

of the bunch, with many of the initial problems sorted and without the more severe vibration problems that affected the unit construction Bonnie of the following year. Others plump for the 1970 Bonneville as the best ever – once again, the last of an era and the summation of several years' development. The arguments will no doubt continue.

Meanwhile, there were few changes for 1962, though in pursuit of taming vibration, the crankshaft's balance factor was increased to 71 per cent from engine number D15789; then again to 85 per cent from D17043. The second change involved a new unit, still based on the same format of a one-piece forged crank, but with a wider flywheel. The 85 per cent balance figure blunted the throttle response, but did reduce vibration, and would stay with the T120 Bonneville for the rest of its long production life.

A Lucas RM19 alternator replaced the RM14 (still with reduced output to prevent overcharging), while the oil tank had new rubber mountings – the brackets had been fracturing due to vibration. The Girling shocks were stiffer, and the T120R had slightly lower gearing overall, with an extra tooth on the gearbox sprocket (now 22 in total).

The truth was, despite its earlier problems, the 1962 Bonneville was settling down and now well-sorted. In America, the Bonnie had proved an easy match for the Harley Sportster, in a street racing duel that would carry on right through the '60s. The Hog might be slightly quicker over a quarter-mile, thanks to the sheer power and stomp from its bigger engine, but the lighter, nimbler Triumph would always have the edge along twistier roads. In competition, who won the Harley vs the Limeys debate depended on the event. In desert racing, British bikes (and especially Triumph) dominated, but in AMA Class C racing on circuits and flat tracks, Harley

Garish grille-style badge stayed with the Bonnie until 1966.

The Triumph Bonneville Bible

> ### The 230mph Bonneville
> The Bonneville was named in honour of Johnny Allen's 214mph speed record set at the salt flats, which in August 1962 was broken at the same venue. Allen had returned to the flats in 1959 with the support of Johnson Motors, but crashed at 220mph, though he survived with a few broken ribs.
>
> Three years later a young man named Bill Johnson (no relation to the Bill Johnson who founded Johnson Motors) came to have a go. Like Allen, his bike was a long, low streamliner with Triumph power, but taking everything one stage further. It was built by Joe Dudek, with advice from aerodynamicists who had a hand in the X-15 rocket plane at North American Aircraft, where Dudek was chief mechanic. The power unit was from a Bonneville, bored out to 667cc and featuring a specially developed cam, using Triumph R racing tappets.
>
> It all worked. On 24 August 1962, Johnson set a new petrol-powered motorcycle speed record, averaging 205mph over two runs. Then his team drained the petrol, changed the jets, filled the streamliner with nitromethane and sent him off again. The result (after changing a blown piston) was an average 224.57mph, a new World Motorcycle Speed Record, though Bill Johnson had actually made that 230.269mph over a measured mile.
>
> His wouldn't be the last Triumph-powered streamliner record breaker, either.

1962; final year for the pre-unit Bonneville.

ruled the roost. Any Triumph rider would tell you that this was down to Class C rules, which allowed 750cc side-valve engines but restricted overhead valve motors to 500cc.

Whatever the truth, Triumph needed success across the Atlantic because the motorcycle home market was looking grim. An increasingly affluent public was abandoning bikes as daily transport in favour of cars, and within two years of 1960, the UK motorcycle market had halved in size. More than ever, bikes were the preserve of the young, and the antics of coffee bar cowboys (not to mention their accident rates) was turning general attitudes against motorcycling. The Bonneville, it has to be said, was the perfect machine for a 19-year-old pulling up outside the Ace Café. It had style, glamour and speed – not only was it one of the fastest bikes you could buy, it looked the part as well. What teen or early twenty-something could ask for more? Unfortunately, there weren't enough of them to keep Meriden humming at a profitable level, and Triumph hadn't made big inroads into mainland Europe. Only the USA remained a golden goose, and one on which it was increasingly dependent.

Signature point of all Triumph twins – the triangular patent number plate.

That face wouldn't change for several years.

Amal Concentrics are non-standard on this '62 Bonneville – they should be Monoblocs.

Smiths speedometer read up to 140mph from 1961.

Although improved, the brakes were still a weak point.

3

1963-70: Prime time

1963

Models:	T120 Bonneville/T120R Bonneville/T120C Bonneville/T120TT Bonneville TT Special
UK price:	£318
From engine number:	DU101
Tank colour:	Alaskan White

Nineteen sixty-three was a landmark year for the Bonneville with the arrival of unit construction, the engine and gearbox housed in a single alloy case. The real puzzle was why it had taken Triumph so long: the little 150cc Terrier had it back in 1953; the 350cc Twenty-One in '57, and the 500cc twin a couple of years later. Yet Triumph's 650cc flagships had stuck with a separate gearbox.

Actually, in this they weren't out of step with the rest of the British motorcycle industry – Norton, BSA and the rest had separate gearboxes, too – and the motorcycle-buying public was essentially conservative; suspicious of radical change. But by the early 1960s, there were good reasons why the move to unit construction couldn't wait any longer.

First and foremost, BSA was going this route. To the outside world, Triumph was part of the BSA group, having been bought by the 'Beeza' back in 1951, so one might have expected any inter-brand rivalry to have been concocted by the marketing men. In truth, a genuine arch rivalry still existed between the two, and

Period early '60s artwork, underlining Triumph's weekend racing heritage – what's the betting the towcar's a Lotus Cortina?

would do right to the end. Their bikes, although superficially similar, shared no components – R&D, production, dealerships: all were kept completely separate. It didn't make economic sense, but getting Meriden and Small Heath to co-operate seemed to be a job the BSA board wasn't willing to tackle.

So when Triumph's Jack Wickes learnt that BSA had a unit construction 650 under development in late 1960, it wasn't long before

1963-70: Prime time

Far left: Some tachometers read anti-clockwise.

Left: Classic Smiths instrument set from the early 1960s.

THE HEART OF A TRIUMPH IS ITS FINE ENGINE

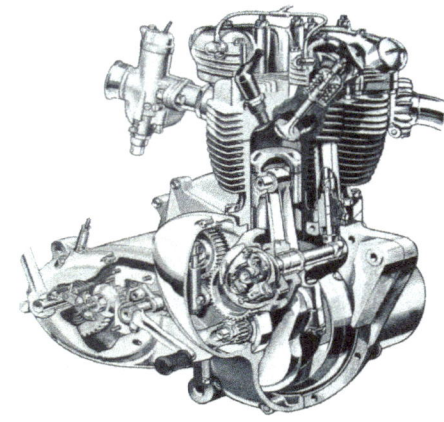

UNEQUALED SINCE TRIUMPH FIRST PRODUCED THE VERTICAL TWIN OHV

NOW COMPLETELY REDESIGNED FOR 1963

Far left: You'd think there was nothing new about the '63 Triumphs: the lamp gets a bigger billing than the bikes.

Left: Unit construction 650 – Triumph twins would follow this same format until the very end.

Unit construction laid bare, claiming less weight and greater rigidity than the pre-unit.

Triumph was doing the same. As the 1960s wore on, there were attempts to get BSA/Triumph to co-operate, with good economic reasoning, but the internecine rivalry remained fierce, almost bitter, right to the very end.

There were other reasons why it was a good time to go unit construction. In America, some dealers wanted the engine/gearbox to have a cleaner look, and going unit would achieve that, but the clincher was, perhaps, that Lucas was about to cease production of magnetos, so a major change to the crankcases was inevitable anyway.

Edward Turner, fresh from his trip to Japan, and long-serving design engineer Bert Hopwood got to work, and drew up what would be Triumph's best-selling model of all time. They made a good team, as Bert Hopwood was a skilled engineer who could make up for Turner's deficiencies in that department, limited only by the fact that ET was the boss and had the final say. In just eight months the design was complete

The Triumph Bonneville Bible

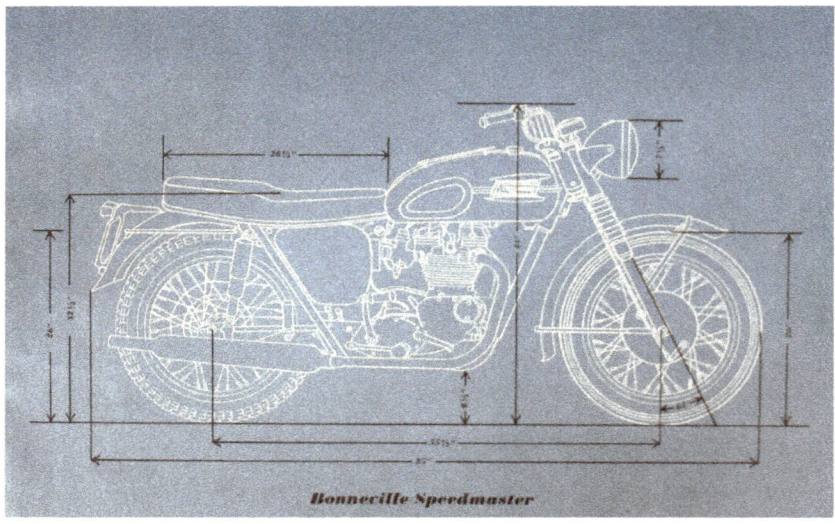

Chic blueprint for an early unit construction Bonneville.

> ### Performance parts for the 1963 Bonneville
> • 8.5:1 pistons machined to accept 3/32in oversize valves, deeper D/24 compression and oil control piston rings, larger valve seats
> • Cylinder head with 1 1/8in diameter inlet ports, carburettor adaptors and oversize valve seats
> • Nimonic exhaust valves
> • E2879 double-lipped roller main bearings, 1 1/8in
> • Amal Type 389 carburettor and 14/624 carburettor
> • E3134 camshaft and followers
> • Close-ratio gears and appropriate speedometer drive gear

and ready for production (ET's last in-house design for Triumph before he retired in 1964).

Edward Turner's engineering ability might have been flawed, but at the age of sixty his styling instincts were as sharp as ever. The unit construction BSA engine was smooth and rounded: like an egg – very clean, but somehow soulless. The new Triumph, on the other hand, was a clever blend of old and new. On the right-hand side, the triangular timing cover and upswept gearbox cover had a distinct family resemblance to the pre-units, which must have pleased traditionalists. The primary drive side, on the other hand, looked modern and substantial, with a backswept flute that suggested speed – it was classic Turner. As for the engine itself, deeper finning, with strong angles on the head, reinforced the tough, bulletproof look.

Fortunately, there was more to the unit 650 than aesthetics. The primary drive was now by duplex chain between fixed centres; chain adjustment taken care of by a rubber-faced tensioner. The clutch now had six plates (increased from five) and new cushdrive rubbers. With the magneto banished, ignition was by twin contact breakers driven off the end of the exhaust camshaft, with twin coils mounted under the fuel tank: ostensibly an advance, but the new system brought problems of its own.

Elsewhere in the engine it was a mix of old and new – new camshafts but pistons carried over – the crank was basically the same but lighter. Perhaps the biggest improvement was that spacing out the cylinder head studs allowed the addition of a ninth stud between the cylinders. The Amal Monobloc 1 1/16in carburettors carried on, but late in the '63 season the Bonneville finally acquired an air filter; a single item that supplied both instruments: standard in the USA, but UK customers had to pay extra!

There was a new frame as well, with the 1960-62 duplex ditched in favour of a far more substantial item with a single downtube that split to a duplex cradle underneath the engine. The headstock was beefier and the rear end made more rigid with substantial mounting plates to join the swingarm pivot, subframe and rear of the gearbox.

There were lots of other detail changes, but this was the gist of the unit construction Bonneville. According to Triumph, the new unit engine/gearbox was lighter than the old separate set-up: more rigid and more compact. Vic Willoughby tested one of the new Bonnevilles for *Motor Cycle* in November 1962, and loved the throttle response ("legalized violence") and brakes ("killed speed as quickly and safely as if I'd run into a glue patch"). There was nuanced criticism of vibes ("the tremor at the grips was tolerable") but it was clear that the Bonneville was still one of the fastest bikes on the market, capable of 90mph cruising and 110mph flat-out. The surprise was that the new frame, stronger and more rigid though it was, had brought about a return of the old handling problems with a high speed weave. According to Mr Willoughby, Doug Hele was already working on a solution, reckoning all would be sorted by the time the new Bonnie went on sale (it actually took a couple more years).

In fact, although the unit construction Bonnie got a good reception, all was not well within the factory, where it was recognised that

The TT Special

The TT Special was a new Bonneville variant for 1963, sold alongside the existing road-going T120R and street scrambler T120C. It was aimed specifically at US West Coast off-road and TT steeplechase racing (hence the name), underlining how important the North American market had become for Triumph. Today, the TT is a collector's item, so much so that some of the surviviors are actually fakes, something relatively easy to do as the TT didn't have its own engine prefix code until 1967, its final year of production.

For 1963, it had very few special parts, and was little more than a stripped-down Bonneville with no lights, no passenger footpegs or speedometer – the tachometer was mounted on the right, and its single-carb equivalent, the Trophy Special TR6SC, had no instruments at all. Ignition was AC with energy transfer coils, so that the bike didn't need a battery. The engine was mildly tuned, with an 11.2:1 compression ratio and larger 1 3/16 in Amal Monobloc carburettors with 330 main jets. The exhaust was by high-level straight through pipes without silencers.

The TT was a successful model in its own right, with 3500 built over five years – some say more than that have survived!

No lights, a 2-into-1 exhaust, and some mild tuning summed up the TT Special.

the extra rigidity of the engine/gearbox and frame had actually made vibration worse. Neale Shilton, Meriden's hard-riding super-salesman who did so much to sell Triumph twins to police forces all over the world, was not impressed. "Within five miles of leaving the factory," he later recalled, "I was regretting the change [to unit construction]. Vibration had arrived and smooth power transmission had gone." Even Bert Hopwood described the motor as a "real shaker," adding that Frank Baker's development work had "managed to compromise with a passable degree of roughness."

The vibration was a fundamental problem, but some less serious issues arose once the bike was in production and being ridden. Fourth gear could be difficult to select, due to insufficient clearance between the gearbox shell and gear selector quadrant. The clutch cushdrive rubbers could break up (resolved by fitting softer rubbers with chamfered edges, coloured green to differentiate them from the older rubbers). More serious was the odd failure of the driveside main bearing, something else that was attributed to the stiffer crankcase: a looser-fit bearing was specified.

The new coil ignition system should have been an advance over the old magneto, but in practice the twin contact breaker system (one set of cb points for each cylinder) was a headache. Altering the points gap for one cylinder changed the ignition timing on the other, so setting it all up was a compromise between the two: if one cylinder was spot on, the other wouldn't be, and the problem only got worse as the components

Eyebrow flash on the primary drive cover wasn't necessary, but did look good. The Triumph 650 was no bland-looking 'power egg.'

Adspeak 1963

"Completely New. Full Powered 40cu in (650cc) ohv Vertical Twins with Twin Carburetors
"Again Triumph leads in the high performance group with its famous Bonneville Range of Twin Carburetor 40cu in machines that are demanded by the expert and highly experienced rider for highest possible performance. Riders will wish to carefully compare and choose between the maximum performance of the Twin Carburetor Bonneville line and the great reliability and smoother running at lower speeds in traffic afforded by the 40cu in (650cc) Single Carburetor Models that are set out further on in this catalog."

The Triumph Bonneville Bible

Competition riders didn't need lights, so the TT didn't have them.

Some TT/T120Cs didn't have passenger footrests, though they all had the full-length seat.

wore. Inaccurate timing meant poor starting; less than optimal running … and more vibration, leading more riders to bemoan the loss of the old magneto. It wasn't until 1967 that the problem was solved, with Lucas 6CA cb sets that could be adjusted independently of each other.

Although unit construction was a step towards modernity, the '63 Bonneville was a flawed machine, and it would take a few years before some of the problems were ironed out. In the meantime, although it was more modern than the pre-unit Bonnie, it still lacked certain big ticket features that Honda had shown riders wanted.

Remember how, in America, Honda succeeded in attracting new blood to biking, and that some of these riders later traded up to a Triumph? It sounded perfect. Honda had given motorcycling a new, clean-cut image, and as a result expanded the market by attracting new customers. The trouble was, some of these new riders were asking some very pertinent questions: If their little Honda had an electric start and a five-speed gearbox, why couldn't the big Triumph, which, after all, cost about twice as much? This sort of question got louder and more persistent as the 1960s wore on, and as the Japanese began offering big bikes of their own.

1964

Models:	T120 Bonneville/T120R Speedmaster/T120C Bonneville/T120TT Bonneville TT Special
UK price:	£320.8s.0d
From engine number:	DU5825
Tank colour:	Alaskan White/Gold

After the flurry of changes in 1963, '64 was a quiet year for the Bonneville, and changes were very few. There were slightly larger valves (up to $1^{19}/_{32}$in inlet and $1^{7}/_{16}$in exhaust), and the Amal Monoblocs were bigger, too, now $1^{1}/_{8}$in, still without chokes, but with a balance pipe between the inlets and safety-wired float bowl cover screws. The kickstarter acquired an oil seal and the oil tank a drain plug (which saved disconnecting a pipe to drain the oil). The front forks were redesigned with shorter, wider springs which sat outside the stanchions, locating in a chrome cup that held the allegedly more effective oil seal, with a bigger gaiter to cover everything. There was a major change in the instruments, though, with Smiths magnetic speedometer and tachometer replacing the chronometric items.

Handsome, indeed: 1964 T120 in Gold over Alaskan White.

US-spec Triumph twin in a very English setting.

It was a quiet year for the TT Special as well, which had larger carburettor adaptors with $1^{3}/_{8}$in threads. An air filter was standard and the gearbox sprocket went down to 18 teeth. The road bikes' new forks were fitted, plus new upper covers that did away with the headlight mounts (not needed on the lightless TT). Tyres were changed to Dunlop Gold Seal K70s. As for '63, the tank colour was the same as the road Bonneville, but with polished alloy (not painted) mudguards.

Triumphs had always been stylish, and Meriden did seem to be waking up to the possibilities of metallic paint, sometimes painting the solid colour over a silver, which gave a beautiful sheen. But colours that weathered well in England would sometimes fade in the sunnier American states, and US dealers often thought that the factory tended to ignore their requests.

'Triumphs are fun': this was the message for 1964.

The bike became the T120R 'Speedmaster' in the USA.

TT Special was intended purely for competition use.

The Triumph Bonneville Bible

Above: American Beauty. The TT Special was a US-only Bonneville.

Above, right: TT Special engine wasn't radically tuned, but didn't need to be.

Later in the '60s, Triumphs arrived in the States with curvaceous scallops of contrasting colour, an idea that actually originated in the USA. A custom car painter based in Detroit named Gurley became known for custom painting scallops onto Triumph tanks brought in by customers. Detroit Triumph dealer Bob Leppan noticed, liked the idea and commissioned another sprayer to paint new Triumphs in the same way. A scalloped tank became quite the thing to have for Detroit-based Triumph riders in the mid-1960s, and from 1969, Meriden began finishing tanks like this: another Triumph trademark.

Meanwhile, *Motorcycle Mechanics* was certainly impressed with the standard 1964 Bonnie: "… goes like a bomb, handles like a dream, and as a status symbol ranks in the bike world like an Aston Martin does to the four-wheel boys." *Motor Cycle* echoed this sentiment: "Think of a superlative, double it … but no, don't even try. Words alone cannot amply describe

BSA/Triumph get close

In 1962, BSA Chairman Eric Turner (no relation to Edward) had commissioned management consultants McKinsey & Co to write a report on likely future sales in North Amercia, and consider the group's strategy for BSA vis-a-vis Triumph. When the report duly arrived, Turner dismissed the sales projections as too pessimistic, and announced that, from now on, the firm's accountants would set the targets. McKinsey had compiled its own figures by talking to the dealers, who had a far better idea of what it was feasible to sell. It was just one sign that BSA was increasingly fixated on maximum short-term profits.

But if Eric Turner didn't like McKinsey's sales projections, he was a lot more enthusiastic about its other idea. Coming from outside, the suited researchers saw two separate companies – Triumph and BSA – under the same corporate roof. These two marques built bikes that were in direct competition with each other, and very similar in layout, yet which maintained separate sales organisations, management, R&D and marketing. Using good economic reasoning, McKinsey argued that a lot of money could be saved by pooling resources – having a common R&D facility for example, or having dealers sell both ranges of bikes, which would, in theory, dramatically extend the dealer network. In many ways, this made sense – sharing components would save money through bulk orders and simplify the parts operation – and during the 1960s some of these economies of scale did happen.

Of course, what this clear-headed economic reasoning didn't take into account was that BSA and Triumph, despite having been part of the same group for over a decade, were still bitter rivals. There was a real family feeling at Meriden in particular, whose workforce saw itself as quite distinct (and probably better at the job) than BSA's sprawling plant and workforce at Small Heath, and Meriden was certainly profitable, with production soaring through the '60s. This tribalism extended to the dealers, and attempts to force American Triumph dealers to sell BSAs caused a lot of resentment.

Then there was brand loyalty which, in the case of BSA and Triumph riders, was quite partisan – any suggestion that a Triumph should use, say, a BSA engine, was tantamount to sacrilege. But it happened: the Triumph Trident and BSA Rocket Three were essentially the same bike with different badges, and Triumph's 250cc TR25SS was BSA-powered.

In short, the BSA/Triumph situation was complicated, and attempts to get the two working as one happy family underpinned a lot of the events of that decade.

1963-70: Prime time

the Bonneville 120; cold figures can but hint at the performance ... Given its head, it will whistle up into treble figures, smoothly and safely. But there is also a fair helping of sweetness and humility down in the lower reaches of the rev band ... must not be far short of the ultimate in super-sports luxury." Even allowing for the hyperbole of the day, there's no doubt that the Bonneville did impress the pressmen.

1965

Models:	T120 Bonneville/T120R Speedmaster/T120C Bonneville/T120TT Bonneville TT Special
UK price:	£362.13s.3d
From engine number:	DU13375
Tank colour:	Pacific Blue/Silver

Proof that Triumph sold Bonnevilles to the Spanish.

This was another year of consolidation for the Bonneville, and there was a good reason for not embarking on any radical change just yet. Sales in the USA continued to soar upward – 6300 machines had been sold there in 1963, but just two years later this had more than doubled to over 15,000. In the next two years, they would again almost double. Of course, it was still peanuts compared to the number of lightweights the Japanese were selling (Japanese bikes outsold British in the USA by more than ten to one in 1965, albeit smaller, cheaper ones).

This all came not just on the back of booming interest in motorcycling (thanks in part to Honda's PR campaign), but on the fine reputation that Triumph enjoyed in the States. Focusing on the Bonneville's problems, it's easy to forget that Triumph in general, and the Bonnie in particular, were highly desirable marques at the time. The flagship 650 was accepted by many to be the best British sports twin: Harley-Davidson, despite the Sportster, still offered nothing comparable, and apart from Kawasaki's outdated Meguro (a licence-built BSA A10), the Japanese didn't either.

However, there was a warning on the horizon in the form of Honda's CB450 Black Bomber (Black Hawk in the States), Honda's biggest bike yet, which was faster than a 500cc Triumph, and came with electric start and didn't leak oil. Triumph's US importers certainly took it seriously, and Johnson Motors' sales manager, Don Brown, compiled a confidential five-page report on the bike which was sent to BSA Group Managing Director Harry Sturgeon. This wasn't exactly industrial espionage, as many Triumph/Honda dealers were already selling the CB450 alongside Bonnevilles and Trophies. Brown rode an early example of the new Honda, and his report concluded: "On the surface it would appear that we are now badly outclassed with the present 500 Triumph and BSA. Now, really for the first time, we have serious competition for the big bike market."

In the meantime, selling every bike it could produce, it is at least understandable why Triumph spent 1964/65 tweaking the Bonneville rather than applying itself to designing something new. To counteract main bearing failure, and reduce primary chain wear, the fixed end of the crankshaft was swapped from the timing (right-hand) side to the drive (left-hand) side by butting the drive sprocket up against the inner spool of the drive-side main bearing. It was swapped back the following year.

Ride a Triumph, make friends, and patronise swish outdoor cafes.

Highly-polished 1965 Bonnie in non-standard colour and with later twin leading shoe front brake.

Left: Triumph's trademark parcel grid; not good news for everyone.

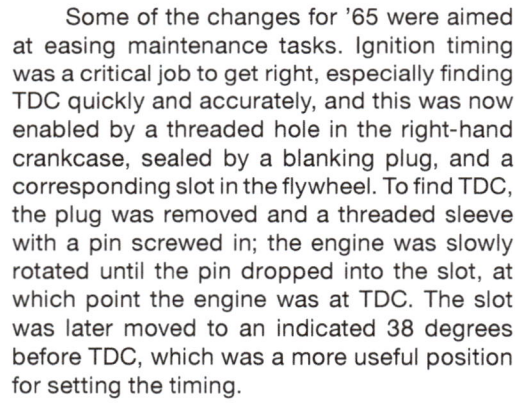

Polished bellmouths were beloved of coffeebar cowboys, with or without wire mesh.

Seats changed in style, along with the colour.

Nice picture, with some artistic licence on the orange tank badge.

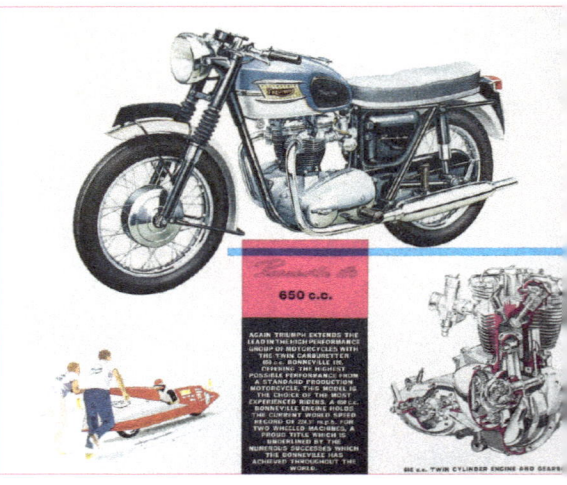

1965 brochure – Triumph was never shy about flagging up those Bonneville speed records.

Some of the changes for '65 were aimed at easing maintenance tasks. Ignition timing was a critical job to get right, especially finding TDC quickly and accurately, and this was now enabled by a threaded hole in the right-hand crankcase, sealed by a blanking plug, and a corresponding slot in the flywheel. To find TDC, the plug was removed and a threaded sleeve with a pin screwed in; the engine was slowly rotated until the pin dropped into the slot, at which point the engine was at TDC. The slot was later moved to an indicated 38 degrees before TDC, which was a more useful position for setting the timing.

To reduce oil leaks, the pressure relief valve was modified and the oil pressure indicator button (if it poked out when the engine was running, then you had pressure!) was deleted. The screw-in exhaust stubs were changed from mild steel to aluminium; the steel ones tended to unscrew themselves, due to the alloy head they were screwed into expanding more rapidly with heat. It was a good theory, except that aluminium is a softer metal and often crushed by tightening the exhaust downpipes, so they would lose their grip on the head and loosen off anyway. Steel stubs returned at engine DU39464. In the transmission, a longer alternator cable nut was

A bike for all reasons, and all nations? Not quite a global brand, but on the way ...

1963-70: Prime time

Racing usually featured in the detail of publicity material.

fitted in the primary drive to protect the cable from the whipping chain.

The frame, too, saw only minor changes. Owners complained that the propstand angle was too steep, leaving the bike likely to topple over on a camber, so that was reduced. The brake rod was straightened out by routing it inside the engine plate, and in another bid to reduce service times, the swingarm pivot bolt swapped sides so that it was withdrawn from the right-hand side, which was easier. The forks did get more significant change, gaining longer travel from longer stanchions, sliders and springs, while the axle cap was now machined. For the electrics there was a new taillight; the horn was moved to a far more audible spot on the lower frame rail, and the battery mounting was changed to prevent over-tightening of the rubber retaining strap, which transmitted vibes through to the battery and did it no good at all.

TT Special

None of this was very earth-shattering, but the TT Special saw some bigger changes for '65. The compression ratio was reduced marginally

TT Special was quite a success – 3500 were sold.

to 11.0:1, and a small batch of bikes sent to the eastern US were fitted with experimental tuftrided camshafts (tuftriding was a hardening process in which the cam was submerged in hot cyanide). It was more expensive than conventional induction hardening, but did not stress the component. The TT now had folding footrests as well to comply with US legislation.

The most obvious change was a new downswept exhaust system, the stubby straight-through pipes ending just behind the gearbox. These not only looked great, but very neatly tucked into the frame, making them less

The Triumph Bonneville Bible

"Cor, look a' tha'! Blinged-up Thruxton does its stuff at a motorcycle show.

P1, the Trident that Triumph could have put into production as early as 1966.

and the blue riband event was at Thruxton, the rural racing circuit just outside Andover in Hampshire, England. The attraction of Production Racing was that the bikes were very closely related to those available in the showroom, with only minimal modifications allowed. By the early '60s, the Thruxton round had become the 500: a 500-mile mini Le Mans, and a win here carried great prestige.

Hence the Thruxton Bonneville, announced in May 1965 as a limited run of 50, the minimum necessary to qualify for Production Racing. In the spirit of the series, the Thruxton was a lightly modified Bonneville. Touring E4220 camshafts were fitted, but with 3-inch radius cam followers; a combination that gave extra valve lift and vulnerable to damage. As with the road bikes, there was a new magnetic tachometer and new forks, plus a big new killswitch on the right-hand side of the bars.

The Thruxton Bonneville

Production racing was becoming increasingly popular in Britain through the 1950s and '60s,

Trident prototype

The three-cylinder 750cc Triumph Trident was launched in 1969, but existed as a fully working prototype in '65, housed in a Bonneville frame. In fact, its genesis went back even further. Bert Hopwood and Doug Hele had worked on the idea of a 750cc triple based on the existing Triumph engine layout as early as 1961, but it wasn't until news came through that Honda was developing a four-cylinder 750 – the CB750 – that the project got serious.

Given the green light by BSA/Triumph's dynamic MD, Harry Sturgeon, Hopwood and Hele forged ahead, producing a workable prototype in a short time, which as far as Hopwood was concerned, would only ever be a stopgap until a genuinely new generation of bikes was ready. As for the prototype, that showed great promise, producing 58bhp at 7250rpm. It was not much wider than a Bonneville, only 40lb heavier, and of course much smoother. If productionising the prototype Trident had continued, it might have been on sale for 1966.

Sadly, this early momentum was lost when, tragically, Harry Sturgeon died of a brain tumour and was replaced by the far less dynamic Lionel Jofeh. From 1966 on, the company seemed to lose its way; top-heavy with management and committees and lacking the direction it urgently needed. In this atmosphere, the Trident was delayed, restyled ("minced about by committees" in Hopwood's memorable opinion), and eventually launched three years later than it could have been.

1963-70: Prime time

> ### What did owners think?
> *Motor Cycle* magazine regularly quizzed owners of particular bikes about what they thought of their mounts, and in May 1965 it was the Bonneville's turn. It got high marks for reliability (an average 91 per cent) and acceleration (a faultless 100 per cent), but owners hated the horn (16 per cent) and were less than happy with the mudguards (45 per cent). Almost everything else got high marks, though vibration did get a mention, and the electrics seemed to be a particular weak point: in four years, 22-year-old Lawrence Gatehouse's bike (most Bonnie owners were in their early twenties) had consumed five batteries, three rectifiers, two alternators and no fewer than 19 ammeters. Several machines suffered from boiled batteries, but this was cured by changing to 12-volt electrics, something Triumph was already working on.
>
> Overall, 99 per cent of respondents thought the Bonnie was a good buy, and 90 per cent said they would buy another Triumph. Given that sort of press coverage, top management complacency becomes a little more understandable, even if not excusable.

duration. A direct oil feed to the exhaust cam prevented rapid wear (added to production Bonnies the following year), and the twin-carbs reverted to the single remote float chamber used on the early Bonnevilles. There were long, upswept, straight-through silencers, and the entire engine was blueprinted: that is to say, carefully assembled with matched components to ensure maximum efficiency. The result was 54bhp against the standard Bonnie's 47bhp.

The frame was standard apart from a steeper head angle, and the 8-inch front brake gained an air scoop to keep things cool. Wheels were bigger 19-inch items and the bars were flatter, though mounted in the standard yokes, as per the regulations. The tanktop parcel grid and tank badges were removed for safety reasons.

The Thruxton remained the rarest Bonneville of all (just 56 were assembled over 1965/66), and its customers were selected as carefully as the engine was put together – Triumph wanted to be sure that anyone who bought one was a potential race winner. Ironically, soon after the bike was launched, the race organisers announced that the 500-mile would move to nearby Castle Coombe – the 'Castle Coombe'

Bonneville doesn't have quite the same ring, does it? Still, it didn't matter, because the name lived on, becoming a legend in its own right: so much so, that it was revived for a new-generation Bonneville in 2004.

1966

Models:	T120 Bonneville/T120R Bonneville Road Sports/ T120TT Bonneville TT Special
UK price:	£349.7s.1d
From engine number:	DU24875
Tank colour:	UK – Grenadier Red/ Alaskan White. USA – Alaskan White/Grenadier Red stripes

After a couple of quiet years, the Bonneville was due some bigger changes, and 1966 certainly delivered them, but here's a word of caution for restorers. Because of the urgent need to churn out more and more bikes for the Triumph-hungry American market, changes were often introduced on the hoof, partway through the model year, so not all 1966 bikes have all of the changes detailed here. For reasons of space, only the bigger changes are discussed here in any case. However, all changes have a starting

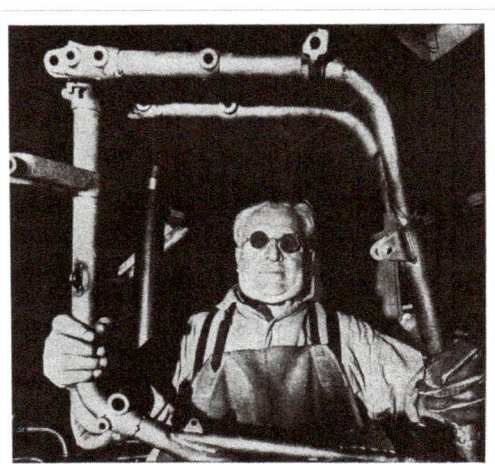

12-volt electrics with zener diode (later 1968 version shown) were a big step forward.

Welder as superman. Some Triumph ads were strong on technical background.

The Triumph Bonneville Bible

Right: Bonnevilles dominated Production Racing in the mid-'60s.

Below: 1966 UK Bonneville in Grenadier Red over White – later twin leading shoe front brake was a common modification.

Bottom: Front view had barely changed since 1960.

engine number from when they were introduced, so reference to a bike's engine number is a good indication of which features it has.

With one eye on the opposition, the Bonneville got a major power boost for 1966, now peaking at 53bhp, only slightly short of the previous year's Thruxton. The cause was a higher compression ratio of 9:1 and sports cams (E4819 intake, E4855 exhaust), plus R-type racing tappets and shorter valve springs. Taken together, these gave longer valve opening duration, and combined with bigger 1 3/16in carburettors (the latter only from engine DU29738), delivered those extra horses. On their own, the racing tappets would wear more quickly, so following the Thruxton, the Bonneville now had positive feed lubrication to the exhaust tappets and followers.

The bike had always been praised for its throttle response, and this was now honed even

A clean sweep for TRIUMPH at Brands Hatch

FOUR OUT OF FIRST FIVE PLACES
in the 'Motorcycle' 500 mile G.P.
captured by 650 cc Bonnevilles

1st **TRIUMPH** D. Degens & R. Butcher
2nd **TRIUMPH** P. N. Tait & P. W. Read
3rd **TRIUMPH** P. J. Dunphy & R. Pickrell
5th **TRIUMPH** D. Chapman & R. Avery

PRECISION · POWER · PERFORMANCE

TRIUMPH

FOR FULL INFORMATION WRITE TODAY TO: TRIUMPH ENGINEERING CO. LTD., MERIDEN WORKS, ALLESLEY, C

Eyebrow tank badge was fitted for three years only.

1963-70: Prime time

further by shaving a whole 2.5lb off the weight of the flywheel by turning down the sides. Despite the reduced weight, this narrow flywheel retained the 85 per cent balance factor of the old version, and was now supported by a heavier-duty roller bearing on the drive side.

This was all very well, of course, but the inevitable result was greater vibration; the last thing the Bonneville needed. According to Service Manager John Nelson: "Many at Meriden [felt that they were] transforming a high-speed tourer into a disguised production racer." Disgruntled customers, thinking something was at fault, would return rough-running Bonnies to the Meriden Service Department, where it wasn't unheard of to fit a milder inlet cam and lower compression pistons, the result of which was that the bike might lose some of that 5000rpm-plus kick in the back, but would be smoother and more pleasant to ride.

There was no attempt to ameliorate the vibes for production, though the other bugbear – oil leaks – was addressed via remodelled pushrod tubes. The speedometer drive moved to the rear wheel, and that for the tachometer was a neater unit at 90 degrees to the exhaust cam, which allowed a much easier cable route. The front brake was widened, gaining 50 per cent more surface area.

These days, all 1960s Triumphs have a reputation for superb handling, and they're certainly good, but the old problem of high-speed weaves and front end lightness was still there in 1965. Drawing on his experience with the 500cc racing twins at Daytona (and by close observation of Percy Tait demonstrating the handling problems on high-speed bends), Doug Hele came up with a solution. He found the gremlins were really down to weight distribution, which he resolved by increasing the trail by half an inch and reducing the head angle to 62 degrees. Bonnevilles now had high-speed handling to rival that of a Norton 650SS. The modified frame (fitted from engine DU25277) could be easily identified by lugs on the downtube for fitting a fairing.

In the electrical department, the biggest news was a move to 12-volt electrics, first with twin 6-volt batteries and then a single 12-volt from engine DU32994 (some say 34174). A zener diode was fitted to dissipate surplus charge and hopefully draw a line under the old problem of over-charging at high speed. On the Bonneville, the diode was initially fitted inside the left sidepanel, where it could overheat, and was later moved underneath the nose of the fuel

Rear numberplate would later acquire a more pleasing shape.

For once, the ads weren't over-selling the bike – there really was a lot new for '66.

tank. A new Lucas headlight now incorporated ignition and main beam warning lights, each side of the ammeter.

There were lots of other detail changes to the 1966 Bonneville, but one of the most obvious was a new slimline fuel tank for US models. It was a graceful thing, tapering back to the rider's knees, its sinuous shape lending itself well to the scallop paint job beloved of many US Triumph owners. It held a mere 2.5 US gallons (2.1 gallons Imperial), cutting the realistic fuel range to less than 100 miles – but who cared about that when it looked so fantastic?

Thruxton and TT

Triumph made seven more Thruxton Bonnevilles in 1966, and in the 500-mile race that year, Meriden twins came first, second, fourth and fifth, so the strategy worked, successfully challenging Norton dominance of Production Racing.

In fact, Triumph had won the 500-miler

The Triumph Bonneville Bible

Keen, cravat-wearing type guns his Triumph, but in a couple of years he'd be riding a Honda ... or driving a car.

The TT only received its own 'T120TT' engine prefix from 1966.

the previous year, and would do again in '67, '68 and '69.

Triumph was beginning a golden era of competition success in the States as well, partly because, after years of lukewarm support, the factory began putting real resources into developing race winners. Even by '66, the company had already won more US scrambles, TT and cross-country championships than all other makes combined, and now moved into other branches of the sport. Doug Hele's 500cc twins won at Daytona that year (and did again in '67), while Triumphs claimed three AMA Grand National Championships, plus 32 National level wins on the flat tracks. As icing on the cake, Bob Leppan raised the motorcycle world speed record to 245.56mph with his Triumph double-engined Gyronaut X-1: so aerodynamic that it needed only 4hp to maintain 100mph (though a lot more to go faster), and Leppan found that at the end of the run he could coast for seven miles, engines off.

No one could stroll into a showroom and buy one of these machines; nor a Thruxton Bonneville or a 500cc twin capable of winning at Daytona (though 1966 did see a twin-carburettor 500, a real mini-Bonneville named after the eponymous race). US customers, on the other hand, could buy a TT Special, ready to race right out of the crate and as competitive as ever. For 1966, it enjoyed many of the same improvements as the road-going bike, plus slightly altered gearing (17-tooth engine sprocket; 46-tooth rear). The new slimline tank meant it lost the parcel grid, but most TT owners removed these straight off anyway. With the slim tank in Alaskan White, and a wide Grenadier Red sports stripe, plus polished stainless steel guards, the TT was more of an eyeful than ever. It was made in far smaller numbers than the standard Bonnie, and 798 were built that year, but later in the season the bike belatedly got its own T120TT engine prefix, replacing the previous T120C.

As if to mark a year of change, all Triumphs came with a new tank badge, abandoning the old grille (a gaudy thing that had been around since 1957) in favour of a large new emblem with an eyebrow, again emphasising the extended 'R' that underlined the name. This would remain Triumph's calling card for just three years.

1967

Models:	T120 Bonneville/T120R Bonneville/T120TT Bonneville TT Special
UK price:	£355.0s.10d
From engine number:	DU44394
Tank colour:	UK – Aubergine/Gold. Later US – Aubergine/Alaskan White

Triumph continued to ride the crest of an export wave to North America as the 1960s progressed, with Johnson Motors (West Coast) and Triumph Corporation (East) taking a bigger proportion of production than ever before. Since JoMo had been bought by BSA in 1965, both were now subsidiaries of the parent company, though still had their own ideas about how the Bonneville should be developed.

They also, despite being well aware of the bike's flaws, wanted more and more of them, as demand continued to outstrip supply. Output had certainly been dramatically ramped up, but the problem was that Meriden was approaching its production ceiling: the company had done well by squeezing ever more units out of the existing plant, only to have Triumph dealers sell out early and demand extra bikes. To do much more, BSA would have to invest in significantly increased production facilities at Meriden. So busy was the factory that it was known locally as 'The Mint' because the pay was good and overtime plentiful.

1963-70: Prime time

Left: West Coast-based Johnson Motors knew the value of pushing Triumph in flat-track racing.

power, stress and revs on the air-cooled twin. Camshaft wear was a particular problem, and the lubrication system for the exhaust cam introduced the previous year hadn't been working as it should, because a new system was added. This system retained the type R tappets, and a metering jet was added which contained a wire screen filter and jiggle pin in the jet. The idea was to provide a steadier supply of lube, the filter removing impurities and the jiggle pin keeping the jet free of blockages. However, this, too, was ditched later in the year when timed tappets were fitted from engine DU63043, which opened up oilways in the tappet block. Because there was more oil around the tappets, rubber O-rings were fitted around the base of the tappet block. The inlet cam didn't have this direct lubrication but, like the exhaust cam, was now copper-plated, and the spec was changed to E3134. Still on lubrication, a direct oil feed to the rockers was added.

Other engine changes were beefier con-rods of thicker cross-section, and a new oil pump with increased scavenge capacity. The old pump sometimes couldn't return oil to the tank fast enough if the bike was ridden flat-out for extended periods,

"… the handsomest in modern design …" – true in 1960; not so obvious by '67.

Still, for the time being there was a little room before Meriden's production ceiling was reached. In 1967, 28,700 Triumphs were sent across the Atlantic and, of those, the Bonneville was clearly a best seller (see table, below right). But there was one clear distinction between east and west coast preferences. In the west, JoMo – based on expected sales – ordered the same number of Bonnevilles as TR6C Trophy 650s, making these joint best sellers. On the other side of the country, TriCor asked for nearly 9000 Bonnies, more than twice that of its second best seller, the TR6R Trophy. It's interesting that the westerners tended to prefer off-road models – the TR6C and Mountain Cub – reflecting the popularity of off-road racing in the western states.

Meanwhile, there were yet more changes to the Bonnie's spec for 1967, some of them dealing with the consequences of increased

Discounted or not, a Bonneville was slightly cheaper than a BSA Spitfire.

Triumphs ordered in USA – 1967	
Bonneville T120	10,900
Trophy TR6R	5500
Tiger T100R	3300
Trophy TR6C	2800
Mountain Cub T20M	2700
Tiger T100C	1600
Bonneville TT Special	900

The Triumph Bonneville Bible

Top: Racing successes kept coming, even with dangerous competition on the horizon.

Above: The Bonneville notched up plenty of Production wins.

with the result that the sump would fill with oil – wet sumping – causing smoky exhausts. Hepolite pistons were fitted for the first time (Meriden had always made its own), but some suffered from crown failure. A more noticeable change was the move to Amal Concentric carburettors (from engine DU59320) in the new 30mm size. These had a narrower body than the old Monobloc, with a central float chamber, and two key advantages were claimed: more even fuelling at extreme lean angles, and the fact that they could be adjusted from either side. They also came with a choke.

The Trophy 650, of course, stuck with a single carburettor, but it's worth noting that, increasingly, this was becoming a single-carb Bonneville in all but name. It kept its milder inlet cam, but now had the E3134 exhaust cam, bigger valves, slightly larger 1³⁄₁₆in carburettor, and the Bonnie's 9:1 compression. It was a clever piece of tuning by Meriden, partly the result of experience with the successful 'Saint' police bike (acronym: Stop Anything In No Time), which combined tractability with good acceleration. In the real world, the single-carb Trophy was easier to live with than the Bonneville, and suited the needs of many more riders, but it was consistently outsold by its twin-carb cousin because it lacked the glamour that went with the name.

Across the range, Triumph began the move from British Standard and CEI threads to UNF – not something that would bother most owners, but a big deal for the Meriden spares department. The Bonneville gained an encapsulated alternator rotor, while the headlight switch moved from the sidepanel onto the headlight itself. There was a 150mph speedo, and, in an attempt to prevent vibes, new spongy handlebar grips were introduced, while the exhaust downpipes were steadied by two short brackets instead of one long one, and UK market Bonnies now had a bigger, 19-inch front wheel.

Adspeak 1967
Big Wheel

"Ride a Triumph and you're on a *real* motorcycle. It's a good feeling. The exhilaration of knowing you've bought the best on the road; a machine that's a household word wherever motorcyclists meet. There's over sixty years of experience in every kind of motorcycling behind the Triumph tradition. It's given us a reputation for sterling British value, reliability, rugged good looks and high performance which is quite simply unbeatable.

"*And what a range!* Zippy little lightweights like the 200cc Super Cub, or the new 500cc Tiger 100T Daytona, the high-powered new sports machine, or the hefty 650cc Bonneville 120, the most powerful standard production twin money can buy.

"*Yes*, you're certainly a big wheel when it's a Triumph you're riding!
PRECISION • POWER • PERFORMANCE"

Adspeak 1967

"This is the top of the line. And with Triumph that means something. A really responsive mount, it's the one that set, and still holds, the world speed record. A true champion in every sense, the Bonneville is greater than ever in '67 – the smoothest ride on the road. If you demand the best motorcycle on the road today, then your choice has to be Bonneville. Available either in the road sport version for road riding or in competition trim for the race-minded."

'Precision • Power • Performance' was Triumph's strapline for the mid-60s. The bike is a 500cc Tiger 100.

1963-70: Prime time

Far left: "Ride a Triumph and you're on a real motorcycle."

Left: In the brochures UK riders always looked more serious than their American cousins.

Right: 1967 T120R (US-spec) Bonneville in Aubergine and Gold – the Gold was changed to Alaskan White later in the year.

US-spec but UK-registered T120R.

Triumph didn't want anyone to forget the source of the Bonnie's inspiration.

The Triumph Bonneville Bible

The slim tank held just 2.5 US gallons.

One pancake air filter for each carburettor from 1967.

Bonneville (left) and single-carb Trophy.

More immediately noticeable to most were new, flamboyant colours: Aubergine – a deep purple – overlay the top of the tank, with Gold in the supporting role with White pinstriping. Bonnies hadn't been this bright since the original Tangerines. US bikes later abandoned the Gold, which tended to bleach in American sunshine, sometimes even before bikes left the showroom, and reverted to Alaskan White.

This was the final year for the TT Special, a bike that was tailored to American tastes and, given its limited competition market, had sold well. American TT and cross-country racing had helped create Triumph's image in the States from the 1950s on, but in the late '60s there was more emphasis on short track and other circuit racing.

As ever, the road testers loved the Bonneville. "A man-sized machine designed for he-man motoring," declared *Motorcycle Mechanics*, which, presumably, wasn't 'he-man motoring' (whatever that was) when averaging 58mpg or 68mpg while "touring." Only in town, according to this test, did the Bonnie ever dip below 50mpg. Figures like these made the new generation of Japanese big bikes – whether two-strokes or four-strokes – look like real gas-guzzlers.

1968

Models:	T120 Bonneville/ T120R Bonneville Road Sports
UK price:	£355.0s.10d
From engine number:	DU66246
Tank colour:	Hi-fi Scarlet/Silver

Motorcycles, like fine wines, can have especially good years, and many argue that the Bonneville's best vintage was 1968-70 – the engine might still be over-tuned, but many of the bike's flaws had now been addressed, and the old high-speed handling problems finally banished. In fact, much of this was in place for 1968, and that year, ignition timing became easier to set up and keep accurate, thanks to independently adjustable Lucas 6CA cb points and a strobe light facility. The electrics were more reliable, thanks to a better-sited zener diode.

1963-70: Prime time

sintered bronze to sintered iron early in the year, but were soon changed back again. A new, longer swingarm with beefier mounts stiffened the rear end; also becoming thicker in mid-year from engine DU81196 (from 14 SWG to 12 SWG), and identified by an 'X' stamped onto the tube. To ease greasing of the pivot bearings, a small breather hole was added to prevent airlocks.

The twin leading shoe brake was yet another plum from the tree of racing development. Ostensibly no bigger than the old SLS brake at 8 inches, it looked much larger thanks to a polished extension. One cable pulled both brake levers, which were linked by an adjustable rod. The right-hand cover sported a big air scoop with a mesh covering, plus an air outlet. On the left side was a chrome cover plate, stamped with a series of air slots. The new brake was extremely powerful, as long as it was set up correctly, and its only fault was the long cable run, which could lead to cable flex under hard stopping. The cable's pin attachment to the

Left: Triumph liked to keep plugging that racing success, and emphasized its claims of 'Precision • Power • Performance.'

1968 Bonnie and Trophy, nicely posed.

But the 1968 Bonneville's real steps forward were in the chassis: a new, twin leading shoe front brake; much improved damping for the forks, and a stronger swingarm – the TLS brake was probably the best British drum brake ever, and the fork and swingarm finally eradicated those high-speed handling woes and made all Triumph 650s some of the best handling bikes on the market. The fact that the forks and TLS brake were adopted by all of the Triumph and BSA twins – plus the Trident – says much about how well they worked. And being shared across the range simplified production and brought economies of scale.

The fork damping was another dividend of Doug Hele's ongoing work, partly as a result of efforts to turn the 500cc twin into a race winner. Externally, the forks looked the same as the previous year's, but a shuttle damper valve was threaded into the bottom of each stanchion, which now had eight bleed holes to allow oil through. It was a great improvement, bringing precise damping control, and preventing the forks from pitching up and down through bumpy bends. Stanchion bushes were changed from

The Triumph Bonneville Bible

Twin leading shoe front brake was an advance for 1968.

brake arm could also jump out if the cable itself was very badly adjusted: soon cured by adding a splitpin. But no matter, the TLS brake was far superior to the old 8-inch SLS item, not to mention better than the conical hub stopper which replaced it in 1971.

For the engine, the long-running problem of accurate ignition timing was finally addressed in a two-pronged effort. Each set of Lucas 6CA contact breaker points had its own backing plate, so now you could adjust one without upsetting the other. To make room for the new points, the condensers were relocated to new rubber mountings under the fuel tank. The new points were still prone to rapid wear, but at least setting them up correctly was easier. Much later, the ultimate answer appeared in the form of electronic ignition, which Triumph itself fitted from 1978, with many owners following suit.

The other big ignition advance (no pun intended) in '68 was an inspection plate in the primary drive cover, which allowed the timing to be set up with a strobe light while the engine was running, by aligning a mark on the alternator rotor with one on the cover. The factory had been setting up bikes by strobe for a couple of years, but many dealers now had this equipment as well. And remember the TDC slot in the crankshaft, accessed via a threaded hole on top of the crankcase? Another slot was cut to signify 38 degrees BTDC (the fully advanced point), with a new access hole low down on the front of the crankcase. Unfortunately, this did a better job of draining oil from the case, so from engine DU74052 the access hole was returned to its original position and the flywheel slot moved to suit.

Compared to all of this, changes to engine internals were minor. The cylinder base nuts were now 12-pointed, which gave more clearance and made a spanner less liable to slip, while the Hepolite piston crowns were strengthened, and the inlet valves gained Stellite tips. Exhaust cam lubrication, despite the many changes, was still insufficient, so Meriden diverted the feed to first the rocker arm ball pins, and then the rocker arms themselves, down to the cam.

In the 12-volt electrical system, the Zener diode's job was to dissipate any surplus charge through heat: difficult to do when it was tucked away behind the toolbox cover. Now it was moved right into the airflow, underneath the headlight, and given a handsome finned heatsink into the bargain. The ignition switch moved, too, onto the left-hand fork upper cover, while the warning lights and silicone-damped ammeter were moved to improve visibility – the lights had previously been hidden by the instruments. That tidied up the left-hand toolkit cover, now with no electrical parts involved, though it did have a tendency to drop off, even after Triumph beefed up the knurled fixing nut.

Motorcycle Mechanics editor Charles Deane wrote about the latest Bonneville in May 1968, but his road test didn't start well as the left-hand headlight bolt dropped out on the M1, shortly after he'd collected the bike from Meriden. Then a lighting wire to the re-sited ignition lock pulled out when the bike was on full lock, plunging the bike into darkness.

Deane was remarkably cheerful about events, recounting how he took off the tank, removed a wiring clip to give the harness a little more freeplay, and fitted a new connector. But it wasn't a good omen. Over at *Motor Cycle*, the tester had the front numberplate come loose, thanks to vibration, and the new TLS brake didn't work well until the cable had been cleaned and lubed.

These weren't the sort of things that should happen to any brand new bike, let alone one loaned to the press, and they were indicative of three things. Although the Bonnie had been gradually improved over the years, it still lacked attention to detail, sometimes in the improvements themselves. Secondly, the rush to maximise production was taking its toll on quality control. Finally, bolts loosening and dropping off were another sign that this was an over-stressed machine that was suffering from inherent vibration at high revs.

That said, both road tests went on to praise the Bonneville's performance, brakes and handling in no uncertain terms, and particularly liked (and this was a constant in almost every Bonneville road test) the fact that high power didn't mean peaky delivery – useful power was available from 2000rpm, and throttle response was excellent.

1963-70: Prime time

A few months after Charles Deane published his Bonnie test, Honda launched the CB750 and the world would never be the same again ...

Production Racing

In the early 1960s, Production Racing was dominated by Norton, but Triumph's fightback began with Percy Tait's 1964 victory in the Thruxton 500. The Thruxton Bonneville evolved from that win, giving selected riders a ready-made racer developed by Doug Hele. Privateer racers who weren't part of these select few felt let down, as they didn't have access to the same parts.

But from Triumph's point of view, the strategy worked, with Bonnevilles winning the 500-miler every year between 1966 and '69. Not only that, but John Hartle won the new Production TT on the Isle of Man, at an average 97.87mph – quite something, as the Island was traditionally a Norton/BSA stronghold. Norton won the Production Race in '68, but Malcolm Uphill snatched it back on a Bonneville the following year, riding the first 100mph lap of the TT on a production bike in the process. In fact, 1969 was a good year, as Bonnevilles won the Swedish Grand Prix and Barcelona 24-hour race as well.

It turned out to be the bike's racing swan song, at least in international high-profile racing, as from 1970 production events were dominated by the new generation of 750s, and BSA/Triumph concentrated on the Trident for race victories. A late flowering, then, but a glorious one.

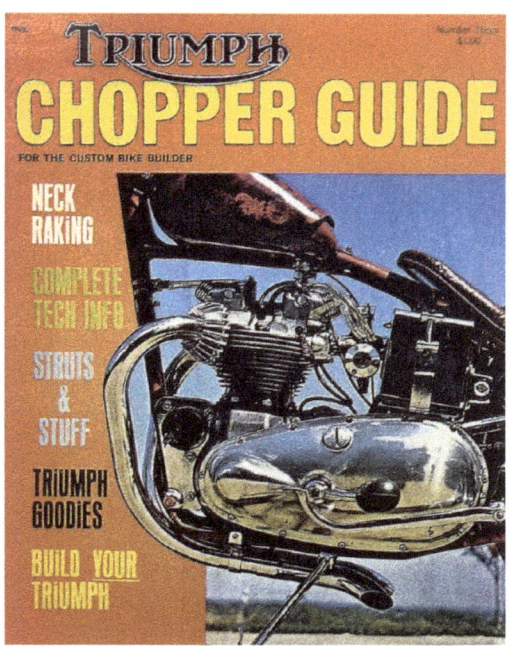

Chopping Triumphs was so popular in the States that the practice even got its own magazine.

dealers in the USA, who imported nearly 33,000 British bikes that year, most of them Triumphs. And they could have sold even more, though it's worth noting that Honda sold over 30,000 CB750s alone in the same period. Moreover, the Bonneville, now in production for ten years, and with a decade's evolution behind it (most of it good), was – just like the factory production – reaching a high point.

As David Gaylin and Lindsay Brooke put it in *Triumph Motorcycles in America*: "Triumph was at its absolute peak in the US during 1967-70, and everything the marque stood for – excitement, race victories, versatility and desirability – was exemplified by the T120R Bonneville. Among all the lovely late 1960s Triumph twins, the Bonnie was by far the most coveted – a lean racehorse, equally adept at humbling Corvettes in stoplight drags, or cantering along a country road."

Or, as Peter Egan wrote in *Cycle World* magazine, the Bonneville had become "a cultural icon ... as much a part of the American scene as James Dean, '51 Mercs [Mercury, not Mercedes] and Lucky Strikes."

Given all of this, it may have been understandable why BSA/Triumph had a tendency to rest on its laurels, but one didn't have to look far behind the adoring surface to see the warning signs. The new generation of big Japanese bikes – not to mention the Triumph Trident and Norton Commando – were creating a new superbike class of 750s, which

1969

Models	T120 Bonneville/T120R Bonneville
UK price:	£373.19s.9d
From engine numbers:	DU85904-DU90282 and JC00101 on
Tank colour:	Olympic Flame/Silver

On the face of it, Triumph – and the Bonneville in particular – sailed through 1969 on the crest of a wave. Production at Meriden had been ramped up yet again, and was now flat-out at 900 bikes per week. Most of these were taken by

Adspeak 1968

"Surely the most potent, fully-equipped road machine in standard production today. Holder of the world motorcycle speed record, the Bonnie added to its laurels during 1967 with a series of outright wins in the International 500 miles GP d'Endurance (for the third year running); the Hutchinson 100 National Production Race (second consecutive year), and the 1967 Isle of Man Production TT. These major international events were all won during 1967 with the same bike – proof indeed of the speed and consistent reliability of this famous machine."

Perfect for the getaway generation? The Bonnie was reaching its peak.

Once again, British Triumph riders were focussed, serious ... and male.

Changes for '69 were minor – Triumph was refining the Bonnie rather than coming up with anything really new.

eclipsed the flagship 650s and meant the Bonneville was no longer the fastest bike you could buy. BSA/Triumph appeared to have no long-term product plan to meet the Japanese threat, and were ready to sacrifice quality in order to meet demand and make short-term profits. Finally, part of the Meriden ethos was keeping in touch with what customers wanted, but the early Trident, with its breadbin styling, seemed to kick that into touch.

There were still plenty of worthwhile improvements to the Bonneville that year, however: continuation of the battle against long-standing problems such as vibration, oil tightness and camshaft wear. Mid-year, the engine numbering system was changed for the first time since 1963, the two-letter prefix in the new system denoting month of manufacture, and model year (not always the same as the calendar year).

The move to UNF threads on engine and gearbox was completed, and the heart of the engine reverted to the wider, heavier flywheel that had been fitted pre-1966, retaining the 85 per cent balance factor. This didn't put a stop to vibration, but did make delivery less peaky. There were new con-rods of RR56 aluminium alloy, and the Hepolite pistons were changed again; this time with domed crowns and bigger gudgeon pins. The camshaft wear problem (especially the exhaust cam) which had been the subject of so many R&D efforts over the years, was finally defeated by nitriding the cams from DU87105. Sensibly, it was also applied to replacement cams for older bikes, and nitrided camshafts were stamped with a capital 'N.' The oil pump now had a larger feed plunger, and the oil scavenge pipe was shortened to allow more oil to stay in the bottom of the crankcase.

Oil leaks remained a problem, but Triumph claimed to have finally nailed the old bugbear of leaky pushrod tubes with a new design of tube

1963-70: Prime time

650cc BONNEVILLE T120

Surely one of the most potent fully equipped road machines in standard production today. Holder of the world motorcycle speed record the "Bonnie" has proved its superiority time and again on race circuits all over the world. Illustrated right Rodney Gould in the 1968 Hutchinson 100 establishing a new record lap speed for production machines at 86.10 m.p.h. Proof indeed of the speed and consistent reliability of this famous machine.

Holder of World Motorcycle Speed Record 224.57 m.p.h. set up at Bonneville Salt Flats, Utah, 1962

Even in 1969, Triumph could still claim that the Bonneville held the motorcycle world speed record.

and seal. This now had a castellated top end, with Viton O-rings at both ends, later supplemented by a rubber washer and steel sleeve at the lower end. The change to UNF necessitated a new timing cover, and Triumph took the opportunity to give it a second oil seal behind the contact breaker points, and wider mating facings, again in the interests of oil tightness.

Another change to the timing cover was the provision of an oil pressure switch, connected to a low pressure warning light. On the face of it, this seemed like a welcome move to reassure nervous riders, but it could have the opposite effect – it was set to light up below 7psi, though the Triumph twin would happily run at 5psi once it was hot. The pressure switch was also apt to give a false reading in hot weather!

As well as the oil warning light, the wiring harness now included a front brake light switch, and provision for indicators. Not the flashers themselves, though, which BSA/Triumph didn't fit at the factory for another two years. This was a half-hearted acknowledgement that the Japanese were fitting indicators as standard. The alternator was now a higher output RM21 and there were twin Windtone horns. The front brake cable, as well as its new switch, was also much-improved: reinforced by a cast-in abutment, it ran straight down the fork leg and pulled on the front lever arm, which was bellcranked to give a straight pull. This answered criticisms that the twin leading shoe front brake could be spongy, and brought out its full potential.

The gearbox had some minor changes with major implications. As well as a statically balanced clutch basket (identified by the lack of cast in pockets) and a new gear quadrant, the gears themselves were treated to a new hardening process. This meant their diameter changed, so the shafts had to be made bigger to suit – only very slightly different in size to the previous shafts, but definitely not interchangeable, and with part numbers to prove it.

One of the most noticeable changes for '69 was the introduction of a balance pipe between the exhaust downpipes, just in front of the outlet stubs. It made removing and refitting the exhaust more complicated, but was otherwise a success in both improving performance and quietening noise. It also allowed UK-market bikes to be fitted with shorter, US-style sports silencers. The Concentric carburettors got smaller main jets, and their inlet adapters now tapered from $1\frac{3}{16}$in down to $1\frac{1}{8}$in, which improved airflow. The 'eyebrow' tank badge was replaced by a neater squared-off item, and US market Bonnevilles gained the elegant scalloped two-tone paint finish pioneered in Detroit.

Finally, amongst several other detail changes, UK Bonnevilles waved farewell to the long-running tanktop parcel grid which had already disappeared from US bikes as a result of one rider being emasculated by one and suing the company as a result. This was the only known incident of its type but enough for BSA/Triumph to play safe. In any case, have you ever seen a Bonneville rider actually *using* his/her parcel grid to carry parcels?

The real question was whether or not all of these detail changes were enough for the Bonneville to compete with the new generation of Japanese challengers? *Motor Cycle's* test in March acknowledged the challenge, but still thought the Triumph was up to it. "Though other, more exotic machines are appearing on the 1969

The Triumph Bonneville Bible

Picture frame tank badge, but several detail changes under the skin.

Leave it all behind?' This Trident would have been fast, but Bonneville sold faster.

Okay, it's a Trophy 250, but this was the rugged image Triumph wanted all of its bikes to portray.

> ### Adspeak 1969
> "Of course Triumph motorcycles are a lot of fun. But make no mistake – they're not to be taken lightly. Triumphs are for men with a strong taste for power, speed and excitement – and with the skill to match. Start with the 250 Trophy if you want to take your two-wheel fun seriously. Then grow up through the big Triumph range. One day, you'll make Bonnie or Trident.
>
> "That's when you'll know you've really made it.
>
> "Triumph – motorcycles for men."

motorcycle stage, the Bonneville can still hold its own. It forms an attractive package in which the ability to top 110mph is allied with race-style handling and touring-style manners, and – big point – it doesn't break the £400 price level."

If the standard Bonneville wasn't racy enough then a fully-equipped Dunstall was the answer. It was a complete package, the 650 twin opened out to 744cc, thanks to Dunstall's own aluminium alloy barrel, plus bigger polished ports and 10:1 compression ratio. The Dunstall Triumph used the Bonnie's standard frame, forks and rear shocks, but added Lyster twin hydraulic disc brakes, rear-set footrests, clip-ons and a racy set of glassfibre bodywork. *Cycle World* tested one in June 1969, and was honest about the bike's shortcomings: "... the weird noises; oil puking ... the prospective buyer in America would do well to come prepared with Loctite, extra screws and wire – and be a halfway competent mechanic." Despite this – and the way the glassfibre half-fairing was already cracking due to vibration, the magazine absolutely loved this ready-made café racer; it's "excellent handling" and braking that "must be experienced to be believed." The writer concluded: "It is a serious machine capable of genuine ferocity. Not given to merriment, but to hard challenge, it will slip through the wind at better than 120mph, and rage over the landscape with choleric haste." Nicely put.

1963-70: Prime time

Make the Trident a Bonnie

Remember how the 1959 Bonneville looked just like a touring Thunderbird? So much so, that the bikes piled up in American warehouses – riders who would have loved the storming performance couldn't live with the touring style. It was put right the following year, but ten years later Triumph made a similar mistake with the Trident!

What potential Trident 750 customers wanted (especially in North America) was something that looked like a Bonneville, with the now-classic tank shape and general lightness of touch. But BSA/Triumph evidently saw this as old-fashioned and commissioned automotive stylists Ogle Design to give the Trident a new look. It was a disaster: a slab-sided boxy thing that emphasised the bike's bulk and weight.

So in 1969, Tridents (and BSA Rocket Threes) were sitting in warehouses unsold, just as Bonnevilles had been ten years earlier. Fortunately, as with the Bonnie, Triumph reacted reasonably quickly, giving the Trident Bonneville-like styling in 1970, and offering dealer-fitted kits (fuel tank, side covers, silencers and so on) to beautify the triple. It worked.

Triumphs weren't just fun, they were smart, at least in this North American brochure image.

Don those sunglasses. Scalloped tank finish was standard on 1969 and '70 US-spec Bonnevilles.

1970

Models:	**T120 Bonneville/T120R Bonneville**
UK price:	£420.5s.3d
From engine number:	JD 24849
Tank colour:	Astral Red/Silver

For many, 1970 marked the year of the last 'real' Bonneville. It was certainly the end of an era, for '71 would see the launch of the much-changed BSA/Triumph range, with new frame, forks, brakes, and lots of other things. In fact, it wasn't so much that the '71 Bonneville had a lot of new parts, but that these were Group products from the joint BSA/Triumph design facility at Umberslade Hall. The 1970 Bonneville, by contrast, was a pure Meriden motorcycle.

With big changes in the offing (and BSA/Triumph giving the Trident a lot of attention), modifications to the Bonnie for 1970 were few, and the only big change to the engine was to the breather system. The Triumph twin needed a crankcase breather because the two pistons

The Triumph Bonneville Bible

Bell helmet, panniers, screen and crashbars – everything the East Coast rider might need for touring.

Large primary drive breather was part of the simpler crankcase breather system.

An access cover in the primary drive allowed ignition timing by strobe.

rose and fell in unison; a breather allowed excess pressure to vent from the crankcase as the pistons descended. For years, this had consisted of a timed disc on the inlet camshaft, but the new system was simpler. Three holes were drilled through to the primary chaincase, just below the main bearing. Pressure was vented from the chaincase via an opening high up at the rear through a large plastic pipe that exited underneath the top of the rear mudguard. This worked well, as the pipe's elevation prevented excess oil escaping via it, and there was enough heat in the chaincase to warm any cold, damp air sucked in through the pipe by the pistons' upstroke (if unwarmed, this would have mixed with the oily exit fumes to form a sludge). The system also maintained the primary chaincase oil at a constant level, so this no longer needed checking and topping up.

There were other minor engine changes: two tapped holes in the timing gear meant this could now be removed with a standard puller, and a new O-ring at the top of the pushrod tube was employed as part of the ongoing battle with oil leaks. In the gearbox, the camplate, plunger and indexing spring were ditched from engine ED52044 in favour of a precision pressing and leaf spring. This turned out to be a mistake, being very tricky to replace, and wasn't rectified until mid-1973.

The forks were improved, with stanchions now hard-chrome-plated and precision ground to give a longer oil seal life, and the engine was bolted to the front downtube via two small plates instead of a lug, which made assembly easier on the production line. Front mudguard mounting lugs were also a thing of the past, replaced by a welded-on pressing, and the Girling shocks gained a small collar to protect the adjusters from wet and grit. The speedo and rev counter went from grey to black faces mid-year, and

1963-70: Prime time

the propstand now had an adjustable stop to prevent it banging against the frame.

This year's colours were Astral Red (a deep maroon) and Silver, but there was a marked difference between US and UK bikes. US Bonnevilles carried over those beautiful scallops from 1969, with Astral Red as the main colour and the scallops in Silver. UK Bonnies looked dowdy by comparison, the previous sweeping curves of the two-tone tank replaced by an unimaginative oval of Silver – a sad note to end an era on, especially when the tank finish had long been so central to the appeal of a Triumph twin.

The first 750

Ask Triumph enthusiasts when the Bonneville 750 was launched, and most will reply 1973. That was the year of the Meriden 750 twin, but three years earlier, Triumph's US importers produced their own. The motivation was the AMA's new 750cc racing formula, which finally allowed overhead valve 750s to compete in short-track events. It was good news for everyone except Harley-Davidson, but only production 750s were eligible, which meant at least 200 had to be built.

Short-track racing, whether the half-mile or mile dirt tracks, were a major pull in the USA, and success here brought prestige and, hopefully, sales. The Trident was a 750, but thought to be too heavy and cumbersome for the flat-tracks, so the importers decided to arrange for their own America-only 750 twin. Big-bore kits were already available from a company named Webcor, and Rod Coates of TriCor ordered 200 of them.

The Webcor kits were already well-proven, and consisted of new, cast-iron barrels, 10.5:1 pistons, rings and gudgeon pins, and would bolt straight onto the standard Bonnie with few modifications. The kit actually came in four sizes, and the biggest (3-inch bores with 76mm oversize pistons) gave 750cc. Minor changes were made to make the Webcor barrels look like genuine Meriden items, and the 200 kits were fitted by West and East Coast importers under AMA supervision.

Freshly-imported T120Rs were partly de-crated, the kits fitted and a 'T' suffix added to the stamped-on engine number. Re-crated, they were directly despatched to dealers – only the biggest volume dealers got the chance to sell the 750, which was named the T120RT and cost $1599 ($150 more than the Bonnie 650). The AMA did approve, and Triumph was able to go flat-track racing, though customers had to sign a disclaimer – officially, these 'production' bikes were for racing only, making the usual warranty void.

At the same as the first Bonnie 750 was taking shape, the 650 was facing yet more competition. Thus far, the new Japanese big

A new breather system was the only significant mechanical change for 1970 – the exhaust balance pipe had featured from '69.

Picture frame badge was simpler than previous tank adornment.

Right: 1970 UK Bonnie lacked the lovely scallop paint job of the US model.

From some angles, not much had changed.

Above, right: Padded grips sought to combat vibration.

bikes hadn't tackled the Bonneville head-on – Honda's CB750 was bigger, heavier and more expensive, as was the Suzuki GT750, while Kawasaki's wild two-stroke triples appealed to a different type of rider. But the Yamaha XS-1 launched in spring 1970 was different. Yamaha's first four-stroke, it was clearly aimed directly at the Bonnie, itself a 650cc twin but with overhead cam, electric start and five-speed gearbox. With 54bhp, it offered an extra couple of horsepower and, despite all the modern equipment, weighed only 6lb more than the Triumph. The hammer blow was that it was over $200 cheaper into the bargain.

Tellingly, Yamaha majored on the fact that the XS-1, with its horizontally-split crankcase and well-machined covers, was oil-tight. But was it actually better than a Bonnie? *Motorcycle Sport Quarterly* tested the two bikes head-to-head, and found it was slightly quicker over the standing quarter-mile, and had better torque.

Adspeak 1970

"There's only one way to know what *good* is. Steer your training wheels to your nearest Triumph dealer and tell him to roll out the T120R. This is the 650cc twin carb scorcher that runs faster than anyone in his right mind would ever want to go. With a streamlined shell, it soared to 245.667mph to win the AMA-approved world speed record at Bonneville, Utah.

"Up front, we put a full width 8in brake with twin leading shoes and real air scoops to keep the wild horses under control

"Down under, we put a sturdy, 2-piece frame that's a masterpiece of strength and lightness.

"In the guts, we put a potful of other engineering wonders to boggle the mind.

"All over, we left off the gingerbread that would made it look like anything else but The Triumph.

"That's what *good* is."

The Bonnie had better handling and brakes, and testers actually thought it was smoother! On every other count (including a 115mph top speed) there was little to separate them. The Yamaha didn't have the Bonnie's classic elegance, but you couldn't argue with a $200 saving. "The first round is over," concluded the testers. "The titans have met, and Triumph has been forewarned."

1963-70: Prime time

Some think the 1970 Bonneville was the best of the bunch.

Nicely-restored 1970, pictured during a New Forest winter.

BSA heads for the rocks

By 1970, the BSA Group, which included Triumph, was heading for trouble. The story has been told many times, and it's a depressing one of mismanagement, lack of vision and industrial strife, but it's worth recounting the main points here, as a backdrop to the Bonneville story.

As we've seen throughout this chapter, Meriden struggled to keep up with demand for its twins right through the 1960s. The Bonneville certainly had its problems, but generally it was a well-respected and much lusted after bike – fast, good-looking and desirable. And it made profits; hence the pressure at Meriden to constantly increase production.

The Triumph factory paid its workforce well, ever-higher wages an inducement to build more bikes. Top level management was inclined to acquiesce to wage demands, just to keep the production lines humming.

There's often a tendency to blame all of this on too-powerful trades union, but it was no more than human nature: who, in the same situation, would not demand higher wages, usually supplied without question? Meriden was certainly more prone to strikes than Small Heath, but it was also more productive and profitable, which the workforce made possible. Still, with hindsight, a factory-based profit share scheme would probably have been a fairer means of rewarding Meriden, without committing the company to high basic wages.

In fact, it was the BSA Group's top management – particularly those brought in from outside the motorcycle industry (Harry Sturgeon was the exception: he had no bike background but swept through the Group like a breath of fresh air) – who appeared to make the biggest mistakes.

Although the Group made profits through the '60s, much of these were squandered on ill-advised projects. Huge sums were spent on the computerization of Small Heath (£750,000), the race programme in the USA ($1 million in 1970 alone), and the infamous Ariel three-wheeler moped (around £2 million). But it was Umberslade Hall that came to symbolise all that was wrong about BSA. This was the Group Research and Development Centre, opened in 1968 and home to 300 staff: an idyllic country mansion, set in its own grounds, which cost an eye-watering £1.5 million to run each year.

Even that wouldn't have been so bad if it had done good work, but Umberslade (known to some as 'Slumberglade') was notoriously inefficient, many of its incumbents cut off from the real world of motorcycle production. It was mired in the Group's burgeoning committee system, which slowed decision-making, and was especially tardy when it came to urgent production changes. Significantly, several key engineering staff, including Doug Hele and Bert Hopwood, refused to move there, electing to stay at Meriden.

Uncharacteristically, Lionel Jofeh asked Hopwood, now looking forward to his retirement, to spend some time at Umberslade and report back on how it was working, which he did in November 1969. His report didn't make for pleasant reading. "Unless we are able to implement important changes," Hopwood wrote, "our 1971 model year will be a disaster." Hopwood criticised the Centre's "poor organisation and poor choice of manpower," in which people without motorcycle experience held senior positions. This was anathema to Hopwood, an immensely experienced design engineer who had spent his working life in the motorcycle industry. "Never have I personally experienced such a mass production release of parts for new models, many of which have not even been given an assembly check, let alone any sort of test." When Bert presented Jofeh with this damning report, the boss appeared to accept most of its findings ... yet did nothing.

With profits invested in white elephants such as Umberslade, or share deals or as dividends, it's hardly surprising that the Group as a whole was increasingly reliant on bank loans, while profits slumped.

Inevitably, Meriden began to feel at odds with its supposed masters at BSA – there had always been rivalry, but the feeling now was closer to contempt. And there is evidence of this on both sides, with Chief Executive Lionel Jofeh being "fiercely pro-BSA" according to author Steve Wilson (*British Motorcycles since 1950*). Nor was that the extent of the Chief Exec's failings from Meriden's point of view. He was not a motorcyclist, had no empathy for bikes, and was apparently lacking in social skills into the bargain, choosing the annual Meriden Christmas party to warn staff that anyone who favoured Triumph over BSA would be sacked! It was in this atmosphere of mutual distrust – and an accounts ledger sliding towards the red – that BSA/Triumph launched its new range for 1971.

Opposite, top: Triumph trumpeted the Bonnie's 100mph lap of the TT, and quite right, too!

Opposite, bottom: From 1970, race wins were increasingly down to the Trident.

1963-70: Prime time

Catch us if you can

Triumph Bonneville smashed the 100 mph lap in the 1969 Production TT Race with an incredible 100.09 mph from a standing start!

'Bonnie' was overall winner of the 1969 Thruxton 500 mile GP D'Endurance at 84.3 mph. Triumphs also took 2nd, 5th, 6th and 7th places. In America at the Bonneville National Speed Week the Triumph Trident captured 15 of the 17 classes entered — and a sixteenth record went to an enlarged 650 cc Triumph Twin. All at speeds of from 132.804 mph to 169.331 mph. Triumph still holds the world motor cycle speed record at 224.57 mph ratified by the F.I.M.

Write for full details of the 1970 Triumph range to: Triumph Engineering Ltd., Meriden Works, Allesley, Coventry

Are you man enough for Triumph?

Triumph Race-bred power.

Firsts
Bol d'Or 24-hour race 1970.
Hutchinson 100 1970.
North West 200 1970.
Isle of Man TT Production 1970.

Write for full details of Triumph's all-new race-bred power range for 1971. Triumph Engineering Co. Ltd., Meriden Works, Allesley, Coventry CV5 9AU.

1971-74: Fall from grace

1971

Models:	T120 Bonneville/T120R Bonneville
UK price:	£558
From engine number:	HE30001
Tank colour:	Tiger Gold/Black

If certain years of the Bonneville are regarded as peaks – 1962, and '69-'70, say – then '71 was the nadir, as this was the year that everything changed, when the Bonneville was transformed from a pure Meriden Triumph into a BSA/Triumph hybrid. Nineteen seventy-one was the year of the 'new range' of bikes, that was supposed to justify the Group's investment in computerisation, reorganisation and Umberslade Hall, but, instead, it brought a disastrous launch, thousands of lost jobs, and the beginning of the end for the BSA Group.

Oddly, the months before the launch were optimistic (as long as you weren't a production worker at Meriden – see below). 1970 had proved yet another record year when Britain exported £10 million worth of motorcycles and Meriden production hit a high of 38,000 bikes. As ever, the USA was still the biggest single market for Triumph, with dealers enjoying their best-ever year. Trident sales were disappointing but, despite the Japanese, the Bonneville in particular was still popular, and Triumph's USA dealers were predicting sales of 50,000 machines in '71.

American dealers were also fired up by the promise of that 'new range' and the

1971/2 Bonneville: not the exciting new start that BSA/Triumph had hoped for.

The conical hub front brake didn't work that well.

1971-74: Fall from grace

Wire headlight mounts replaced the old wing brackets.

Far left: Finally, indicators were fitted as standard.

Left: Instruments came in rubber cups – this speedometer is the old type.

Left: Latest Lucas switchgear won few friends.

The rear hub was conical as well.

plus a 'new' Bonneville, maybe anticipated sales of 50,000 units wasn't so fanciful.

Certainly, the official launches (on both sides of the Atlantic) seemed to vindicate the optimism. The UK event in October 1970, held at The Royal Lancaster Hotel in London, was a particularly lavish affair involving a sumptuous lunch and dinner, a long guest list, and high-profile entertainment from the likes of comedian Dave Allen and the Young Generation dancers. Sixteen new bikes were unveiled, each mounted in a three-dimensional picture frame under intense spotlights.

The US launch was no less extravagant, based at the La Quinta Hotel in Palm Springs the following month, with journalists invited for four days of hospitality and riding. Except for the new 350, which was unveiled along with the other bikes, but apparently wasn't yet ready for test rides: here was the first inkling that 1971 might not be the breakthrough year after all.

So what was all the fuss about? Contrary to the epic nature of the launches and build-up of anticipation, the 'new range' for '71 wasn't the radical break with the past that many were

all-new 350cc twin, the Triumph Bandit/BSA Fury, commissioned from Edward Turner (now working as a design consultant) in the mid-'60s. US dealers were shown a prototype in late 1968; it looked just the thing to rival the Honda and Yamaha 350s, and *Popular Mechanics* magazine stoked anticipation by reporting that the prototype had lapped a British race circuit faster than a Trident. With this promised for '71,

UK-spec Bonnies, available from later in 1971, had this slab-sided tank.

Sky-high seat was symptomatic of how the '71 bikes were developed.

hoping for, and the 500cc twins were carried over almost unchanged, apart from the addition of indicators. The Bonneville, along with all BSA and Triumph 650 twins, did get more significant change in the form of an all-new frame, new forks, brakes, styling, and switchgear. But crucially, the engine and gearbox – the same pushrod vertical twin descended directly from the 1937 Speed Twin – carried on with very little change, though there was talk of an optional five-speed gearbox.

The new frame was a product of Umberslade Hall, with input from Dr Stephan Bauer, who had designed the Norton Commando's frame. Code named P39, it consisted of a thin-walled steel spine which contained the engine oil, doing away with a separate oil tank, and a duplex cradle. Of all-welded construction with no lugs, it was claimed to be stronger and lighter than its predecessors, while replacing both BSA and Triumph frames with one common item simplified production and brought economies of scale (at least, that was the theory). Using the main spine to hold the engine oil was new for a road bike – Rickman had done the same on its competition scramblers – though the disadvantage was a smaller, 4-pint capacity.

The new alloy forks were Ceriani-style with exposed stanchions, which looked up-to-date and proved comfortable, though without the protection of gaiters they did allow grit in to damage the oil seals and cause leaks. The new twin leading shoe front brake was housed in a distinctive conical alloy hub with a big forward-facing air scoop. It did look good, but like so much of the '71 Bonneville, brought problems of its own. The air scoop tended to take in rainwater as well as cooling air; the cam levers were too short, and the brake itself proved prone to fade under hard use. And it had to be kept well adjusted to be up to scratch.

What with the new forks and brakes, the '71 Bonneville looked quite different to the '70. In fact, the entire bike had been re-styled, with slimmer, squared-off sidepanels (made possible by the absence of an oil tank), skimpy mudguards, and fat, 4.00x18in rear wheel. All early bikes had the US-style fuel tank and high-rise bars, and the whole thing was clearly aimed at the sunny West Coast rather than the wetter climes of northern Europe.

It was in the style of the time, with a vaguely chopper-like look, but author Steve Wilson described the '71 bikes as, "a bit like a child's [or young American's] idea of a motorbike." Said long-time US Triumph dealer and speed record

1971-74: Fall from grace

Spine frame (on a later bike) showing the large oil-bearing spine – once the teething troubles were cured, it would remain part of the Bonneville to the very end.

As launched, the US-spec '71 Bonneville with the new frame, new front brake and indicators.

holder Bob Leppan: "As soon as I saw these photos [of the 1971 range] I knew we were in trouble … The one thing Triumph didn't have to change was the appearance of its motorcycles – that's why people bought Triumphs!"

The electrical system was modified to include indicators as standard, operated by new Lucas switchgear, and the headlamp lost its ammeter (a new-found confidence in Lucas electrics?). There were new instruments on the rubber-mounted bars.

And that was it, the result of two years' R&D, innumerable meetings, much investment, and 1200 modifications to the frame drawings alone. But if BSA/Triumph were expecting an instant rapturous reception, they were disappointed.

Jack Wilson of US Triumph dealer Big D Cycles was forthright (quoted in the book *Triumph Motorcycles in America*): "Nobody asked us dealers, or Triumph owners, if we wanted any of that stuff! If they'd just put a front disc brake on the old forks and kept the 1970 frame, fixed the oil leaks and a few other things, we couldn't have sold enough of 'em."

Months before the launch, there were doubts in the company at the highest level about the new range. The BSA board was given a preview of the proposed '71 range, and afterwards board member Jack Sangster asked Bert Hopwood what he thought of it, adding glumly, "I cannot think that these machines are going to be very successful." Hopwood's predictable riposte (in his book *Whatever Happened to the British Motorcycle Industry?*) was that Sangster should have voiced his doubts at board meetings "long ago while there was still time to do something about it."

The decision to stick with a drum front brake was especially puzzling. Honda had been offering an hydraulic front disc for two years, and it was rapidly becoming the must-have item on big bikes, yet Triumph's latest brake was a cable-operated drum!

These initial reactions to the '71 model launch were just the start of a disastrous 12

The Triumph Bonneville Bible

Was Triumph cutting its advertising budget? Low-key black and white ad from 1971, apparently pictured on the A45 a couple of miles from Meriden!

BSA Fury and near-identical Triumph Bandit were part of the new range, but never reached production.

months. Usually, production of the new model year would begin after the August summer holiday, and the finished drawings had to be received by the factory well beforehand so that it could make the tooling for any new parts (which in this case, was almost everything except the engine/gearbox). But by October, even as the new bikes were being unveiled at The Royal Lancaster, the drawings still hadn't arrived, and it was obvious that the '71 range was going to be late.

For Meriden, this meant three months of enforced idleness. The factory kept busy for a while by building up its entire stock of 1971 500cc twins, while Bonneville and Trophy engine/gearbox units were also assembled, and stacked up wherever there was space. But they soon ran out of parts, and as a result the assembly workers were kept on with nothing to do for those three months – though in the meantime they still had to be paid.

Some passed the time by playing chess (using oil pumps for pawns) but the end result was mounting frustration that they couldn't get on with the job. This had a particular impact at Meriden – which, of course, had been working at a pace for many years just to keep up with demand – and having nothing to do for three months was a shock that did nothing to improve faith in top management. A young welder named John Rosamond reported for work in mid-November for the first time, only to find he had nothing to do! (Rosamond, of course, went on to lead the Meriden workers' co-operative.)

Eventually, in November, the drawings arrived, and the factory had to get on with producing the jigs and tooling as fast as possible. It must have been a chaotic couple of months, in the midst of which Lionel Jofeh addressed a meeting in the Meriden canteen, not to explain why the drawings were late, or encourage the Meriden men in their vital task of getting the Bonnie into production, but to warn that any wage rises would have to be based on increased productivity, and if that didn't happen the factory would close! He clearly distrusted the workforce, thinking it would use this desperate situation to hold the company to ransom, but, according to John Rosamond, nothing could have been further from the truth.

Meanwhile, tooling was completed, the first new frames built – and now came the time bolt in a Bonneville engine for a pre-production test. It wouldn't fit, and one can only imagine the reaction in the factory when the news spread.

In fact, some ex-Triumph people, such as John Nelson, have drawn the conclusion that the new frame was never intended to fit the Triumph engine, and that there were contingency plans

1971-74: Fall from grace

to close Meriden and concentrate production at Small Heath.

Fortunately, Meriden was good at getting things done, though had to make eighteen changes to the cylinder head, rocker boxes and other parts before the engine would fit. This all took more time, and Bonneville production finally restarted just before Christmas 1970, late for the vital US selling season, which, on the East Coast, was quite short. All US Triumph dealers had to offer were the '71 500s, the Trident, and a single-cylinder 250. The Bonneville was the big seller, and that's what they didn't have.

Even when the production bikes finally arrived at dealers on both sides of the Atlantic, yet more problems became apparent, the first and most obvious of which was that the new frame was immensely tall, giving a seat height of over 34 inches! For those who did not have very long legs, this made the bike virtually unrideable unless a high kerb could be found to assist starting and stopping. BSA testers had pointed this out to Umberslade but had gone unheard.

Another crash programme had to be instigated, this time to reduce the seat height, and once again it was Meriden that took the lead. Doug Hele and Bert Hopwood cut the seat height by lowering the rear subframe mounts on the main spine, fitting shorter shocks and forks, a thinner seat and other parts. But this, too, took time, and wasn't finalised until April 1972.

The new frame had other troubles, too. In the production process, swarf collected in the oil bearing spine – obviously a disaster for any engine – and the factory began flushing out spines before bikes were shipped, which resolved that. The spine also proved prone to fracture, partly because of stress caused by the centre stand, which was mounted directly on the spine. A cure was concocted, but not before some frames had fractured, causing serious oil leaks. The oil-in-frame bikes (as they became known) also tended to run hot, partly because the oil reservoir was tucked away from any cooling breeze, and partly because, at 4-pint capacity, it was quite small (the old-style tank held 5 pints). The prototype spine had a larger capacity, but this was reduced when the filler point was moved from the steering head to just in front of the seat nose to combat oil frothing.

All-in-all, the first months of the 1971 range were a fiasco, but what did the press think? Well, surprisingly, quite well, certainly when it came to the Bonnie. The good news about that new frame (and there was some) was that it steered and handled very well. *Cycle World* tested a

The Bonneville for 1971 shared a brochure with the new 350s.

T120R Bonneville and, apart from criticising the high seat and the new Lucas switchgear (the blades were too short), was impressed, praising "... an excellent set of brakes," and "one of the best operating fork assemblies available." It continued that the engine "starts easily, vibrates only mildly, and has good power available through a wide rpm range."

Not every owner of a '71 Bonneville would have agreed, however, and warranty costs mounted alongside the problems with day-to-day running. As well as those frame oil leaks, the new forks also leaked, a bad batch of valve seats fell out when the engine was hot, and some batteries split or even blew up after Lucas supplied them with blocked breather holes. The road testers praised the low level of vibes, but judging by the fractures and breakages, these were still getting through to the machine.

These problems and the long delay in production meant that 1971 was a financial disaster for the company. Sales were lost due to the late arrival (BSA/Triumph's combined market share in the USA slumped to 6.9 per cent), and as the US selling season came to an end, 11,000 unwanted bikes still sat in warehouses. In July, the company announced a whopping loss of £3.3 million. Motorcycle production ceased at Small Heath (though it carried on building Trident engines) where nearly 3000 jobs were lost. Lionel Jofeh resigned (though not before ordering that the tooling for the new 350s be destroyed), as did Chairman Eric Turner and Peter Thornton, President of the US operation. BSA Inc continued with its lavish spending habits right to the end, typified by a race programme

The Triumph Bonneville Bible

Down-at-heel '71 Bonneville – front disc brake is non-standard.

Adspeak 1971

"The Legend! High performance twin cylinder twin carb engine, race bred and race proven. Ready for hard, fast riding anywhere. Rigid twin tube frame with large diameter top tube carrying oil."

Adspeak 1971

"1971 is a good year for Triumph followers! New machines with Triumph's race-winning flair for performance and handling. All with refinements gleaned from our racing success. That's the Triumph Power Plan for 1971.

"The Bonnie is a legend in its own time. Development has made this machine the world's most consistent production race victor for its class. Now that same development has produced an even better Bonneville. New brakes, a new spine frame (lightness with extreme rigidity), new competition-style frame for even better handling, straight handlebars, large tank, and other exciting features."

that cost $1 million for 1971. The triples did claim a 1-2-3 victory at Daytona, but it didn't come cheap, and cost money that BSA didn't have.

The company also pulled the plug on the new 350, as there weren't the funds to launch it. Ironically, the Triumph Bandit/BSA Fury was actually quite close to production, with some tooling ready, and the bikes had even featured in the 1971 brochures as production models. With the 350 dead, the old 500s looking outmoded and Trident sales disappointing, any chance of a recovery in 1972 rested with the 650cc twins – could the Bonneville do it?

1972

Models:	T120R Bonneville/T120RV Bonneville
UK price:	T120R – £569; T120RV – £629
From engine number:	HG30870
Tank colour:	Tiger Gold/White

If 1971 had been a disaster, an attempt to turn things around was made the following year. There was new blood at the top of the company with Lord Shawcross replacing Eric Turner as Chairman and ex-GKN man Brian Eustace taking over from Jofeh as MD. A new board brought in people with long experience of the motorcycle industry; notably Bert Hopwood in charge of engineering design. This new regime also inherited borrowings of £22 million, and it says much for the determination of its members that these had been halved by April 1973. Umberslade Hall was closed, and some non-motorcycle parts of the BSA empire were sold off, as were parts of the vast – and now rapidly emptying – Small Heath factory.

In the States, Dennis McCormack (who had headed TriCor in the early days) was brought back to head-up the operation, his first job being to clear the warehouses of leftover '71 bikes. He did make a start, although some 1971 and '72 bikes were still unsold into '73, by which time he had gone, replaced by one Dr Felix Kalinski. Kalinski had no motorcycle background, and at his interview admitted he knew nothing about bikes, but promised to become an expert in six months! He certainly managed to carry on the clearance of unsold stock, spending a lot of money on magazine ads and giving generous discounts (nearly 50 per cent) to dealers if they took old-spec machines. Dealers who off-loaded the most bikes received a trip for two to England and France – a hundred qualified!

In short, the company was having to spend money to save itself, and over £4 million of its

1971-74: Fall from grace

Ray Pickerell, Paul Smart and Percy Tait (L to R) lend weight to the Bonnie's racing pedigree in a 1972 ad.

1972 bikes held out some hope that Triumph might recover from the '71 debacle.

budget was devoted to the big task of factory reorganisation and rationalisation. Even in March of 1972 it was close to its £10 million overdraft limit – needing to make £1 million profit just to pay the interest – and hadn't broken even by July. The Meriden workforce, now making all of the company's bikes, didn't help by repeatedly disrupting production through strikes.

On the surface, it looked as if Lionel Jofeh's worst fears of workers holding the company to ransom because they thought it couldn't do without them were being realised. But it's also true that the Meriden workers had seen many years of flat-out production and profitable working – as far as they were concerned, the last eighteen months could just be a temporary blip. They certainly had a more determined streak than their cousins at Small Heath, who had voted overwhelmingly to accept redundancies rather than stage a sit-in or strike. Meriden production for 1972 was just 65 per cent of the target figure, but there's evidence that this wasn't all due to strikes. There were parts shortages, too, as Dennis Poore of NVT (see below) admitted when later asked why he had decided to close the Meriden factory. This, he said, was down to management's inability to properly organise parts supply.

Meanwhile, the immediate job was to make the Bonneville saleable again. Coopers, the company's management consultants, had recommended that the Bonnie be enlarged to a 750 as quickly as possible. From a marketing point of view, this made a lot of sense – the 650 class was rapidly being overtaken in sales by the 750s, and a 750cc Bonneville would have a better chance of competing. Advocates pointed out that there were already big-bore aftermarket kits on both sides of the Atlantic, and that, for years, tuners in the USA had been boring out Bonnevilles to 750cc and winning flat-track races with them.

But Bert Hopwood was having none of it, and one of his first actions as the new engineering chief was to put a hold on the Bonnie 750's imminent production. "I felt like a criminal," he wrote later, "in vetoing the mass production schedule," adding that it made him unpopular with a lot of people. But he explained that the 750 conversion was untested (there was no real prototype), and if any lesson had been learnt from 1971, it was that new bikes should not go into production without thorough testing. As for the American 750s, these performed well on race tracks, but at the cost of frequent crankshaft breakages – a road-going Bonnie 750 would have to be made of sterner stuff.

While development of the 750 went on, just as urgent was the need to resolve the problems that arose from the 1971 'new range.' Fractured frames – and resultant oil leaks – were attributed to the stress of operating the centre stand, and a beefier mounting for the stand to pivot on cured that. The sky-high seat was a serious detriment to showroom sales, but the lowered version was finally in production by April 1972. In fact, Hopwood maintained that the lowered bike was ready to go over six months earlier, but a BSA management meeting voted against it. Most of the folk at the meeting, according to

The Triumph Bonneville Bible

1972, and already a legend – according to the copywriters.

> Bonneville ... the most famous Triumph of them all.
>
> ## Bonneville 650
>
> The legend. The world's most consistent production race winner of its class, race bred, race proven. The high performance twin-cylinder, twin-carb engine is tough and rugged, ready for hard fast riding anywhere.
>
> Competition-type forks, enormously strong frame are two features of a bike that has proved its worth time after time. Now in new colours for '72 with polished forks.
>
> *Bonneville is available in large tank (4 gall.) as main illustration or small tank (3 gall.) specification – shown (right).*

New colours for 1972.

Whatever else was said about the oil-bearing frame, it did deliver good handling.

Hopwood, "... were trying to learn the ABC of the world of motorcycles."

Because of the urgency, it was decided to introduce fixes throughout 1972, as and when they were ready rather than wait, and package everything together for '73. Late in 1971, a UK-spec 4-gallon fuel tank – less elegant than the 2.5-gallon US tank, but more practical – had been introduced, and from early 1972 had lower UK bars and kneegrips to go with it. Later in the year, a slimline 2.1-gallon US tank was introduced. Gradually, Triumphs were regaining the classic good looks they'd lost in 1971.

The '71 front mudguard stays were prone to fracture, so in '72 the mudguard received a central reinforcing stay. A new cylinder head followed which replaced the four rocker box inspection caps with a pair of larger flat covers. These made tappet adjustment much easier,

1971-74: Fall from grace

though reduced sales of the old circular covers as spares, which had a tendency to vibrate loose. The exhaust pipes were now push-fit directly into the head, rather than over stubs, though they were less secure and more likely to pop out.

A five-speed gearbox became standard on the Trident, and officially available as an option on the Bonneville since June 1971, though in practice was only available later. Costing an extra £60 in the UK ($200 in the States) it was based on a cluster developed for racing by Rod Quaife, and fitted into the existing box with only minor modification. Some thought that the five-speeder was simply pandering to fashion, and that four speeds were perfectly adequate for a 650 twin. For a mildly-tuned 650 out of the 1950s, perhaps, but the new five ratios were well chosen and suited the Bonneville; closer ratios also meant there was less need to rev out the engine in each gear. At the same time, a new, three-ball clutch lever was fitted.

As well as it worked, even the five-speed box wasn't without its problems. The layshaft first and second gears had not been carburized, making the teeth very brittle and prone to fail, the chips of steel being ground through the gearbox works and causing a lot more damage – they could even blow a hole in the casing. Sometimes gearboxes even failed as the new bike was ridden away from the dealership for the first time.

According to the authors of *Triumph Motorcycles in America,* Lindsay Brooke and David Gaylin, the Americans sorted out their own fix: with 1000 five-speed 650s sitting in warehouses, they needed to. Makeshift assembly lines were set up at both West and East operations, with the offending gears removed, the replacements heat-treated and carburized by a specialist in Los Angeles before fitting. Meriden, now reacting more quickly to problems with the corporate committee system gone, also introduced carburizing for those gears.

The Motor Cycle tested a T120RV Bonneville (as the five-speeder was known) in August 1972, and, contrary to earlier tests of the Bonnie's broad spread of power, thought that this one only really delivered beyond 5000rpm. The official limit wasn't much higher up the range at 6700rpm, but this particular bike was clearly free-revving and undergeared, since with wind assistance it pulled 7700rpm in top gear for a best top speed of 117mph. It was a 2000-mile test – plenty of distance to show up any flaws – and there were some. Testers complained about vibration (an exhaust pipe bracket fractured), and oil consumption of 160 miles per pint. Even with the flatter, swept-back bars, they didn't like the riding position (both bars and footrests were too far forward), but loved the handling and poise delivered by the frame and forks – Umberslade had got some of the basics right after all.

The Motor Cycle of course, was one of Britain's longest-running bike magazines, but the new monthly magazine *Bike* was a different kettle of fish, regarded as an irreverent upstart (in its own eyes, anyway), and very different to the gentlemanly motorcycle press of old. *Bike* also tested a Bonnie – in the dark time of late 1971 – but wasn't that much more critical than the mainstream press, despite having the indicators fail after 150 miles, followed by the taillight and pilot light bulbs. The magazine found the switchgear "inefficient," and thought the front brake good, though requiring "constant adjustment." Overall, *Bike* appeared impressed, liking the handling and "a spirit of pervasive, effortless power," plus a quality finish. And, it was "also better than the good old Bonneville you've always wanted."

The Bonnie might be outmoded, but Triumph could always point to its racing record, as this ad did.

1973

Models:	T120R Bonneville/T120RV Bonneville/T140R Bonneville/T140RV Bonneville
UK price:	T120 – £434.53; T140 – £625.34
From engine number:	T120 – JH15366; T140 – JH15435
Tank colour:	Hi-fi Vermillion/Gold

In the dark days of late 1971, Bert Hopwood had come up with a three-stage, product-based plan to revive Triumph as a serious motorcycle manufacturer. The first stage was to correct the worst mistakes of '71 – the high seat, the frame troubles, the many details that were wrong – and by mid-'72, this had been achieved. The second stage was to update the bikes with a front disc brake and standard five-speed gearbox, and

The Triumph Bonneville Bible

Standard five-speed gearbox, front disc brake and (almost) 750cc – this is actually a '76/'77 bike with left-foot gearchange.

Stage 3 never happened, however, because it required an investment of many millions which the company did not have. Stage 2 did, though, as stated previously. Hopwood – along with others at Meriden – was reluctant to produce a 750 Bonneville, thinking it a step too far for the already vibration-prone 650. Most of the pressure to do this came from the USA, where the 750 class was increasingly dominant; Europe, of course, was going the same way. As a sign of the times, 750s now had their own racing class – 750 Production. Honda, Harley (if you counted the 883cc Sportster), Norton, Suzuki: all offered 750s, and Yamaha was about to join them. The Trident was a 750, too, but sales were hampered by its low production and high price. What US dealers wanted was the Bonneville's classic looks and relative affordability with a 750 badge.

Doug Hele had his own answer in the form of an all-new 750 twin, with single overhead cam and a balancer linkage to iron out vibration. It was

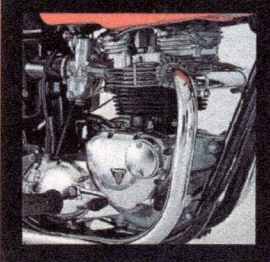

Scratch, tour, overtake trucks: adaptability seems to be the message of this 1973 brochure.

bore out the Bonnie to 750. The final stage, envisaged for 1975 on, was a completely new generation of bike that would share many components to reduce costs. This modular range would cover everything from a 200cc single to a 1250cc V5, and would finally replace the ageing Bonneville and Trident.

a far better long-term solution than a bored-out Bonneville, but it only existed on paper, and in any case the company had neither the time nor the money to take it any further. The only practical solution was to get on with a Bonneville 750.

"It was a horrible form of engineering" said John Barton, who worked on the project. "Our

1971-74: Fall from grace

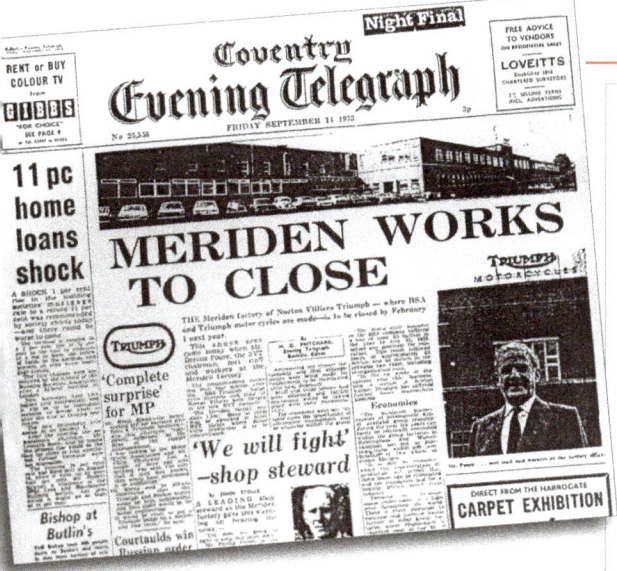

Far left: Shock headline – many Meriden workers first learnt of the planned factory closure from the front page of their local paper.

Left: Tax changes (the introduction of VAT) allowed a price cut in the UK during 1973.

hands were tied in so many ways." The first prototypes would run to over 120mph, but it wasn't long before crankshafts began to break and the engine had to be de-tuned so that its bottom end (designed for a 650) could cope. So milder camshafts were fitted and the E3134 cam profile finally abandoned. As a result, the Bonneville's character changed from a raucous sportster that loved to rev to a more laid-back bike with an emphasis on mid-range torque.

Fortunately, the budget did run to some strengthening, and the 750 benefited from a stronger triplex primary drive and a heavier-duty timing side main bearing; thicker con-rods and shorter, more solid cylinder block. The new block also featured better lubrication, thanks to bigger internal oilways to take advantage of a larger oil pump. The new cylinder head that was part of the package was held down by ten studs instead of nine. There were stronger

Final spec of the old regime: five-speed T140V, but still with right-foot gearchange.

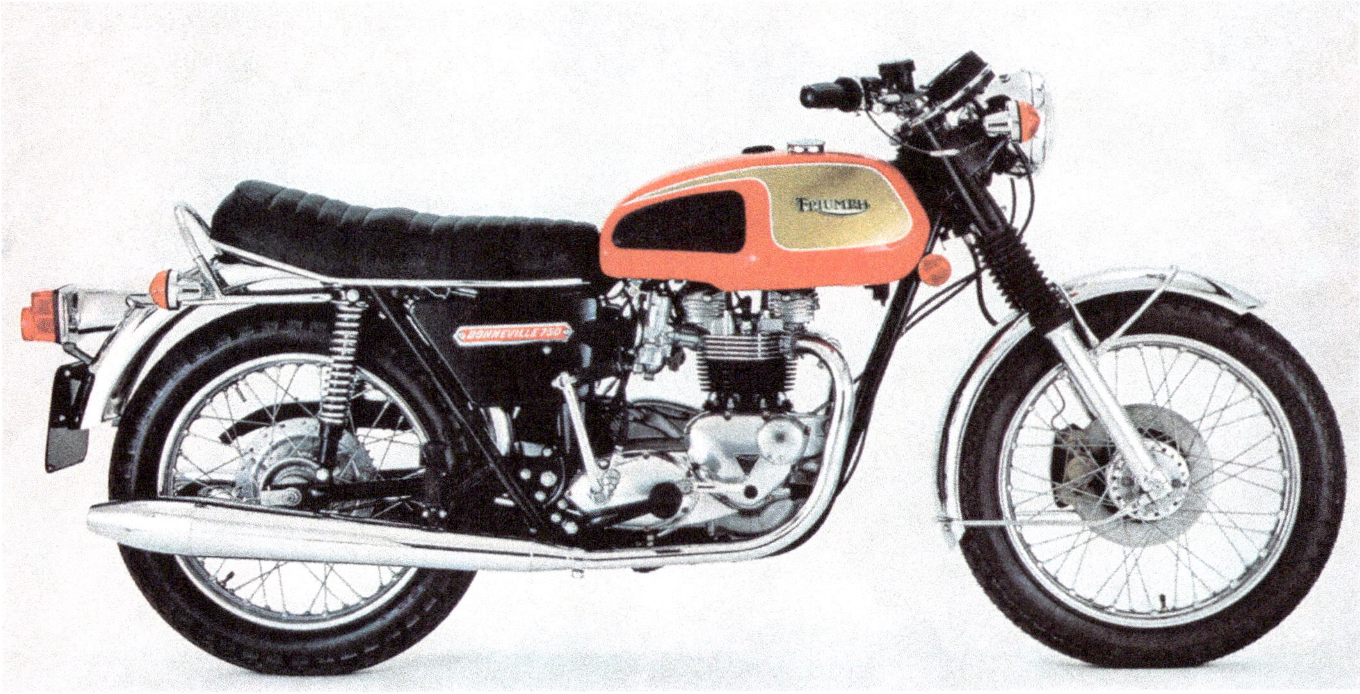

By now, Bonnie sales were attributable to its 'legend' status.

USA was actually short in 1973. In the July 1973 issue of *Motorcycle Week* Doug Hele was interviewed about the new 750, and made it clear that this was a stopgap. "One can only stretch a design so far," he said. "As far as I see it, to get still more performance is going to become increasingly difficult and costly … We have new designs on the way, but the twin is likely to be with us for two years ahead." Little did he know that Meriden would be building Bonnie 750s for another 10 years!

The five-speed gearbox was standard on the 750, but now came with a new high gear and layshaft assemblies. The T150 Trident camplate and indexing plunger were adopted in lieu of the tricky-to-replace leaf index spring.

Compared to the bigger engine other changes were minor, but the Bonneville did finally get the front disc brake it needed, a 10-inch Lockheed item with opposed pistons. The oil filler cap now had a dipstick – with that marginal 4-pint capacity, it was more important than ever to keep the oil topped up.

And there were further moves to reinstate Meriden, rather than Umberslade, styling. More substantial chrome mudguards also reverted to 1970-type brackets, the headlight was closer to the classic teardrop shape, and gaiters returned to the forks of UK bikes. The alloy was polished (not painted) on the rear hub and rear light mounting, and the 4-gallon UK fuel tank was lightened up with two-tone 'comma' panel.

By and large, the road testers liked the 750. Vibration always got a big mention now, and *The Motor Cycle's* test bike lost its left-hand front indicator, while the numberplate fractured. *Motorcycle Mechanics* complained about mechanical noise as well as vibration, and noted that the Bonneville lacked Japanese convenience features such as an electric start, helmet lock, and even a seat lock. But what it agreed on was that the 750 handled just as well as its little brother, and loved the recipe of extra torque in a package that weighed about the same. The single disc brake always came in for praise, and all of the testers commented on the absence of oil leaks and clear improvement in quality control.

So, having begged for a Bonneville 750, what did the Americans think of it, and its single-carb equivalent, the Tiger 750? *Cycle World* hated the Lucas switchgear and noted more vibes that you'd find on a Japanese four or Ducati V-twin. Ironically, it didn't like the US high-rise bars either, but that's what the customers wanted. Everything else, it loved. The T140V was

clutch springs, and gearing was raised to take advantage of the higher torque, not to mention keep revs down at cruising speeds. Even so, the capacity increase came in two cautious stages, launched as 724cc in September 1972, and out to 747cc four months later.

The result still wasn't a serious competitor to the modern 750s, but it was close enough to please Triumph aficionados. Knowing their market, the American dealers had been right – the Bonnie 750 sold well, and supply in the

1971-74: Fall from grace

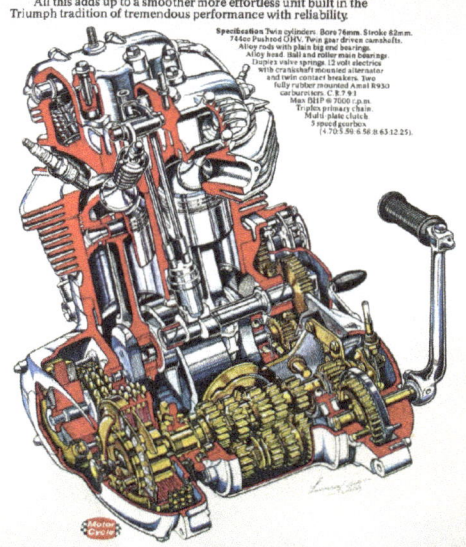

Far left: Overhead cam Trident was another early 1970s prototype that never made it into the showroom.

Left: 'Big Bonnie' equalled the 750: a marketing necessity.

decidedly faster than the 650, running a 13.65sec quarter-mile at nearly 94mph. Interestingly, the Tiger was just as quick, confirming that the new, softer Bonneville didn't really take advantage of its twin carburettors – the old single-carb Trophy had never been far behind the 650cc Bonneville, but now there was virtually nothing in it. There was more good news, according to *Cycle World* in the shape of better quality control, and "... one of the best balanced chassis available anywhere."

Best of all, the Bonneville had lost its price premium. A better dollar/sterling exchange rate and a more aggressive pricing strategy meant that the new 750 cost about the same as the old four-speed 650. It was the same in Britain, where the bike cost a few pounds less than the 1972 650 five-speed. The 650 was still available in '73, and a bargain at £434, but were there any takers? True, some still regretted the move to 750, and a deputation of dealers actually visited Lord Shawcross, asking him to bring back the 650. But, in practice, the 750 was here to stay

Forward to the future, but could the Bonnie hang on until the new generation was ready?

Adspeak 1973

"When you buy a Triumph you open up a whole new chapter in your life. Because Triumph make big bikes. Nothing else. Bikes you can get your teeth into.

"Bikes that perform, handle and respond like nothing else on the road. That's why we call it the big ride. "And here's how we do it.

"When we make a motorcycle a lot goes into it. A lifetime of engineering skill. We've been making motorcycles longer than anyone else in the world. Look at the very first one we made. This gives us the right to know what we're doing. In design, in development, in manufacture, in assembly, in testing. "Everything must be right. We think we owe you that."

The Triumph Bonneville Bible

and would survive until the very end of Meriden Triumph.

1974

Models:	T120V Bonneville/T120RV Bonneville/T140V Bonneville/T140RV Bonneville
UK price:	Unavailable
From engine number:	GJ55101
Tank colour:	T120 – Purple/White; T140 – Cherokee Red/White

1973, for all its difficulties, had been a year of continued recovery for Triumph and the Bonneville. The BSA parent group was still heavily in debt, but this had been drastically reduced, and the 750cc Bonneville, despite the misgivings of many at Meriden, had been well received. In fact, it was once again in demand in the USA, and Triumph dealers found themselves still with unsold stocks of '71/'72 bikes, and customers clamouring for the '73s. The exception was the TR5T Adventurer, a trail bike based on the 500cc twin, which was not a success.

Bert Hopwood was quite enthused by the new regime, as he later recounted in an interview: "[We had] a marvellous team ... Brian Jones, Chief Designer, Hele in Development, Ernie Webster, Horace Watson and Harry Summers, all assistant Chief Designers in charge of a particular section, and a tremendous stylist, Jack Wickes ... I believe they all felt that, at last, they were going to make something of it. The people who had brought us to this unhealthy state had all gone ... we had got plans and a board that would come round and have a look."

The plans Hopwood referred to were his modular range, the ambitious scheme for an all-new line-up of bikes which would take over from the Bonneville and Trident. The engines for the new range consisted of 200cc, single cylinder modules (stretchable to 250cc), which could be doubled up (and tripled, and quadrupled), so a common cylinder could be built up as a 400cc twin, or 750cc triple, or that 1250cc V5. It would be air-cooled, with a single overhead cam and two or four valves per cylinder, all based on modern, straightforward practice.

The engineering department never got as far as building prototypes, but some of the individual features were built and tested on their own. The rear transmission, for example, was drawn up as a swingarm with integral oilbath chaincase on one side, and quickly detachable wheel on the other. This set-up was built into a Bonneville, and due to begin testing in July

Hundreds of Bonnies like this were trapped at Meriden when the blockade was imposed.

1973. Work also continued on developing a rotary-engined bike, and £129,000 was spent on licensing fees to NSU – that machine would eventually come to light as the rotary Norton of the 1980s. On Hopwood's timetable, this new range would be ready for production in three years, with the old Bonneville phased out in 1976.

It was a hugely ambitious scheme, but one that was well thought through, and offered the prospect of BSA/Triumph surviving as a mass production manufacturer. The alternative appeared to be struggling on with the old Bonneville for as long as this could find buyers and meet emissions and noise legislation. Unfortunately, for the new range plan to move any further than the drawing board and limited rig testing, it would need a large injection of cash which the company didn't have.

Lord Shawcross decided to apply to the Department of Trade and Industry (DTI) for help. Writing this in the early 21st century, when free market economics is resurgent (though facing a major economic crisis), it's easy to forget that, back in the seventies, it was accepted that governments had a duty to lend failing businesses a hand. With the correct investment, it was thought, the state could save jobs. The philosophy was not one of subsidy without end, but short-term finance to enable companies to stand on their own feet, as BSA/Triumph would discover. British Leyland was just one of the highest profile recipients of state aid (and there were many others). At the time, there was much talk of 'lame ducks' which should simply be allowed to fail; never mind the consequences of mass job losses. But to take British Leyland as an example, the company carried on, returned to private ownership, and survived in slimmed-down form for another 30 years.

By comparison with a giant like Leyland, Lord Shawcross' request for help was comparatively modest, and at first the reaction was positive. In fact, the DTI indicated that up to £20 million would be available, but for the whole motorcycle industry, not just BSA/Triumph. In effect, this meant Norton Villiers, the only other major survivor of a once-huge industry.

This is where Dennis Poore comes into the picture. Poore was Chairman of Manganese Bronze Holdings, a group of engineering companies that had taken over the bankrupt AMC group (including Norton) back in 1966. Under his leadership, Norton had made a success of the Commando, whose rubber-mounted engine gave a smoother ride than any other British parallel twin. Behind the scenes, Norton suffered from many of the same problems as Triumph – a lack of investment over many years, and making the best of an ageing design. The company had made a small profit in 1972, but this had fallen into loss by early '74, as the Commando began to suffer from more modern competition. It also made far fewer bikes than Meriden, averaging 10,000 a year, and taken together, BSA/Triumph had between four and eight times the capacity.

But in government circles Norton was considered a successful private enterprise. As author Steve Wilson has pointed out, Dennis Poore's background probably helped plant that idea. He was of the Establishment, ex-Eton and Cambridge, a merchant banker who could speak the same language as Conservative politicians and top civil servants.

So when the DTI considered Lord Shawcross' request, it said yes, but only if BSA/Triumph merged with Norton-Villiers with Poore as Chairman. It soon became clear to Shawcross that this was the only game in town – Triumph could not survive without an injection of funds from outside, and this was the only way to get it. He was already being accused of dragging his feet, so the BSA board agreed and the merger was, in Wilson's words, "hustled through."

Secret negotiations got under way, and by March 1973 the two sides had a draft agreement. But on March 14, just as the proposals were being printed, there was a run on BSA Group shares. A Stock Exchange broker, probably acting on a leak from the negotiations, staged a 'bear raid,' that is, he encouraged mass sales of BSA shares which he could then buy at a low price, and later sell to make a fat profit. Amoral, perhaps, when businesses and jobs were at stake, but that's the way the Stock Exchange worked in the seventies.

As an experienced financier, Dennis Poore immediately used the plunging BSA share price as a lever to renegotiate his terms. Now, Manganese Bronze would buy BSA's profitable non-motorcycle businesses (which included Carbodies, maker of the London black cab) at the knockdown price of £3.5 million. The DTI approved, and the newly-merged Norton-Villiers-Triumph was to receive £4.8 million in state aid. This was far less than the £20 million originally mooted, but was the maximum available without needing a debate in Parliament.

It soon became clear that Dennis Poore's vision of NVT was very different from that of the BSA Group. Hopwood's detailed plans for a new generation of bikes was dismissed as too

The Triumph Bonneville Bible

Confidence? You'd need plenty to corner like that on wet cobblestones ... even on a Bonnie.

ambitious, but Norton had nothing comparable on the stocks. Cosworth, the racing engine concern, had designed a water-cooled, twin-cylinder engine with which Norton planned to go racing. There were less definite ideas for it to power a road bike, a four-cylinder engine possibly being used instead.

Poore was also convinced that NVT's three factories – Wolverhampton, Small Heath and Meriden – were one too many, and on a visit to Meriden on 14 September, announced that the Triumph factory would close, with Bonneville production moving to Small Heath. This was a reversal of BSA Group policy, which was running down Small Heath to concentrate work at the more productive Meriden.

1971-74: Fall from grace

'When you buy a Triumph, you open up a whole new chapter ...' – aspirational words from an American brochure.

There was good economic reasoning behind closing one of the three factories. Selling one site (valuable in the crowded West Midlands) would drastically cut costs and bring in another injection of cash to fund future plans. On the other hand, choosing Meriden for closure made little sense. It was efficient, and contained many highly skilled people who had a real loyalty to Triumph, plus there was room to expand on its 22-acre site if need be. It's more likely that Poore was influenced in this decision by Meriden's volatile industrial relations, which he didn't want as part of NVT.

The reaction of the Meriden workforce was immediate. The unions set up a partial blockade of the factory, which soon turned into a complete lock-up with nothing allowed out. This was serious for Poore – not only did the supply of Bonnevilles cease (there were 2650 machines trapped inside), but Meriden held all the tooling and drawings for the Trident, and Poore could not go ahead with his plan to restart Trident production at Small Heath without them.

Either stubborn or determined (take your pick) he spent £500,000 on having new tooling made so that Trident production could restart. In any case, it went both ways, with Small Heath still holding some tooling needed for the Bonneville.

In theory, the Meriden pickets (well-organised on a round-the-clock rota) were acting illegally, and Poore could apply for a legal writ, backed by the police, to take back the tooling and unsold bikes. In practice, the DTI discouraged him in this, while the Meriden men were supported by local MPs Leslie Huckfield and Geoffrey Robinson, and (after the new Labour government came to power) new Trade and Industry Minister Tony Benn. Negotiations dragged on into 1974, and a plan emerged that NVT would pay the Triumph workers' redundancy money, which they would then use to buy the factory from NVT, forming a workers' co-operative. The co-op would go back to building Bonnevilles, which would all be sold through NVT.

Tony Benn was central to the whole idea, throwing his ministerial weight behind it and assuring Dennis Poore that more government

The Triumph Bonneville Bible

T120V in modern clothes, but the 650cc Bonneville was nearing the end.

money could be forthcoming to support a three-factory plan.

Meanwhile, the Meriden factory ticked over, surviving on contributions from well-wishers – Chrysler car workers paid the electricity bill after NVT had the supply cut off – and there was even development work going on with the Bonneville. US legislation would require a left-foot gearchange from 1975, and a Bonnie was converted inside the factory. With no road insurance, tester Chuck Knight was restricted to the Meriden car park, in which he managed to cover 11,000 miles and make 93,000 gearchanges! The new system worked.

Examples like that illustrate the sheer determination of those from the Meriden workforce who stayed (many left to find other jobs) to secure a future for the factory. But there was some destructive behaviour as well. Long-time Meriden employee Hughie Hancox, who came back to the plant to clear his office, found that his riding kit and tools had been stolen. Down in the Service Repair Shop, fuel tanks, forks and mudguards were being smashed, apparently for the hell of it. And of the many finished bikes sitting in the factory, some were left outside, exposed to the winter weather. After years of anger and frustration, some were evidently taking the opportunity to get their own back, still seeing Meriden as part of NVT, and not their own future.

After 13 months of negotiations, another General Election in October 1974 returned Labour with an increased majority, which strengthened the co-op's hand. Benn agreed that Meriden would receive just under £5 million in state aid, mostly in the form of a loan which was expected to be repaid. Meanwhile, between July and November '74, Meriden's doors were opened to allow out some Bonnevilles to be sold by NVT (engine numbers JJ58080 to KJ53067 (T120) and KJ59160 to NJ60037).

But resentment was building at NVT, where it was feared that Benn would not support both

1971-74: Fall from grace

the co-op (which chimed with his political ideas) and the private enterprise of NVT.

All this uncertainty – with, at best, just a trickle of machines coming through – was a disaster for Triumph dealers around the world. Many, having nothing else to sell, faced bankruptcy, and 68 US dealers gave up their franchise in November 1974 alone.

Meanwhile, those in the factory still worked on developing the Bonneville, in the expectation that production would restart. As well as the left-foot gearchange, the Bonnie's compression ratio was reduced to 7.9:1 (8.6:1 was still an option in the UK; standard in the USA). The rocker box fixings were improved (two extra screws and better gaskets); the oil pressure release valve received a finer mesh filter gauze, and the oil pressure indicator switch was new. There were other minor changes, but the most noticeable was the new-shape silencers on UK bikes. And for the first time, the US-spec Bonnie, with its high bars and teardrop tank, was offered on the home market.

But all of this would be for nought if an agreement could not be reached with NVT. Dennis Poore thought keeping Meriden open made the whole industry unviable, as it would absorb government funding that should have gone to NVT. The unions at Small Heath and Wolverhampton were also against the idea – the blockade had prevented them restarting Trident production, and Poore's plan would have transferred Bonneville production (far greater than either Commando or Trident) to Small Heath. And since Meriden was still NVT's property, the co-op could not go ahead without the company's say-so.

In the end, Tony Benn and Bob Wright (convenor of the shipbuilding and engineering unions) managed to break the impasse. Wright persuaded the Small Heath shop stewards to withdraw their objection to the co-op, which they did by Christmas 1974. NVT's management needed a bigger stick, and Tony Benn was holding it. Like Meriden, the company was overwhelmingly dependent on exports.

Desperately short of cash (it made a loss of nearly £3.7 million in the year to July 1974), it could only ship bikes abroad with the support of the government's Export Credit Guarantee, a widespread practice, offered by many governments, to aid exports. The state would underwrite the value of the goods, guaranteeing to pay for them if the overseas customer defaulted. NVT had been promised £8 million of Export Credit Guarantee, but now Tony Benn would not release it unless Poore agreed to the Meriden plan. Faced with growing stocks of Tridents and Commandos, the NVT boss had no choice but to agree.

Finally, in March 1975, it was all made public. The co-op received a loan and grant of just under £5million, £3.9 million of which went straight to NVT as payment for the factory, tooling and work in progress. So Meriden was now independent of NVT and back in business, but it was hardly a golden dowry for the co-op, which faced the reality of running a 22-acre site, persuading component suppliers that it was a good risk, and supporting a payroll of 700 people. In the memorable words of Geoffrey Robinson, who would become one of the co-op's strongest supporters, "It was like rescuing a drowning man in the middle of a lake and leaving him up to his neck in quicksand." Still, the new venture had £1million in working capital and a plan to make over 200 bikes a week. Meriden Triumph, the co-op era, had begun.

Visit Veloce on the web – www.velocebooks.com
Details of all books • Special offers • New book news • Gift vouchers

5

1975-78: Yes, we can

1975

Model:	T140 Bonneville
UK price:	Unavailable
From engine number:	DK 61000
Tank colour:	T120 – Purple/White; T140

Nineteen seventy-five was a year in limbo for the Bonneville. Because of the turmoil at Meriden, the 1974 bikes had only very slight changes compared to those of '73, and there were no changes at all for '75. All the blockaded factory could do was assemble batches of machines from parts already sitting on the shelf.

Production had restarted in a small way in February 1974, in anticipation of the agreement between NVT and Tony Benn, but didn't officially get going until March 10, a day after the agreement was announced and the 18-month blockade finally lifted. Both 650cc T120s and 750cc T140s were built (though mostly the latter), and they made up the Bonneville's shortest ever model year, which finished in June '75. All of them were 1974-spec machines. Through February and March, the work mostly consisted of completing assembly of unfinished bikes, but on April 9, the first Bonneville wholly built by the co-op (engine number DK 61000) left the production line.

On June 25, the last 1975 bike was completed, the final T120 having engine number NJ 600070 and the last T140, EK 62239. A couple of weeks later, the first 1976 Bonneville, complete with that left-foot gearchange developed in the midst of the blockade, was ready for dispatch.

In July, *Cycle World* decided to run one of those mega-tests that magazines sometimes get round to organising. In this case, it wanted to find the best tourer on the market, putting ten of them together for ten weeks. The latest T140V Bonneville was pitted against the Honda CB750, Harley-Davidson FLH, BMW R75, Suzuki GT750, Yamaha TX750, Norton Commando 850, Kawasaki Z1, Moto Guzzi 850, and Triumph Trident T150V. It was a mammoth affair, all the test bikes covering at least 1500 miles under 12 different riders, taking in the Sierra Nevadas, Death Valley and downtown Los Angeles, as well as a complete performance test.

And what did the magazine find? Well, the Harley was a letdown and "the testers were woefully disappointed," while the Honda was "the great machine for the basic American rider." The verdict on the R75 was unsurprising: "No one can deny the adaptability of the BMW for touring." The Z1 had "shattering but controllable power, immaculate construction, engineering excellence," and the Moto Guzzi was uneven: "... bulletproof engine, shaft drive, superb comfort ... lumpy performance, cumbersome controls." The Commando obviously impressed, "... an enthusiast's tourer ... spirit without complexity, smoothness without complication, sophistication without mystery." Suzuki's GT750 was the only two-stroke, and was thought an ideal tourer, "... ox-strong engine performance ... amazing engine dependability and a totally unique touring experience." The Trident was

1975-78: Yes, we can

Some 1974/'75 Bonnevilles escaped the factory blockade.

Early 1970s instruments on this 1975-registered T140V.

Left: US-style Bonnies were now available in the UK as well.

really far too sporty – "less of a long distance tourer than the others" – and it was telling what was said about the Yamaha TX750, a vertical-twin with balance shafts, electric start and overhead camshafts: "Never in the history of motorcycling has a vertical twin four-stroke of such sophistication been available." Interestingly, the TX, though it made more power than the Bonneville, was slower and far heavier. The bike also suffered from serious reliability problems in its first year, showing that the Japanese weren't infallible after all.

By contrast, the Triumph's assessment was mixed: "Rock-steady consistency with Triumph's most famous traits, good and bad. Though not best at any one thing, the Bonnie has so many close top placings that the potential for a really great sporting machine is obviously inherent in the collective make-up. All it would take is the loving care of an enthusiast."

The T140 was praised for its handling: the lightest bike on test it offered the second best fuel consumption, plus fine brakes. On the other hand it was only midfield on performance, with a 14.01sec standing quarter, and reading between the lines it would need a good dollop of TLC. Oh, and it used a whole four quarts of oil on test, even more than the two-stroke Suzuki!

You could tell that the testers had a soft spot for the Bonnie, mentioning its sporting heritage and the fact that it remained *the* vertical twin for most American riders. The trouble was, buying into that needed some commitment from the rider, certainly more than if they had bought a Honda.

Meanwhile, back in the Midlands, the remainder of 1975 was to be an exciting – if challenging – year for the Meriden co-op, but NVT fared badly. Only two months after Meriden restarted production, there was a cabinet reshuffle, and Tony Benn was replaced by Eric Varley. The co-op had never enjoyed 100 per cent support within the Labour government, and there's little doubt that Eric Varley would not have supported the plan as strongly as Benn had, if at all. He was also disinclined to help NVT. Dennis Poore had been calling for a far greater government investment – he thought £30-£40 million was needed – but Varley's response was to withdraw NVT's vital Export Credit Guarantee, and in this he was supported by the department's civil servants, who had never backed the co-op idea.

This signalled the end of NVT as anything more than a low-volume manufacturer. Small Heath, the Experimental Department at Kitts Green (to which Doug Hele had moved) and the Norton factory at Wolverhampton closed. The Wolverhampton workforce attempted a Meriden-style sit-in, but without a Tony Benn to champion their cause, this came to nothing. This wasn't quite the end of the NVT story, however, as the government did rescue it from complete oblivion in December 1975, allowing it to continue on a small-scale, assembling mopeds and 125/175cc trail bikes from imported components, eventually launching the rotary-engined Norton that BSA/Triumph had been working on back in 1972/73.

Eric Varley's decision was based in large part on a report on the prospects of the British motorcycle industry by the Boston Consulting Group, commissioned by Tony Benn in March and published in July. It was a damning take on a once-proud industry, and not for nothing were the authors known as the 'Boston Stranglers' at NVT. Dennis Poore disputed some of the figures (notably stocks of unsold Commandos and Tridents, and future sales) but the Boston report was a very thorough appraisal of what was left of the industry in 1974/75, when it sold 20,000 bikes and Honda sold two million, and it's worth looking a little more closely at what the findings were.

Triumph, BSA and Norton had suffered a catastrophic collapse of market share in just a few years. In the USA in 1969, the British held 49 per cent of the big bike market which, within four years, had plummeted to just 9 per cent. The sheer speed of this collapse seems astonishing, but the report made clear that the seeds had been sown many years before. The British industry had concentrated on short-term profits. Faced with small, newly competitive Japanese bikes, rather than attempt to compete it had retreated, abandoning first the moped class, then the 250s, then the 350s, then the 500s, and so on. The superbike (750cc+) market had become, in the words of the report, "... the final refuge." Shrinking markets meant shrinking profits, until it was impossible for the industry to invest on the scale needed to match Japanese productivity.

Even now, the report makes for depressing reading, sprinkled with phrases such as, "fundamentally uncompetitive ... low and stagnant production volumes ... mostly old, general purpose, fairly labour intensive equipment." Abandoning the small bikes market was "a fundamental strategic error." Honda and the rest had large, well-equipped R&D centres employing 800 to 1300 people apiece – the entire British industry could muster just a hundred R&D workers. The Japanese were more productive and at a far lower cost, and this wasn't due to low wages, as the report pointed out that Japanese labour costs had actually been higher than British ones for several years. Put all that together and it seemed that BSA et al were a commercial basket case bereft of investment, outdated in product, plant and working practices.

However, the report wasn't completely doom-laden: the motorcycle industry could be revived, it said, and laid out three alternative strategies for doing so, all of them based on a new 'family' of bikes, with interchangeable components as advocated by Bert Hopwood a few years earlier.

The first option was the low-volume one, building 15-20,000 bikes a year which would sell for a 30-40 per cent premium over equivalent Japanese machines. This new family would be 750cc/1000cc bikes only, and investment would be minimised by sticking to labour-intensive production. The second option sought to follow

1975-78: Yes, we can

the BMW model, restricted to two bikes (750 and 1000) still but with more capital-intensive production to produce 35,000 bikes a year, the higher volume production savings allowing a lower price differential to Japanese offerings. Finally, the most ambitious option was to go straight back into mass production, investing heavily in modern tooling to make 70,000 bikes (divided between 500, 750 and 1000cc models), which would cost only 10-15 per cent more than equivalent Japanese machines.

It all sounded great until one looked at the costs. The first option, estimated the report, would require an investment of £4million. The second would need £23million and the mass production option £37million. If development work began now, the new family of bikes would be ready in 1979, and the industry would incur heavy losses in the meantime. Take all that into account, and any government (and in the economic climate of 1975, it was assumed that no private capital would step in to do the job) would not see a return of its money for at least a decade.

Having read the report, it's hardly surprising that, at a time of economic crisis when other, bigger industries urgently needed investment, inflation was rampant and unemployment rising, Eric Varley withdrew support from NVT, and, as author Steve Wilson put it, "... in effect wash his hands of the industry." For the time being, NVT was out of the picture, which made the Bonnie Britain's sole surviving motorcycle.

1976

Model:	T140V Bonneville
UK price:	£874
From engine number:	HN 62501
Tank colour:	Poly-Red/White

In previous years (with the exception of the '71 debacle), each model year's production had begun the previous August, after the annual summer holiday, but for '76 it began in the July of 1975. A final batch of 1500 right-foot shift Bonnevilles was completed by the end of June, allowing the new-spec bikes to take over.

The newest feature of these was, of course, the left-foot gearshift which Chuck Knight had worked so hard to test during the blockade. It couldn't really be called an improvement (having been forced on Triumph by US legislation), but it did have the benefit of familiarity for the new generation of riders who had grown up on Japanese left-foot bikes. Although it sounded like a simple modification, the new gearchange and corresponding right-foot rear brake pedal involved many changes. A steel rod, cranked around the clutch, transferred gearchange operation to the left, and necessitated new inner and outer gearbox covers, plus changes to the operating quadrant and kickstart axle. The

Right-foot shift Tiger 750: really a single-carb Bonneville.

Nicely presented US T140V with left-foot shift.

The Triumph Bonneville Bible

NVT took out full-page ads to reassure an anxious public.

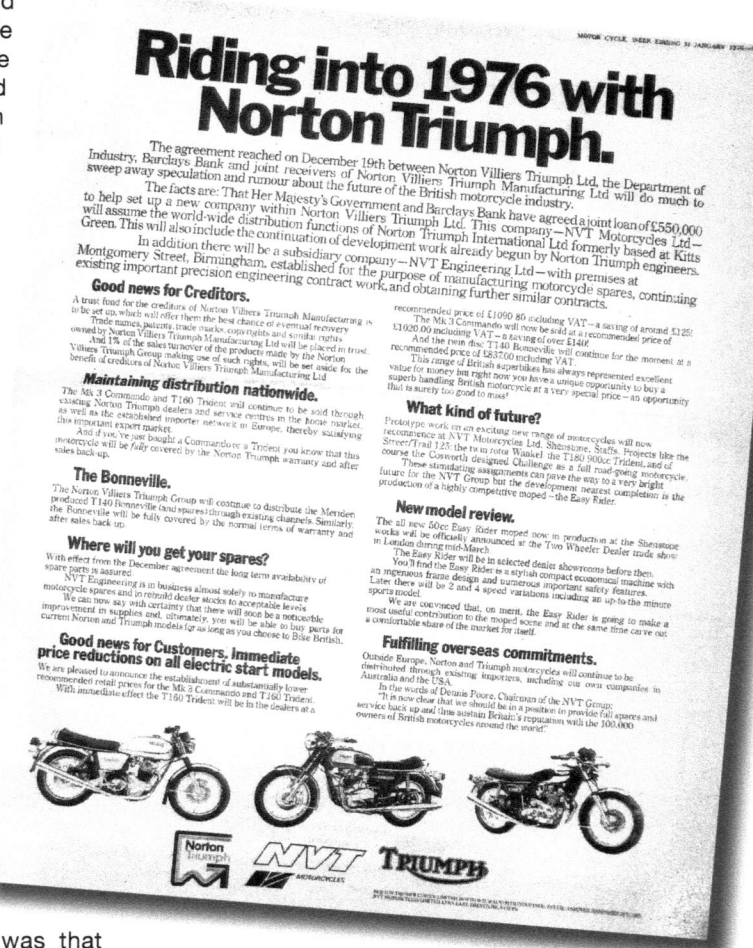

primary chaincase was altered to accept the gearlever spindle and, at the same time, the old timing cover was deleted in favour of a screwed-in inspection plug and fixed pointer.

The new gearchange did the job, though road testers complained that it was too stiff; far harder work then the traditionally slick right-foot shift. NVT (through which all co-op-built Bonnevilles were sold) complained as well, and some brackets were strengthened as a result. It also involved moving the left footrest further forward, which made the riding position uncomfortable on longer rides.

The other major change for the 1976 model year Bonnie was replacement of the old drum rear brake with a disc. Old hands pointed out that the new brake was no better than the old, and some thought it wooden by comparison, but the fact was that buyers of 750cc superbikes expected discs at both ends, so the Bonneville had to have them. The 10-inch disc was chromed, which prevented rust but reduced effectiveness in the wet, and its underslung calliper proved vulnerable to dirt and grit flung up by the rear wheel.

There were other changes that year, including pillion footrests now at a 45 degree angle, something else demanded by US legislation, and with 80 per cent of co-op production heading Stateside, couldn't be ignored. Noise legislation, too, was being tightened, hence internal changes to the silencers and the air filters. To improve oil tightness, an O-ring was fitted to the oil pressure release valve, while the oil pump junction block, feed and return pipes were all revised, and longer fixing screws fitted to the breather stub on the primary chaincase. The front mudguard fixings were changed, and this also lost its holes for a numberplate as this was no longer a legal necessity in the UK. One welcome change was that the clumsy left-hand Lucas switch cluster was improved – now easier to operate but still vulnerable to damp – and there were new Smiths instruments in the shape of speedo and rev counter.

In October, the latest Bonneville finally made it back to the USA, where dealers had been without dependable supplies for two years. NVT's American arm, Norton-Triumph Inc (NTI) celebrated with a major ad campaign, which centred on nostalgia, picturing a Bonneville outside a 1950s-style drive-in hamburger joint. Big news, perhaps, but times had changed since dealers could have sold every single Triumph they could get. In the two years that the Bonnie had been away, competition had got stiffer; many buyers had turned to a Japanese bike and the venerable vertical twin looked older than ever. Reliable spares supply was still a problem, too.

As if that wasn't bad enough, due to the new cash-strapped era – so different from the final profligate days of the BSA empire – US Triumph dealers now found they had to pay for every bike in full before they could take delivery. Then, after just a few months, the Bonnie's price increased by $100 to almost $2000, on a par with that of the CB750, a fact reflected in sales. Some US dealers, despite having stayed loyal through the 1974 blockade, found this all too much and dropped the franchise. One of Triumph's strongest suits – its large and loyal US dealer network – was shrinking year-by-year. NVT America (as the importer was called in its latest re-branding) moved to smaller premises and had its payroll slashed to thirty employees. The days of the $100,000 dealer conventions, as one employee sadly related, were long gone ...

Back at Meriden, things were changing in the factory. The tag 'worker co-operative' was not just skin-deep, and radical changes in the way the plant was run were made. Led by a young Denis Johnson, formerly the works convenor, the co-op paid a flat rate of £50 to everyone, regardless of age, sex or skill level, and that included Johnson and the section leaders. There was no clocking-on, and every worker had a shareholding, so each would benefit from any profits. If anyone left, their shares remained in the co-op, held on behalf of the workforce by trustees. A supervisory board was elected by the workforce, while a management board – which included heads of each department, looked after the day-to-day running. To help keep everyone involved, there were regular Saturday morning mass meetings.

"Critics say we are trying to make capitalism work," said Bill Lapworth of the Transport & General Workers Union, and one of the early directors. "They're right, for if this comes off both managers and workers will share the benefits. The Meriden Co-operative, with the scrapping of restrictive practices and over-manning, as well as a willingness to accept the linkage of pay to productivity, could demonstrate one of the answers to the deeper problems of British industry. It was well worth paying a small sum of taxpayers' money to find out whether it does."

Note that Lapworth made no mention of socialism. For the majority of the workforce, the co-op was not about politics but simply a means of keeping the 'family' together and ensuring that Triumph had a future. And they were making sacrifices. That £50 flat wage was lower than the average in the Coventry area, especially for skilled workers. The sometimes absurd demarcations between trade unions, the source of so many disputes, were swept away. Now, everyone had to be prepared to do any job they were capable of in order to keep the production lines going. Some skilled men found themselves preparing and packing finished bikes: 'unskilled' work that would have been beneath them in the old days.

Of course, things didn't run quite as smoothly as the foregoing might imply. As the workforce grew from an initial 200 to 700, inevitably a minority took advantage of the new lack of supervision, and a commitment to automatic full sick pay had to be rescinded as a result. There was also tension between many at Meriden and Geoffrey Robinson, ex-Chief Executive of Jaguar Cars and Labour supporter, who would do much in the coming years to keep the co-op in business. Approached for help, he agreed to work three days a week for Meriden, unpaid. Robinson had a successful background in conventional management, and became impatient with the early co-op principles, which he thought were hampering its recovery.

And it had to recover, because the co-op, like the eleven other co-operatives formed under Tony Benn's tutelage, came about from a failed private enterprise, something that was obvious to anyone who worked at Meriden. "The factory was falling down around them," recalled Frank Baker, who had worked at Triumph in the 1950s, and came back to join the co-op. "The footings had all gone; the walls were cracking and the roof was leaking everywhere. But they had a good workforce. The co-op would have worked if they'd had enough capital." He could have added that much of the tooling was worn out, which resulted in quality control problems, but without the funding to replace it, the workforce had to make do with what it had.

Variable quality became yet another hurdle to overcome. The first two left-foot shift Bonnevilles were actually sent back by NVT after testing with a damning list of 30 faults. (Worse still, news of the rejection was leaked to the press.) New bikes would be delivered to dealers with faults such as exhaust pipes loose in the head, or badly routed cables. Many suffered from high oil consumption. Worn-out tooling – a perennial problem at Meriden – was partly to blame, but the failings were also down to a lack of supervision, and a general reluctance to take on responsibility.

But Meriden's biggest headache was a shortage of capital – there simply wasn't enough money to maintain and run the place, let alone invest in new machinery or a new Bonneville. Even cash flow from sales was restricted by the two-year agreement to sell every bike to NVT. Dennis Poore was not sympathetic to Meriden, given that, as he saw it, it had undermined his own company's government-funded revival. So he drove a hard bargain, buying Bonnies from the co-op for £450 when the retail price was £874, increased in October to £999, which all but wiped out any price advantage the Bonneville had over the Japanese 750s. Poore's NVT may have been making a loss overall, but it was making a profit on every Bonnie it sold.

Peter Watson tested a Bonneville for *Bike* magazine, and told it like it was. His fingers were numbed from vibration; his rear end by the seat. The gearchange was stiff, the bike blew three fuses, and its indicators went haywire at speed, the front left one persistently coming loose. And yet he thought it was worth buying. The Bonnie handled as well as ever, and braking was superb ("the most sensitive stoppers I've ever tried.") The suspension was firm, but just right, and Watson loved the 750 twin's wide spread of power. "If you want more cubes per greenback, then the Bonneville delivers. End of story."

Dennis Poore appeared to have changed his tune by October 1976, praising the co-op in his annual report to NVT shareholders. This may have been because he wanted to transfer tooling for the T180 830cc Trident to Meriden, so that this new enlarged (and very promising) version of the three-cylinder bike could go into production. But like Meriden, NVT had no cash to fund the transfer, so Poore applied to Eric Varley and the DTI civil servants for the money: the answer was 'no.' That was a shame, because Meriden was now a one-product factory, and the T180 was by all accounts a modern, more torquey version of the original Trident, which would have given Triumph a superbike competitor. But it never reached production, and the Bonneville would just have to soldier on by itself.

1977

Models:	T140V Bonneville/T140V Bonneville Silver Jubilee
UK price:	T140V – £1012; Silver Jubilee – £1245
Tank colour:	T140V – Cherokee Red/White or Polychromatic Blue/White; Silver Jubilee – Silver/Blue with red/white lining
From engine number:	GP 75000

In 1977, Triumph discovered the benefits of the special edition. The changes to the standard Bonneville for that model year were so minor that one blink and you'd have missed them. The front mudguard lost its upper braces, which were replaced by a single flat support underneath the guard, held in place by a Phillips screw. It tidied things up, but the age-old problem of mudguard cracking returned, so the braces

1950s nostalgia to sell a 1970s Triumph ...

1975-78: Yes, we can

THE MOST EXCITING COLLECTOR'S ITEM TO COME OUT OF JUBILEE YEAR!

There's still only one big bike with real breeding behind it – the legendary Triumph Bonneville 750.

Built by men with bikes in their blood, the big beautiful Bonnie is a real man's bike with real character. Prized by enthusiasts for its unique handling and gutsy 112mph performance.

Now, in Silver Jubilee Year, Triumph have added another exciting chapter to over seventy years of motorcycling history. By bringing out a special limited edition of this great British bike in superb Silver Jubilee livery.

Only 1,000 are being built for the UK, each with its own Certificate of Ownership.

You'll spot the differences on the Silver 750 right away. Smart red, white and blue styling on the silver tank, chain guard, and wheel rims. Restyled seat in blue with red piping. Chromed front fork sections, chain cover, timing cover, gearbox cover and rear light. Race-bred Dunlop K91 Red Arrow tyres.

But there's only one way of experiencing its exhilarating performance. Feel the breathtaking surge of power as you slip smoothly through its 5-speed box. Hear that famous Triumph roar as you twist the throttle wide open.

And that's by asking your dealer for a test ride. But make it soon – remember, this is a limited edition.

Only a lucky few will know what it's like to ride this living legend.

SILVER 750 LIMITED EDITION

The Silver Jubilee was unashamedly touted as a collector's item, and, after a decent interval, it became one.

Far left: The Bonneville Silver Jubilee was a clever way of moving on unsold bikes.

Left: Lord Stokes, the super-salesman seconded from British Leyland, came up with the idea for the anniversary model.

made a comeback in later years. The aluminium taillight housing was now painted (black) rather than polished, and UK Bonnies received metal-covered sparkplug caps (these had a tendency to retain moisture, and many owners replaced them). And for the first time, the Bonneville offered a choice of colour: Cherokee Red and White, or Polychromatic Blue and White (more lyrically called Pacific Blue in the USA). The Bonnie had been joined by a single-carb Tiger 750, and this, too, had a colour choice.

But that was it, the sum total of changes to the standard '77 model year Bonneville. It was hardly surprising that some 1977 bikes were shipped to the USA with '76 owners manuals, and that the official parts book (normally updated each year) covered both 1976 and 1977.

So the year would have been a bit of a

The Triumph Bonneville Bible

Even the seat came in for the red/blue treatment ...

... as did the wheel rims.

Jubilee philosophy was: if it's visible, chrome-plate it!

1977-on instruments – the wiggly arrow is NVT's trademark.

And if you were in any doubt ...

... the seat back and rear mudguard continued the theme.

non-event in Bonneville development were it not for the Silver Jubilee. It was Lord Stokes' idea. The ex-British Leyland chairman was helping out the co-op with sales and marketing on an unpaid basis, and he thought that a special edition Bonnie to celebrate Queen Elizabeth's Silver Jubilee would build on the bike's strengths of Britishness and traditional values. It also effectively put an end to any rumours that the co-op was a hotbed of left-wing republicanism!

In the way of these things, the Silver Jubilee was only a cosmetic job. UK- or US-spec bikes were given a base colour of silver, with blue panels on the fuel tank and suitably patriotic red, white and blue pinstriping on tank, mudguards and even the chainguard. The seat

1975-78: Yes, we can

Was the Silver Jubilee overdone? It doesn't look too bad here.

was in blue with red piping, and there was extra chrome on the fork yokes, timing and gearbox covers and primary chaincase. To set it all off, the Dunlop K91 Red Arrows, in 4.10 x 19 front, 4.10 x 18 rear, had pinstriping: possibly the only tyres ever so embellished. And the wheel rim centres were painted blue, with red and white pinstripes. Finally, there were special badges on the sidepanels and the tank mounting plug. The sidepanels were plastic covers, slightly larger than the standard offering and later adopted by the standard Bonnie. There was one mechanical change, in the adoption of 'upside-down' Girling gas-filled shocks with adjusters mounted at the top, but this was simply a precursor to their adoption on the standard Bonneville. The larger section 4.10 tyres became standard issue as well, but without the red stripe.

The overall effect of the Silver Jubilee was a bit like an over-iced cake, and certainly not in the classic understated tradition that Triumph was moving toward. Still, that hardly mattered, because the silver, red, white and blue Bonneville was a great success, at least in the UK and Commonwealth. One thousand T140Js, as the factory code went, were built in UK spec and another 1000 in US. Initially, that was to be the end of this limited edition, but it became a little less limited when demand from Australia, New Zealand and other Commonwealth countries persuaded Meriden to build another 400.

Altogether, Silver Jubilees made up one-quarter of Meriden's output for 1977, buyers encouraged by a stirring TV commercial featuring Rule Britannia, and an extensive advertising campaign in mainstream newspapers like the *Sunday Mirror* as well as the motorcycle press. *The Daily Mirror* ran a spot-the-ball competition, and the BBC TV programme *Tomorrow's World* raffled a Silver Jubilee at the Earls Court Motorcycle Show. Triumph dealers weren't forgotten, either, and given help to promote the bike locally.

It was a masterful publicity campaign which chimed with huge public awareness of Queen Elizabeth's 25th anniversary on the throne, and did much to raise Triumph's profile in a positive way. The co-op had never embarked on such a campaign before, which was the work of Brian Reilly, one of a small management team seconded from GEC. Naturally enough, some at Meriden questioned the cost of all this publicity, but in thoroughly professional style, it had been costed into the price of every bike (£30) and was easily absorbed by the £233 premium over the standard Bonnie. Of course, what the publicity campaign didn't advertise was that the Silver Jubilee was no more or less than a ploy to sell off unsold bikes which were piling up at the factory, which Brian Reilly himself reminded the board of.

But nobody outside Meriden knew or cared

The Triumph Bonneville Bible

Above: Standard 1977 T140V with left-foot shift.

Above, right: There was still a market for the Bonneville.

Right: 1977 twin: little changed from the first '73 750.

Far right: Big, one-piece rocker covers made tappet adjustment less of a chore.

about this. As it was, every buyer was sent a Certificate of Ownership, featuring the first owner's name and signed by the Chairman of the co-op. These certificates could be a while in arriving, and some American Jubilee buyers found theirs turning up after they had sold the bike on to someone else!

In fact, the Jubilee wasn't the success in the USA that it was at home. A few collectors bought the bike as an investment, but some sat in dealer showrooms gathering dust for several years, even into the 1980s. Even those Americans who loved Triumphs had no great affinity for the British monarch, it seemed. In any case, there were other unsold 1977 Bonnevilles available in the USA, and they cost $127 less than the Jubilee.

American dealers, it has to be said, were not having a good year. Not only were the 1977 Bonnevilles not selling well, but spares continued to be in desperately short supply, and when the

1975-78: Yes, we can

new importer, Triumph Motorcycles America (TMA), promised that parts was the number one priority, with enough on the way to fulfil all back orders, some took this with a large pinch of salt. The reality was illustrated by Meriden's decision to strip down 50 stockpiled bikes at the factory in order to sell the parts as spares. The spares problem was finally addressed but, at the same time, it was announced that parts for pre-1973 bikes would no longer be supplied. This came as a serious blow to US dealers who had customers riding 650 Bonnevilles (there were thousands of those alone) and other Triumphs, who were being effectively abandoned by the factory. Jack Wilson of Big D Cycles was bitter: "Discontinuing those pre-1973 parts was the biggest mistake they made," he later recalled. "Boy, that really hurt those of us who stuck with Triumph and still deeply believed in the products." Arguably, this was a short-sighted move by Meriden, as making spares was profitable business, but the provision for 650s was now abandoned to aftermarket suppliers, who lost no time in filling the vacuum.

Triumph's US staff were also unimpressed by two styling suggestions for the Bonneville made at around this time. A custom-style Lowrider was rejected for looking too much like a Harley (though it would later resurface in milder form as the Bonneville Special). The 750FT was more radical: a complete re-working of the Bonneville in flat-track style, designed by Tom Hingham and Jez Bradley of Meriden. It kept the standard engine and frame but added shorter forks and a longer swingarm. A large fibreglass seat/tailpiece also acted as the rear mudguard – extending down to form big sidepanels – and used a Yamaha XS750 rear light. There was a rectangular headlight and instrument panel, Astralite aluminium wheels and fuel tank were from the stillborn Bandit 350. The 750FT certainly transformed the Bonneville's appearance, which lost its classic elegance in the process. The Americans rejected it. A few years later, Honda launched the FT500, which had some resemblance to the Triumph, but it wasn't a great success.

Despite the spares shortage, disgruntled dealers, and lack of interest in the Silver Jubilee, the USA remained Triumph's best market, with about 8000 bikes shipped there in 1977. Back in the UK, the Bonnie was actually the best-selling 750, though this sector was shrinking, having lost its superbike status to a new breed of 1000cc machines. Its following in Britain was demonstrated by winning the *Motorcycle News* Machine of the Year award in both late 1977 (for the '78 model T140D), and in '79.

In fact, the latter part of that decade were really the co-op's best years. By the end of 1976, it had largely found its feet, and the following year saw the injection of some much-needed management expertise, a production increase, and a more sympathetic attitude from the government. It also saw Meriden finally break free of NVT. In November '76, Phil Love had joined the co-op as Chief Executive on a one-year contract, and one of his first jobs was to renegotiate the ex-works price which NVT paid for Bonnevilles. Talks soon broke down, but both Love and Geoffrey Robinson came to the conclusion that the only way out for the co-op was to buy the Triumph name and marketing rights from NVT.

The classic US Bonneville rider's view, which road testers didn't like but many customers did.

> **Adspeak 1977 (Silver Jubilee)**
>
> "There's still only one big bike with real breeding behind it – the legendary Triumph Bonneville 750.
>
> "Built by men with bikes in their blood, the big beautiful Bonnie is a real man's bike with real character. Prized by enthusiasts for its unique handling and gutsy 112mph performance.
>
> "Now, in Silver Jubilee Year, Triumph has added another exciting chapter to over seventy years of motorcycling history by bringing out a special limited edition of this great British bike in superb Silver Jubilee livery. Only 1000 are being built for the UK, each with its own Certificate of Ownership. You'll spot the differences on the Silver 750 right away …
>
> "… but there's only one way of experiencing its exhilarating performance, and that's by asking your dealer for a test ride. Feel the breathtaking surge of power as you slip smoothly through its 5-speed box. Hear that famous Triumph roar as you twist the throttle wide open.
>
> "But make it soon – remember, this is a limited edition. Only a lucky few will know what it's like to ride this living legend."

A price of £500,000 was agreed, but they still had to find the money, not to mention interest payments now looming on the original government loan. But Meriden's friends in high places (notably union leader Jack Jones and Harold Lever as well as Geoffrey Robinson) managed to get the support of Minister of State for Industry Alan Williams and Sir Arnold Weinstock, head of GEC. The outcome was that a share deal between the government and NVT came up with the £500,000 needed to buy the name and marketing rights, which included the USA importer. Meanwhile, GEC lent the co-op £1 million (with 2000 stockpiled bikes as security) to pay the interest and keep things running. And it wasn't just money. A small team of GEC managers and engineers was loaned to Meriden, free of charge.

Not everyone was pleased about these imported managers from private industry, and Denis Johnson actually resigned over the issue, replaced as Chairman by John Rosamond, the welder who had started out at Meriden in 1971 and served his time on the picket line.

The GEC managers, along with Geoffrey Robinson, had a conventional business background, and certainly were less sympathetic to some of the co-op's founding principles, and it was their view that eventually prevailed. They suggested replacing the flat rate wage with a bonus system, which would help attract skilled labour. Managers, too, now received salaries, and the team was strengthened by the arrival of John Nelson as Managing Director and Brian Jones as Chief Engineer. Brenda Price, a long-time Triumph employee, remained on the financial side, later to head-up the US subsidiary while it looked for a new chief exec. It shouldn't be forgotten that all of these people – managers and shopfloor – were earning less than they could have done in private industry, so working at Meriden still required a commitment to the co-op.

But the financial situation was still precarious. John Nelson worked out that even with production now increased to 300 bikes a week, Meriden was barely covering its costs. The first lorry-load of 60 bikes would bring in enough cash to pay that week's wages. The second would pay for next week's materials; the third would cover essentials such as heating and tools – only when the fourth load left Meriden was there any profit, and that was often swallowed up by essential repairs to the creaky factory building.

This meant no money was left over for serious development of the Bonneville. Geoffrey Robinson's vision was that if the Bonnie was gradually developed over time, it could become a sort of two-wheeled MG or Morgan, with classic appeal but modern enough to be acceptable. This plan had to include some way to combat vibration, and a GEC engineer named Paul Morton designed a balance shaft system that had great promise. The tragedy was, it would need a new crankcase, crankshaft, primary chaincase and timing cover, pushing the total cost to £500,000 – and Meriden didn't have the money. A shame, because the Metropolitan Police had tested the prototype and liked it; getting some lucrative police business would make a big difference.

The co-op tried to balance the books by taking on other work. Basically, the low production levels meant only part of the big factory was being used, but it was still necessary to heat and maintain all of it. Puch mopeds were assembled for a while, as were Moto Guzzi 125s, but neither project came to much.

1978

Models:	T140V Bonneville/T140E Bonneville
UK price:	T140V – £1284
Tank colour:	T140V – Tawny Brown/Gold or Aquamarine/Silver
	T140E – Tawny Brown/Gold or Astral Blue/Silver
From engine number:	HX 00100

This was a big year for the Bonneville as it marked

1975-78: Yes, we can

The Bonneville was still held in great affection in Britain, winning MCN's Machine of the Year in 1978.

Left: Rising phoenix-like from the dry ice ... this was the final year for the T140V.

the launch of the T140E: a cleaner-running bike which would comply with new emissions legislation in the USA. The 'E' stood for 'EPA' (Environmental Protection Agency), source of the new legislation. It was actually launched in the USA in January 1978, making it '1978½' in terms of model years. The plain '78 model year Bonneville had been unveiled in August the previous year, and included some changes of its own.

The lower 7.9:1 compression ratio was standardised on all bikes, which blunted performance a little but improved reliability. A bigger step forward was the new metal/composite cylinder head gasket, which, as long as it was fitted correctly, finally made the Triumph's top end oil-tight. Oil retention was also improved with 'self-aligning' fork oil seals and retainers. The wheel bearings finally had rubber seals, which greatly extended their life – failures at less than 10,000 miles hadn't been unknown – so this, too, was a positive move. Gas-filled Girling shocks were now fitted as standard and the rear wheel gained thicker spokes to combat a rash of breakages. There was a move to more imported parts as well, with Japanese Yuasa batteries replacing Lucas later in the year, and French Veglia instruments in place of the familiar Smiths, the latter thanks to Smiths' apparent inability to keep Meriden supplied. There were a few other detail changes, such as a gasket between inner and outer gearbox covers, and a change to painted (not chromed) mudguards on UK bikes.

Late in 1977, there was a morale boost when Ted Simon came home to Britain after a four-year round-the-world trip on a 500cc Tiger 100. Simon, a journalist for *The Times*, had left the UK just before the Meriden blockade began, and he received a warm welcome at the factory. Back then, not many people had ridden around

The Triumph Bonneville Bible

After all the turmoil, the public needed reassurance that the legend hadn't died.

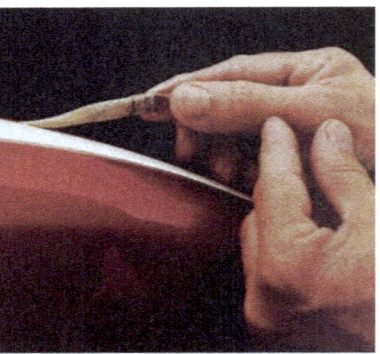

Pinstriping was always hand applied, which became a convenient sales point in an age of mass production.

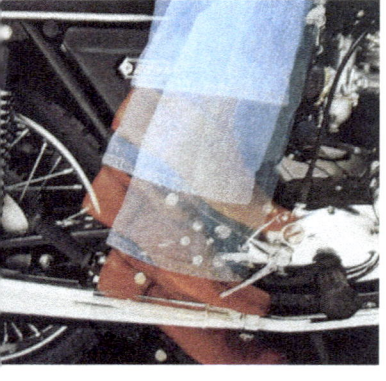

Triumph tried to give kickstarting romantic appeal, but really the Bonnie needed an electric start.

the world by bike, and Ted Simon went on to write the best-selling book *Jupiter's Travels*, based on his experiences. It was a classic of travel writing, and all the attendant publicity did Triumph no harm at all, though Meriden failed to take full advantage of it. [On a far more modest scale, the author rode a Tiger 90 around the coast of England and Wales in the summer of 1983, and wrote to the co-op. He received a nice letter from Brian Jones, who said that Meriden was now being wound up, "but thank you for thinking of 'Triumph'."]

But the really big news came in January 1978 with the launch of the T140E in the USA – it wouldn't go on sale in Britain for another 14 months. Developing the E was one of the first jobs of Chief Engineer Brian Jones who, along with Jock Copeland, faced the challenge of cleaning up the Bonnie's emissions. The pair succeeded, though had to come up with a new cylinder head that allowed the bike to run leaner as well as cleaner. It had parallel inlet tracts (finally losing the Bonnie's trademark splayed out carbs) which allowed the fitting of Amal Mk2 Concentric carburettors. These were an advance on the Mk1, with alloy PTFE-coated slides and improved airflow. The old float ticklers had gone, as US legislation forbade any petrol or vapour to vent into the atmosphere, which also meant that the primary drive now vented into the airbox and the oil tank into a rocker cover, not into the fresh air.

Internally, the crankshaft was more comprehensively machined than before to combat vibration, and the timing side ball bearing was replaced by an SKF roller bearing, which was able to give positive location to the crank, like a ball bearing, but with the greater load capacity of a roller bearing.

One of the biggest advances for the engine was the adoption of electronic ignition. For years, the Triumph twin had suffered from hit and miss ignition timing, which got worse as the miles went by and the contact breaker system wore. It was also tricky to set up with absolute accuracy. The Lucas Rita electronic system, on the other hand, was simple, 100 per cent accurate, and, once set up, would give spot-on timing, providing some auto advance as well. The change was easy to see, as the new system lived in the old cb points chest, which now had a finned cover.

The electrical system itself finally went from positive to negative earth, and gained a Lucas three-phase alternator that boosted output at low revs – especially useful for any low-revving Bonnie that spent much of its time in town, when previously just the brake light and indicators were enough to flatten the battery. The infamous Lucas switchgear finally came good; easier to use now and with proper labelling, though it could still let water in at times. And in a final touch of Japanese-style convenience there was a more visible warning light display between

1975-78: Yes, we can

Amal Mk2 Concentric carburettor mounted on parallel inlets helped make the T140E cleaner running.

Tawny brown was a fashionable colour in the 1970s – ask your parents ...

the instruments (now protected by thick rubber binnacles), even including a neutral light.

In fact, the T140E was, by Triumph standards, positively festooned with modern conveniences. A small rear parcel grid was fitted as standard, and US bikes regained their fork gaiters. All Bonnevilles now had a lockable seat, which contained not one but two helmet locks. No electric start, of course, although the factory had now accepted that this should be a priority. Cornering clearance had been a common recent criticism, and now the footrests were chamfered, straight from the showroom, so that keen types didn't have to do the job in mid-corner.

The gearchange, too, was improved: ever since the shift to a left-foot change, there had been complaints of notchiness and stiffness, which was reduced somewhat by a reprofiled cam plate with a deepened neutral indent. Both clutch and brake levers were redesigned to be less of a stretch away, though the clutch was still heavy, and the UK-spec handlebars were narrowed by a couple of inches. The brake discs were thicker (now 2.54mm) and the standard tyre became the Dunlop TT100, 19inch front, 18inch rear; both of them 4.10in section. Allen bolts replaced Phillips screws in the engine cases, exerting more pressure on the joints and less likely to be butchered by a clumsy home mechanic.

All-in-all, the T140E changes were the most comprehensive the Bonneville had seen since 1971, and unlike the efforts of Umberslade Hall, these were all genuine changes for the better. It was probably the most thoroughly tested update as well, simply because the EPA

The Triumph Bonneville Bible

At a glance, the EPA Bonneville looked the same as its predecessor – half-hidden carburettors are the giveaway.

Not quite as slimline as older Bonnevilles, but the T140E was still lightweight by contemporary standards.

emissions limits required that the engine was as clean at 9500 miles as it was when new. As a result, two prototype T140Es spent much time amassing miles at the MIRA proving ground – they passed the 9500 mark in the nick of time, and passed the test.

All of this was reflected in the good reception that the latest Bonneville received, as well as a noticeable improvement in quality. American dealers contrasted the latest bikes to come out of the co-op with those delivered in the '60s, sometimes deliberately sabotaged by the workforce. "The co-op workers really were conscientious," said dealer John Healy. "They just had little money to work with." Cornering clearance was still a problem (despite those chamfered footrests), as was the vibration: *Cycle Guide* magazine described it as "unbearable" over 55mph. But everyone noticed that the finish was deeper and more lustrous than it had been for years. The frame was now powder-coated and the paint went on in five coats; the chrome was good and the polished cases shone.

Many pointed out that the T140E had lost power compared to its predecessors, and for some the EPA consisted of a bunch of evil bureaucrats out to spoil other people's fun. It was true that the E now made only 49bhp, but

1975-78: Yes, we can

the hard fact was that the Bonnie had long since been left behind in the horsepower race. In any case, the changes to the E had actually fattened the torque curve in the low to mid ranges, which surely suited the Bonneville's new role.

Meriden responded by increasing production, and the 1978/9 season would see 11,999 bikes roll off the line, peaking at 320 a week in the summer of '78. It was the co-op's highest ever production, and it had never seemed closer to profitability and a secure future. The production increases of 1977/1978 actually brought problems of their own, unfortunately, with several key suppliers unable to keep up with demand. At first, Amal could only deliver half the number of carburettor sets needed, though it did establish a small factory in Spain to help fill the gap. Supply of Smiths speedos and tachometers faltered; hence the move to French-made Veglias. And Lucas, the source of so many electrical headaches for Triumph over the years, had difficulty coming up with 300 Rita electronic ignition sets per week, despite having been forewarned of this production target. "We never expected you to build 300 a week," was the reply ...

It was imperative that the first T140Es bound for the USA got there on time, and the factory considered shipping bikes out incomplete, for finishing on arrival. But this was vetoed by the government's Export Credit Guarantee Department, without whose help the Bonnies wouldn't be going anywhere.

Of course, the suppliers had their own problems with Meriden, which was increasingly in debt to many of them, and one can well imagine priority being given to customers who paid on time. Not only that, but to a company like Lucas, used to supplying the car industry with tens of thousands of items, the small quantities of motorcycle-specific parts needed by Meriden were simply a production planning nuisance, and because of the relatively low production, probably low profit earners into the bargain.

Despite all of this, production did peak in the summer of 1978, and this – combined with improvements to the T140E – gave cause for optimism, and even hope that the co-op may have turned a corner.

But it was not to be. Triumph's dependence on the American market had always left it vulnerable to fluctuating exchange rates, and in 1978 the dollar plunged against the pound from an expected $1.94/£1 to nearly $2.40. That meant price increases, except that Meriden had already signed up to supply bikes at the old exchange rate. It was enough to turn a projected profit for the season into a loss of £700,000. And when the US price did shoot up (making the T140D Special $600 more than a Suzuki GS750), buyers stayed away in droves, despite the T140E's good press coverage. TMA had forecast sales of 8000 for the '78/'79 season, but sold only half that figure, and 480 bikes had to be shipped back to England at great expense. According to Steve Wilson, this marked the end of Triumph's American dream: "[It was] the last and final contraction of Meriden's long-time gold-laying goose; American enthusiasm for the twins never really revived, and the market there was only good for around 1000 machines a year from then on." He added that there was still a good demand for spares, but you couldn't run a factory the size of Meriden on spares alone – it had to build bikes.

Visit Veloce on the web – www.velocebooks.com
Details of all books • Special offers • New book news • Gift vouchers

6

1979-83: On the slide

1979

Models:	T140E Bonneville/T140D Bonneville Special
UK price:	£1768 (T140D); £1577 (T140D)
Tank colour:	T140E – Black/Red or Beige/Gold; T140D – Black/Gold lining
From engine number:	HA 11001

1978/'79 would prove to be the co-op's high point with almost 12,000 bikes built, but after that production slumped to 4460, and then averaged little more than 1500 until the end. Meriden had really gambled that the T140E would be its saviour – in many ways it was the best Bonneville yet – and maybe it could have saved the co-op if North American sales hadn't been virtually killed off by that disastrously low dollar. Unfortunately, international exchange rates were something over which the factory had absolutely no control.

In the meantime, although financial troubles worsened through early 1979, there was another new bike: the T140D. The origins of the D, handsome in black with gold pinstriping, lay in Triumph's visit to Daytona the previous year, during which TMA representatives were distinctly unimpressed by the proposals for a flat-track-style Triumph, and a Harley-style lowrider.

The T140D was Triumph's take on the new breed of factory custom, which Yamaha had pioneered with an XS650 Special in 1978. There was nothing radical about it as it was simply a watered-down version of what home-build customisers had been doing for years, including high bars, slim tank, a stepped seat and special paint. Arguably, Harley-Davidson had been building factory customs for several years, but this was the first time the style had broken out into the mainstream. Yamaha's XS650 cruiser sold by the thousand, and Honda, Suzuki and Kawasaki soon jumped in with bikes to suit.

To Triumph's credit, it lost no time in coming up with a Bonneville version – ironic, because some thought the Yamaha Special showed Bonnie influence. In any case, Triumph was already halfway there with the US Bonneville. Based on the standard T140E, the D had the slim US fuel tank painted black, with gold pinstriping, and the simpler Triumph script badge from UK bikes. The sidecovers were finished to match, with a 'Bonneville Special' badge, the 'Special' script in red. What really set the bike apart from previous Triumphs, however, were the American-made, Lester seven-spoke alloy wheels. It was a cheeky move, as they were very similar to Yamaha's, and in black with highly polished rims they set off the bike well. One detail was that the finned electronic ignition cover was also in black/polished alloy. The mudguards were chromed; the front one chopped short in the custom style.

Much work had gone into the exhaust system, a graceful, two-into-one whose downpipes exited straight out of the head, with

1979-83: On the slide

no balance pipe, and joined under the crankcase into a single, two-stage megaphone silencer. It looked good, and the improvement wasn't simply cosmetic. Back at Meriden, Jock Copeland had spent a long time tuning the exhaust to make it as clean as that of the T140E, and to improve ground clearance (always a problem on the T140) and boost mid-range torque. Not only that, but ditching one silencer saved a lot of weight (the T140D weighed 25lb less than the standard Bonneville), and made driveside maintenance less of a chore. The new exhaust also reverted to the old screw-in exhaust stubs that had been fitted in the 1960s – they stayed put more reliably than the push-in downpipes, and made replacing the pipes far easier.

At the rear, to make room for the new silencer the brake calliper was moved to the top of the disc: this helped protect it from road dirt and was soon adopted by the T140E, as were the screw-in stubs. The swingarm was thicker (for cosmetic reasons, apparently), and as part of the custom look a slightly wider, 4.25-inch section Dunlop TT100 (still 18-inch diameter) went on the rear. The fatter tyre was less successful, contributing to a weave at speed. Not only that, it could foul on the rear mudguard when travelling two-up, leading to punctures, so was soon replaced by the 4.10in size.

But that wasn't the extent of the Special's changes. As well as a squared-off rear grabrail, the stepped seat was quite different: much thicker and featuring 'cold cure' inserts to improve comfort. Like that rear tyre, it was one of the T140D's flaws, its bulky looks out of kilter with the lean and hungry effect elsewhere, and it wasn't as comfy as it looked. It was also higher than the standard seat which, for shorter-legged Triumph riders, must have brought back memories of 1971! Partly to compensate for the higher seat, and to increase ground clearance, the footrests were raised by nearly two inches. The Bonnie's tendency to grind its way through corners had become a familiar point in road tests, and the Special certainly had more clearance. It was now fine on the left, but the new exhaust system still touched down early on the right – Meriden couldn't really tuck it away, because it wanted to keep the centre stand.

Viewed as a whole, the T140D was a masterful take on the factory custom craze. It built on the Bonnie's traditional image and, that fat seat apart, looked just right. And although most of the changes were cosmetic, they had been thought through and introduced with the same care as development of the two-into-one

Bonnevilles continued to be used in club and classic racing. This is Alan Bennallick from Cornwall.

exhaust had employed. If the bike had a problem in the States, it was that the exchange rate (plus the expense of those Lester alloys) had pushed the price up to a whopping $3225, $600 more than a Suzuki GS750. The Bonneville Special looked cool, but, for most American buyers, not $600 worth.

In March 1979 the T140D and E received their UK launch. The E had been given US priority in this respect, partly because it complied with legislation, partly because the American market was so crucial to Triumph, and partly because there were still unsold '78 Bonnies that had to be cleared. The D was now also available in UK guise, keeping the alloy wheels and two-into-one, but with lower bars and the larger tank. In fact, referring to the two different styles as UK and US was becoming increasingly meaningless, as a small number of UK-style Bonnies were shipped across the Atlantic each year, and an increasing proportion of British buyers opted for the small tank/high bars version.

Even if they were late, both the T140D and E got a good reception from the British motorcycle press, which was largely sympathetic to Meriden, though these days no longer inclined to gloss over fundamental faults. *Bike* magazine tested a D and clearly liked it. Sure, the choke came loose, followed by a front indicator; the clutch was heavy and high-speed vibration bad. But at a steady 70mph the vibes were just an "offbeat rumbling." The tester loved the handling: "You

The Triumph Bonneville Bible

The T140E was the basis for Bonneville production over the last few years.

can revel in a bike so light and yet so precise and smooth on corners," though he mentioned a high-speed weave (not yet traced to the fat rear tyre), and the silencer had "worn paper-thin" after two weeks of exuberant touch-down cornering.

The Bonneville was slow by 750 standards, failing to reach 100mph, but the testers liked the solid mid-range torque and easy-kick starting provided by the electronic ignition, hot or cold. By this time, an electric start Bonnie was under development, and the magazine writer had seen one in the workshop at Meriden, but thought the extra complexity might actually detract from the Bonnie's lightness and simplicity; features that were becoming key to its appeal.

At that time, nearly all big Japanese bikes had four cylinders. It was the UJM (Universal Japanese Motorcycle) era, when bikes of the big four manufacturers were looking, sounding and feeling increasingly similar. A twin-cylinder Triumph, on the other hand (or Harley, BMW or Ducati), offered something very different.

The Bonneville Special was certainly a hit with passersby, who, after whistling at the price (a steep £1768), plied the tester with questions. "Yes, it may be ageing," he wrote, "but the Bonneville still has a grip on the hearts of more people than would care to admit it." He also wondered whether the small boys wearing 'British Iron' T-shirts would ever get to own a Bonneville – of course, 40-odd years later, some of those boys might well be riding a new Bonneville, albeit the one built in Hinckley.

In that road test there was also speculation about whether the '79 Special would be the last Bonneville of all. Meriden's problems were well known – in the public spotlight and much discussed in the press and at bike rallies and meets on both sides of the Atlantic – which, in itself, was part of the problem: who would buy a bike whose maker might be out of business a year later?

There was certainly plenty to be gloomy about at Meriden, where the financial situation was as precarious as ever. With sales in the US just half of the target figure, interest on the government loan looming again, and a lean winter coming up, matters looked as serious as ever. Geoffrey Robinson, now pursuing a political career as MP for Coventry North East, agreed to come back in December 1978 as unpaid Chief Executive, intending to use his political contacts to obtain some managerial expertise, and even persuade the government to waive interest on the loan. But this time, both GEC and fellow engineering giant GKN declined to lend

1979-83: On the slide

Left: 1979 brochure, with the original dealer's business card (Terry Hobbs of Plymouth).

the Bonnie a cooler-running alloy cylinder barrel had to be dropped, because it would cost the trifling sum (to most businesses of this scale) of £3000.

According to Geoffrey Robinson, the only way out was to reduce production to 200 bikes a week. This was well below the optimum level of 300, but might give Meriden a breathing space in which to find a business partner, increasingly seen as the only means to survive. It also meant 200 jobs would be lost, something that Robinson had thought essential when he rejoined in December. This clearly was the case, but it was heartbreaking for many of the older workers who had served their time on the picket line, and now had to sacrifice their jobs in order to save the co-op. After two mass meetings, the workforce accepted the redundancies.

Meanwhile, stories were circulating about various companies who were managers to the co-op, and the government refused to waive the interest due. It has to be said that high-profile car giants such as BL and Chrysler were getting far more government money, with no suggestion of any interest. They did, of course, employ thousands, compared to Meriden's hundreds, but in terms of cash per job, the sums involved to keep Triumph afloat were relatively small, especially compared to a prestige project such as the Concorde.

Geoffrey Robinson's return did mean a further move away from the co-operative ideal, and toward a conventional management structure. This caused tensions, but the workforce did have great faith in Robinson, who had given a lot of his time to the co-op since its inception, and was generally regarded as a staunch ally. All of his leadership and business acumen would be needed in the coming months as debts mounted. Winter was always a hard time for Meriden, and by May 1979 the co-op owed £1.2 million in interest to the government. Commercial creditors (many suppliers of vital parts) were owed another £1.3 million, Coventry Council was waiting for £100,000 on the rates, and the co-op had a £400,000 overdraft at the bank. Finally, after the poor sales of 1978, 2000 Bonnevilles remained unsold. A proposal to give

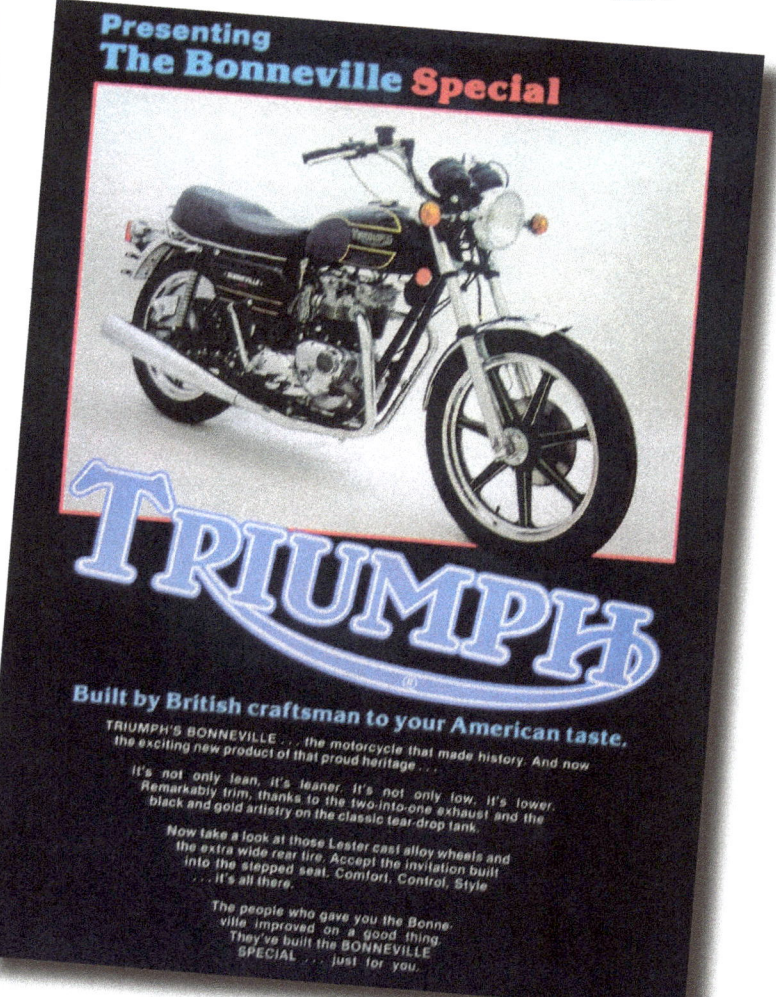

T140D Special was designed to appeal to American tastes – but didn't.

The Triumph Bonneville Bible

The UK-spec T140E was launched more than a year after the US original.

1980

Models:	T140E Bonneville/T140ES Bonneville/T140D Bonneville Special
UK price:	£1797 (T140E); £1897 (T140ES)
Tank colour:	T140D – Black/Gold lining; T140E/ES (UK) – Steel Grey/Candy Apple Red or Black with white pinstriping; T140E/ES (US) – Black/Candy Apple Red, Grey/Black or Olympic Flame/Black
From engine number:	PB 25001 (T140ES: CB 29901)

purportedly interested in buying Meriden. Component manufacturer Armstrong, which would later buy CCM, the low-volume maker of motocross bikes, certainly was, but that would come to nothing.

There was reportedly also interest from Suzuki, the Nigerian government (which was contemplating buying Triumphs), and even Harley-Davidson, but it was the Kawasaki story that had legs, and it emerged in Parliament that there had been top level talks in the Civil Service about a plan to let Meriden go bust and sell Kawasaki the Triumph name and manufacturing rights.

Building bikes at Meriden had no part in this scheme. Kawasaki would probably have sought a factory elsewhere, possibly Humberside, which would entail lower wages, a more docile workforce, and perhaps a government grant to create jobs in one of the Special Development Areas of high unemployment. Either way, nothing came of it.

As for Geoffrey Robinson, he was becoming well known in government circles for his unflagging support for the co-op, and took to wearing his red, white and blue Triumph jacket (a specially made, three-quarter length job) in the House of Commons. Making the case for waiving loan interest, he pointed out that Meriden had supported 700 jobs for three years; exported £10 million-worth of bikes in the same period, and had 30 per cent higher productivity than when under private ownership. Eric Varley remained unconvinced.

Then, in April 1979, the Labour government lost the General Election to Margaret Thatcher's right-wing administration, which had pledged to cut back public spending and allow 'lame ducks' to die. If a Labour government wouldn't help the co-op, the new one looked even less likely to do so ...

For the 1979 model year (1978½, in the case of the T140E) the American market had got priority in the latest-spec bikes from Meriden. But now the tables were turned, with warehouses full of unsold bikes in the US needing to be cleared before 1980 machines could be imported, and the UK and other markets got first dibs.

And there was plenty of new features for 1980, despite the state of Meriden's finances and major changes of the previous year. The Bonneville finally had an electric start option, the touring Executive was unveiled, and all bikes received a four-valve oil pump.

The oil pump alone was a big step forward, with four spring-loaded valves instead of two. Not only was capacity increased, but it was less vulnerable to the grit that could prevent the old pump from delivering any oil at all, with terrible consequences. The brass-bodied pump also had more resistance to wet sumping, but could only be retrofitted if it came with the appropriate timing cover.

Even bigger news was the long-awaited electric start, though this didn't appear until June 1980 when the model year was almost over. Purists held that this was an unwanted complication to the no-frills Bonneville, but the reality was that kickstarting was now unacceptable on a 750cc bike that cost around £2000 in Britain, or nearly $4000 in the States. Critics might also point to the Norton Commando's feeble electric start, but in this case the Meriden boys had done their homework well. Although the starter motor (a Lucas M3, actually made under licence in India) was the same as that used by Norton a few years earlier, it was backed up by a beefy 14.5amp/hour battery. Meriden had taken the trouble to test the

1979-83: On the slide

Bonneville 'American' was a US-spec T140E with fork gaiters, flat seat and plain tank badge, sold in the UK.

Finally available – the Bonnie with electric start, here in US form.

set-up in a cold room, which revealed that the standard 11amp/hr battery wasn't man enough. It also used lower gearing than the Norton (20:1 instead of 15:1), which helped.

The starter was mounted behind the timing cover driving through the timing gears, and used a Borg Warner sprag clutch. Ozzie Oswald, who had been selling his own aftermarket electric start conversion kit for Triumphs, urged Meriden to drive via the clutch. The factory's version

The Triumph Bonneville Bible

Right: Meriden's final years saw a much wider choice of colours.

necessitated fewer expensive casting changes, but put quite a strain on the timing gears. There were a couple of teething problems, one of them literally. Early versions of the starter had thin teeth, which soon wilted under the strain, and the first 200 or so Bonneville Electros had an oil hole in the shaft supporting the starter gears drilled in the wrong place, which led to a few failures. But once sorted, the Bonneville's e-start proved dependable. The surprise was palpable when American magazine *Rider* found the starter, "remarkable, fuss-free and reliable." Although it added 40lb in weight, the electric start cost a modest £100 extra, and about half of all Bonneville buyers ordered it from then on. As the years went by, older Electros did give trouble: yet another case of scarce resources limiting the co-op's capability.

An official launch was held in London for both the Executive (see below) and the electric-foot T140ES. Geoffrey Robinson again made use of his contacts list, allowing the launch to take place at the prestigious Grosvenor House Hotel, and securing the attendance of ex-Formula One World Champion James Hunt, and singer (and long-time Triumph owner) David Essex, both of whom were happy to pose for photographs on a Bonneville. What you can't see in the pictures is that Hunt had his left leg in plaster from a skiing accident – the snappers obligingly took their pictures from the right-hand side of the bike. It was telling, though, that publicity material for the launch was supplied by supportive Triumph dealers (including Reg Allen and Roebucks) as the factory was out of stock and couldn't afford to buy more.

To help feed that big battery (and it was literally bigger, requiring a hollow in the seat pan in order to fit) there was a higher output Lucas RM24 alternator, controlled by a pack of three zener diodes, which were mounted in the airbox to keep them cool. At the same time, the Lucas electronic ignition sensor was beefed up to give a fatter spark at low revs.

There were other across-the-range changes for 1980. The primary chain could now be adjusted without oil running down the adjuster's arm. Some of the features that had worked well on the T140D – such as the high-mounted rear brake calliper, thicker swingarm and raised footrests – now became standard on all bikes, including the single-carb Tiger 750, which was no longer sold in the USA since it couldn't be fitted with the cleaner Amal Mk2 carburettor. The front hydraulic reservoir was now of opaque plastic to allow at-a-glance checking; the speedo drive moved to the left-hand side of the rear wheel, and, in an attempt to prevent blown bulbs and loose stems, the indicators were rubber-mounted. New BAP fuel taps sought to eradicate petrol leaks, and Avon Roadrunners replaced the TT100s as the factory-fit tyre.

As mentioned previously, there was no strict demarcation between US- and UK-spec Bonnevilles, and with American sales dropping rapidly, the factory had an incentive to sell more US-spec bikes at home, thanks to excess stocks of suitable components. Hence the Bonneville American, which was really just the standard US bike with the addition of fork gaiters, a plainer tank badge and a flatter (not stepped) seat.

With its higher prices and better quality, Triumph appeared to be aiming upmarket, and this was confirmed by the Bonneville Executive, launched halfway through the model year in February 1980. With its metallic Smoke Red paint, nose fairing and standard luggage, this Bonneville was clearly intended to have more than a hint of BMW about it, and in that Triumph succeeded. The nose fairing was glassfibre, lined with ABS leathergrain and painted to match the tank, sidepanels and luggage. Colour co-

1979-83: On the slide

ordinated Sigma panniers and topbox (complete with prominent Triumph badge) offered 3.9cu ft of carrying capacity, and the panniers themselves could be quickly unclipped for transportation into the foyer of the swankiest hotel. There were big circular mirrors (which would find their way onto the other bikes), and the stepped seat was based on that of the T140D, but with better padding. Appearing a few months before the ES electric start, the Executive at first came in kickstart form only.

But, as ever, behind the exciting new features, matters were grim at Meriden, once again the result of lack of sales, innumerable debts, and (even after the redundancies) too many workers building too few bikes. The only bright spot was an order for 1300 fully-equipped Tigers from the Nigerian government. This was actually a huge bonus, representing about six months' production for the new low-volume Meriden, and potentially very profitable. Secured against competition from BMW and Suzuki, the deal included sending four Meriden personnel to Nigeria to train mechanics, plus spares and tools support. But there was a tight deadline, and if the first batch of 300 bikes didn't make it on time to the waiting planes, the entire order would be cancelled. One hundred and ten Meriden workers stepped into the breach, offering to work a weekend unpaid to get the bikes finished, and they did it.

Meanwhile, Geoffrey Robinson was trying hard to persuade the new Conservative government to give Meriden more time, rather than insist on having its money back. No fan of state-assisted businesses, still less those that were described as 'worker's co-operatives,' the government was disinclined to help. Geoffrey Robinson's plan was that with breathing space, he would be able to find a business partner for Meriden who would bring in private investment. In a letter dated August 1979, he stated that negotiations were going well, and that the Nigerian order, plus smaller orders from Egypt and Libya, not to mention 400 private orders, were enough to keep the factory busy until the end of the year.

In fact, no fewer than thirteen potential partners were contacted, of which Amstrong Equipment (as mentioned above) and Suzuki were the most serious. Bernard Hooper, boss of Armstrong, was willing to carry on Bonneville production at Meriden, but with a much smaller workforce (about 150 people) building just 100 bikes a week in one section of the factory, the rest of the site being sold off. He also wanted all government debt and interest waived. The co-op workforce actually voted in favour of this drastic plan, but Minister of Industry Keith Joseph refused to write off the debts, so that was that.

Talks with Suzuki carried on through the first half of 1980, and the Japanese were certainly serious about taking on Triumph. They had approached Meriden first, and in January/February John Rosamond put the deal at 9:1 in favour. Suzuki engineers visited Meriden and some Triumph dealers in the USA, and a team led by Geoffrey Robinson flew to Tokyo. It looked like Suzuki (or its giant parent company, Marubeni) was interested in building bikes at Meriden from a mix of Suzuki and UK components, similar to British Leyland's partnership with Honda. But by June it was all off, the failure blamed on the unfavourable exchange rate between the pound and the yen. In fact, none of the partnership talks came to anything, and Triumph was on its own again.

1981

Models:	T140E Bonneville/T140ES Bonneville Electro/T140E Bonneville Executive/T140ES Bonneville Executive Electro/T140AV Bonneville (police only)
UK price:	£1966 (T140E); £2036 (T140ES); £2422 (Bonneville Executive)
Tank colour:	All models (UK) – Black/Candy Apple Red, Steel Grey/Candy Apple Red, Silver Blue/Black, Black/gold lining, Smokey Blue/gold lining, Smokey Flame/gold lining; all models (US) – Steel Grey/Black, Silver Blue/Black, Black/Candy Apple Red, Black/gold lining, Smokey Blue/Silver, Smokey Flame/Ivory
From engine number:	KDA 28001

With the Suzuki deal off, and no money to keep production running at 200 bikes a week, output was cut to 50 a week, which meant two-day working for the 460-strong workforce. In August 1980, Bernard Hooper decided not to go ahead with the Armstrong deal, and with all partnership talks having failed, and no money left, there was no option but to drastically cut the co-op

The Triumph Bonneville Bible

Bonneville Electro in UK guise with flatter bars and big tank.

Royal Wedding UK, missing some parts and in need of some TLC.

in size yet again. The workforce agreed to the board's proposal for 287 redundancies – only four workers had voted against, though others subsequently complained about how the job losses were implemented.

John Rosamond had the unenviable task of deciding who had to go, while keeping a nucleus of workers with the right range of skills to build bikes. It must have been a tricky – not to mention emotionally-charged – job, especially for someone who had been there at the blockade, and when it was done, 150 people remained to work in an empty, echoing shell of a building. "With 300 members missing from the Meriden factory," Rosamond later wrote, "it was just like a vast empty mausoleum, housing 150 guilt-ridden mourners taking part in a family wake." The plan was to move this shrunken set-up into the smaller Butler building before finding a smaller factory and selling off the entire Meriden site. It sounded a lot like Bernard Hooper's plan, with the dubious advantage that it was the co-op's own, rather than being imposed by a new private owner.

One small upside of this move to low-volume production was that the factory was able to build bikes to order and, in fact, buyers could choose any combination of options they wanted: electric or kickstart; UK- or US-spec; six different colour schemes, and alloy or spoked wheels. These special order bikes were labelled Factory Finished Custom, 'FFC' stamped alongside the engine number. If any of these turn up today in original condition, it's likely to be the only Bonneville built with that particular combination of options. Triumph made a virtue of all of this in its publicity material, one brochure describing the bikes as "virtually hand-built."

Then at the end of September 1980 came an unexpected piece of good news, something Meriden had been trying to achieve for several years. The government, realising that it was never going to get its money back, wrote off the debt, which now amounted to £8.4 million. This still left £2 million owing to the Export Credit Guarantee Department, but the unsold bikes in the US (there were 2000 of them) were said to be worth £4.4 million, while the Nigerian order, if it went ahead in its entirety, would bring in another £3 million.

"For the first time since the underfunded Meriden Co-operative was set up in 1975," wrote John Rosamond, "the company would no longer be on a war-like footing, continually battling in day-to-day negotiations to survive."

The debt write-off was certainly good news, but Meriden still faced immense problems. Even for a motorcycle company in good shape, 1981 saw fierce competition in a market that was shrinking amidst a recession. Triumph was paying 16.5 per cent interest on its overdraft, and the exchange rate made its products hopelessly uncompetitive in the USA, where nearly 1300 T140Ds and over 400 T140Es were still sitting unsold.

On a trip to help salvage the situation, various options were discussed with Wayne Moulton of TMA, including shipping bikes back to the UK, where they could be sold for a higher price; this would also avoid US import duty. One intriguing possibility which, according to John Rosamond, was actually discussed, was to build a new, 1000cc lowrider in Meriden, but from US-sourced parts. With a projected price of $3995, it would be aimed squarely at the American market and satisfy those US dealers who thought that Triumph needed a bike bigger than the Bonnie. A 'Triumph Harley' could have been interesting, but even if this Anglo-American hybrid had reached production, would it ever have succeeded in the early 1980s? With hindsight, it seems unlikely, given that Harley-Davidson itself was facing serious problems, and that such a bike would have had less appeal outside the States.

However, two ideas did come out of these meetings. Jack Wilson of Big D Cycles happened to drop in on one of them, and was introduced to John Rosamond. Wilson, of course, was a well-known Triumph tuner, who was very enthusiastic about the 8-valve Bonneville Triumph was currently developing with Weslake. This gave Wayne Moulton the idea of fitting the 8-valve

1979-83: On the slide

engine to the custom-style Bonneville TSX he was currently developing, again as an answer to Triumph dealers who thought the standard Bonneville too slow. The other idea came to John Rosamond from his hotel bedroom TV one morning. An excited news feature announced the forthcoming wedding of Prince Charles and Lady Diana Spencer – maybe this could be the basis for another special edition, and a way of updating a batch of 200 unsold 1979 T140Es?

Moulton was sceptical, perhaps remembering (though he didn't work for Triumph then) the less than enthusiastic response of American buyers to the last limited edition Bonnie with a royalist theme. However, the idea took root, and in July 1981 the Bonneville Royal Wedding was announced as a limited edition, though so late in the model year it is really regarded as an '82 bike

The Royal Wedding would be a cosmetic conversion, but the 1981 model year was a busy one for new bikes, notably the short-stroke 650 Thunderbird (an attempt to produced a budget-priced Triumph, though it wasn't cheap), and the single-carb Tiger Trail in both 650 and 750 forms.

As for the Bonnie, this year did bring more useful improvements. Oil seals were now fitted to the inlet valve guides, which could drastically cut oil consumption (why wasn't this done before?). Gearing was raised slightly, with a 45-tooth rear sprocket replacing the 47-tooth, and the heavy clutch (a long-running complaint from riders and road testers) was made lighter with softer springs and by cutting out one of the bonded plates (now just six). A new, nylon-lined cable

Triumph hoped the Executive would grab a piece of the touring market.

Royal Wedding at Meriden – probably one of the last PR shots taken outside the factory.

helped as well. There were rubber-mounted footrests, and work to quarantine the headlight from vibration allowed the use of a 60/45-watt sealed beam unit. The Amal carburettors that, in one form or another, had been fitted to every single Bonneville to roll out of Meriden, were replaced by Bing CV carbs, though these had been produced in collaboration with Amal.

Poor wet weather braking had been a long-standing complaint about the disc-braked Triumphs, thanks in part to the discs' chrome plating. The factory was reluctant to drop the chrome, because plain cast-iron discs weren't as pretty, quickly discolouring with surface rust. In mid-year it relented, also allowing the latest sintered metal Dunlopads to be fitted, which gave far better performance in the wet. Some bikes now had Dural callipers, and twin AP Racing discs were a new option.

One change brought on by necessity was a switch to an Italian company for fuel tanks, the British supplier having ceased production. The new, 4-gallon tanks came with Monza-style, flip-open caps, but didn't have the beefy appeal of the old 'breadbin' tank; still less the elegance of the slimline US-spec tank.

Meanwhile, work was continuing on a final solution to the Bonnie's vibration problem. Norton, of course, had famously rubber-mounted the Commando's vertical twin back in 1969, and Harley-Davidson followed suit in 1980 with the FLT Tour Glide, eventually extending this successfully to its entire range of V-twins. Now Meriden was working on its own rubber-mount system – AV – which, unlike the Norton's Isolastics, did not require periodic adjustment. Two prototypes were running as early as 1979, and a small batch of rubber-mounted Bonnevilles was built in 1981. There were good reports from some who rode AV Bonnevilles ("smooth as silk" at 70mph, according to veteran journalist Bob Currie) but in practice the AV system had several problems. Rear wheel and sprockets were only kept in line by two inadequate brackets, which led to handling problems. Sprockets, chain and swingarm tended to wear quickly, and if oil leaked onto the lower rubber mountings, these could degrade and even shear. Sadly, the AV system was never fully developed, and never made it onto a production civilian bike.

There was a growing consensus that the quality of standard production Bonnevilles was improving, something noted by dealers on both sides of the Atlantic, and this new faith in the product was underlined by the decision to double the warranty to 12 months/12,000 miles for 1981.

John Smith tested an Electro for *Bike*, opening with the famous quote from Dr Johnson about patriotism being the last refuge of the scoundrel. He wanted to make it clear that he wasn't intending to be swayed by a sentimental attachment to the Bonneville's Britishness. But he did like it, anyway: "From the moment I touched the red starter button on a frosty morning and the motor burst into instant life I knew this was going to be okay." Sure, the 1981 Bonneville had lost some overtaking urge, but the test bike still ran up to 102mph, with a sub-15sec quarter-mile. It gave 50mpg, even when ridden "with abandon," which was a bit of a selling point when petrol prices were rising and equivalent Japanese bikes used at least 10 per cent more fuel.

In fact, the Bonnie's fuel consumption could be improved still further by fitting an SU carburettor. Staple of generations of BMC and British Leyland cars, the SU was a simple, efficient carb, and a conversion kit by Phoenix Motorcycles to replace the Bonnie's twin Amals with a single 1¾in SU was available in 1981. *Bike* tested one, and, apart from grumbles about vague instructions and fitting difficulties, found that it improved consumption from an average 44mpg to 55mpg – exactly 25 per cent.

Going back to that road test, John Smith found the gearchange stiff but with good feel,

1979-83: On the slide

A cheerful James Hunt and David Essex promote the Electro. The ends of Hunt's crutches are just visible behind the bike.

Triumph – a special feeling

The 1981 brochure majored on attention to detail, describing the production process at Meriden:

"… motorcycle assembly is undertaken by Triumph's highly-skilled fitters working in small groups. On leaving the track, all motorcycles pass to the rolling road test cells, where simulated road conditions enable the Triumph high-performance engine and all other motorcycle functions to be extensively checked. Following satisfactory completion of these procedures final adjustments are made; seats and petrol tanks fitted prior to despatch.

"Having spent a great deal of time on attention to detail, Triumph's crowning glory is in its final finish, achieved by highly-skilled paintshop personnel. Over many years of experience, it has been found that there is no short cut to quality; it only comes with painstaking attention to detail, all of which is totally worthwhile, when one views the finished Triumph motorcycle.

"Triumph – 'A special feeling you will never forget.'"

The Triumph Bonneville Bible

and the clutch lighter and nicer to use. As with almost every other Bonneville test ever written, the handling received fulsome praise. There were no oil leaks, and vibration had been reduced by more consistent quality control, particularly for the crankshaft, while the brakes were "superb." After a few asides about how good it was to ride something clearly hand-built, John Smith finished with a wry acknowledgement to his opening quote: "The Triumph pleased me so much that offered a free choice between it and a Honda 750FA – my favourite in the class so far – I'd be on the horns of a dilemma ... Guess I'm just a scoundrel after all."

Triumph's American sales had all but collapsed, and Meriden was reduced to little more than a skeleton staff, but they were clearly doing something right. And there were several new developments. The eight-valve TSS, and the anti-vibration AV frame were being widely talked about in the press, and April had seen the TS8-1 prototype unveiled at the International Motorcycle Show at the NEC in Birmingham in the UK. The TS8-1 put the eight-valve together with the AV frame in a set angular bodywork quite unlike anything Triumph had built before. Finally, and further in the future, there was T2000, an all-new, watercooled parallel twin that would finally replace the old Bonneville. If the co-op could bring these in, sell off Meriden and move to a smaller, cheaper-to-run factory, recovery from the brink didn't seem too much to hope for after all.

Meriden's big hope for 1982: the eight-valve TSS.

1982

Models:	T140E Bonneville/T140ES Bonneville Electro/T140E Bonneville Executive/ T140ES Bonneville Executive Electro/T140LE Bonneville Royal/T140 TSX (from GEA.33528 June 1982)/T140 TSS (from CEA.33027 March 1982)
UK price:	£2025 (T140E); £2075 (T140ES Bonneville Electro); £2449 (T140E Bonneville Executive); £2249 (T140 TSX); £2399 (T140 TSS)
Tank colour:	All models (UK) – Black/gold lining, Smokey Flame/gold lining, Smokey Blue/gold lining; all models (US) – Smokey Flame/Ivory, Smokey Blue/Silver, Silver-Blue/Black, Black/Candy Apple Red
From engine number:	HDA30651

Behind the exciting new model plans – the TSS, the AV frame and the T2000 – Triumph was still in dire straits. Bikes were now built in batches of around 80, because this was all they could afford to make at a time. Only when each batch had been sold and paid for could Meriden put the cash down for the parts to make another batch.

The Meriden factory – although a third of it was now sub-let – was still far too big for Triumph's needs, carrying a rates bill of £40,000 a year. The plan was still to sell the entire site and move somewhere more affordable, but, despite having been in the hands of estate agents since 1981, there was very little interest. Britain (and the entire Western world) was suffering from a savage economic recession, made worse

Right: The TSS motor was powerful and revvy, though troublesome.

The Triumph Bonneville Bible

Several components, such as indicators, now came from abroad.

Above, right: Simple black and gold finish on the '82 TSS.

Red line at 7-8000rpm was no exaggeration.

Twin front discs were standard on the TSS; optional on the other Bonnevilles.

by monetarist policies which insisted that the West's economic ills were only curable by dramatic government spending cuts, with high unemployment a price worth paying. In these times, not many entrepreneurs were looking to buy a factory, still less in Britain, whose manufacturing industry was being devastated. The recession hit the motorcycle-buying public as well, with UK sales down by 63 per cent in 1982.

Meanwhile, the Bonneville Royal was in production, and according to John Rosamond sold well as a limited edition. Ironically, demand was so strong that the co-op (unlike many firms in Britain) wasn't able to give everyone a day off for the royal nuptials on July 29 because all hands were needed to build bikes celebrating the occasion!

Based on the Bonneville Electro, the Royal came with the now-standard Bing CV carburettors and Marzocchi rear shocks. The most striking feature was a chromed fuel tank, with gold-lined black wings on the UK-spec bike; Smokey Blue on the US. The UK bike also had twin front discs, ungaitered forks and Morris alloy wheels. The engine was painted matt black, as was the headlight. US bikes had a chrome headlight, semi-King and Queen seat, polished engine and forks, single front disc and wire wheels. It's thought that only 50 Royal Wedding Bonnevilles actually made it to the States, and with plain black tanks rather than the chrome of UK bikes.

All Royals had a plate on the headstock with the special edition number and the words, 'In celebration of the wedding of Prince Charles and Lady Diana Spencer.' It was, of course, all approved by the palace, and just 250 were made.

1979-83: On the slide

There were few general improvements to the standard Bonneville for 1982, which is hardly surprising given that Brian Jones and the tiny engineering department were fully stretched preparing the eight-valve TSS and custom TSX for launch. Longer sidepanels, now fastened by a single Allen bolt each side, covered the bulkier Bing carburettors; there was a bigger toolkit, and the clutch and brake levers were doglegs, which finally laid to rest the criticism of hard-to-reach controls. Stainless steel mudguards were another change for the better, and there was a new seat with moulded inserts.

But the really big news for 1982 wasn't announced until March. The TSS was Triumph's final throw of the dice; the last major change to the Bonneville. It actually wasn't a new idea at all – Weslake had been offering an eight-valve cylinder head conversion for some time and this latest version was a joint project with Meriden, though, according to Lindsay Brooke and David Gaylin, Jack Wilson of American dealer Big D Cycles also had a hand in it. Wilson had been loaned a development 8-valve motor, with which his team won the Battle of the Twins race at Daytona.

Launched at the Royal Garden Hotel in Kensington, the TSS looked good. Triumph claimed 57bhp, 16 per cent more power than the standard Bonnie, and a top speed of over 120mph. At the same time, John Rosamond was able to announce that the co-op was finally free of all government debt, as the money owed to the Export Credit Guarantee Department had been paid off.

The two years spent developing TSS didn't appear to have been wasted, Brian Jones designing a more robust bottom end to cope with the extra power. The crankshaft was stiffer, with a beefier flywheel and fatter big-end journals. It ran on roller-bearings and was machined all over. All of which, it was claimed, reduced flexing and hence vibration.

There was a new alloy cylinder block with pressed-in steel liners, squared-off and with more fins than the old cast-iron one, the bores set wider apart to allow more air space between the cylinders. The wider-set bores meant there was no room for a conventional head gasket, so sealing was via a pair of Cooper rings, set into grooves in the cylinder head. The head itself came with integral rocker boxes (eliminating one source of oil leaks), the eight valves at a narrow, 30-degree angle. It breathed more efficiently than the old head, and set the 12mm sparkplugs centrally between the four valves.

Flat-topped pistons ran cooler and allowed a 9.5:1 compression ratio.

The whole motor looked very businesslike finished all in black, and although that 57bhp was produced at 6500rpm, the engine was said to be safe to 10,000rpm ... No wonder John Rosamond's quote for the press was a

Standard US and UK Bonnevilles carried on for 1982, alongside the TSS.

Custom TSX was Triumph's final bid for the US market.

The Triumph Bonneville Bible

TSX was designed by Triumph's US importer, though that didn't make it a success.

triumphant: "We're back in the performance business." In road tests, the TSS appeared to live up to its promise, endorsing a claim of 120mph+, backed up by a standing quarter-mile of 14.28 seconds. Journalists confirmed that vibration was much reduced, and that the new motor, despite the rumour of a five-figure redline, was perfectly docile at lower revs. If there were criticisms, these were levelled at the standard Bonneville running gear that made up the rest of the bike – the riding position still placed the feet too far forward, and some thought the suspension too stiff.

It was only after the first TSSs were sold that the bad news began to filter come in. An initial batch of cylinder heads turned out to be porous, allowing oil leaks, after all the hard work to combat leaks! And the Cooper rings could blow if the liners slipped down the barrels, which they frequently did. Cams wore fast; valve springs broke, and the TSS soon became a warranty liability for Triumph. Four hundred and thirty eight were built in all, which, given Meriden's by-now low production, was quite a chunk of the annual total, Just 112 were exported to the States, where the bike received good reviews but was hampered by a price of $3690 (rising to just short of $3900 for '83).

A month after the TSS launched it was the turn of the TSX. This was the brainchild of Wayne Moulton, head of TMA, who had been developing a version of the Bonneville that would appeal to American buyers. Moulton had a track record, having masterminded the popular LTD series when he worked for Kawasaki.

The TSX was in the same factory custom

By 1981/2, the Bonneville had spawned a whole range of variants.

1979-83: On the slide

mould as those Kawasakis, using standard Bonneville running gear but high bars, stepped King and Queen seat, and a welcome return of the Triumph slimline tank. It shared some of the TSS's stronger bottom end, but stuck with the standard Bonnie's four-valve top end and cast-iron barrel. There were stubby megaphone silencers (which looked good and sounded nice but were actually quite restrictive), and a 16-inch rear wheel equipped with a fat Avon Roadrunner, balancing the standard 19-inch Roadrunner on the front. Morris seven-spoke alloys underlined that this was intended to be a modern cruiser, not a classic-look Triumph. If the TSX made a styling gaffe it was in the garish red, yellow and orange stripes that adorned the tank and sidepanels. "A Yamakawahonzuki it ain't" went the Stateside advert, the last magazine ad for Triumph in the USA. True enough, it wasn't one of those, but it did look like one. Even if American customers liked the look, they would probably still have been put off by the official price of $3695.

1983

Models:	T140E Bonneville/T140ES Bonneville Electro/T140 TSX/T140 TSS/T140AV Bonneville Executive Electro
UK price:	£2025 (T140E); £2075 T140ES); £2249 (T140 TSX); £2399 (TSS); £2449 (T140AV)
Tank colour:	T140E/ES (UK) – Black/Candy Apple Red, Burgundy/gold lining, Black/gold lining; T140E/ES (US) - Black/red, yellow, orange decals, Midnight Blue/decals, Burgundy/decals; TSX – Black/red, yellow, orange decals, Burgundy/red, yellow, orange decals; TSS – Black/gold lining
From engine number:	BEA.33001

For the last few months of Bonneville production, history becomes less precise! The factory was so short of money that bikes were assembled according to what parts were available at the time, so differences to the official specification may well have crept in. The TSS, for example, was restyled, and would apparently adopt the

This is how the 1983 TSS would have looked – nicer than the '82.

AV frame, but there's no evidence that any were actually built. Similarly, the Executive was listed with the AV frame, and John Nelson (*Bonnie: The Development History of the Triumph Bonneville*) also provides a starting engine number of GEA.33526 in June 1982, so at least one of those did, presumably escape.

The reality at Meriden was that the money to pay wages ran out in late 1982, so most of the staff were laid off, though the 41 left evidently did still assemble a few bikes: according to John Nelson, the last-ever Bonneville built at Meriden was completed on January 7, 1983, with engine number AEA.34389. Another contender for the

Fitting the eight-valve engine to the TSX was another objective for '83.

final Bonneville is the one owned by Bill Crosby, proprietor of long-time Triumph dealer Reg Allen in London. "In 1983 they were getting short of bits," he remembered, "so I actually had to take some parts up for them to finish it." His bike, a kickstart T140E, is on display at the London Motorcycle Museum.

The 1983 range was actually shown to the public at the April 1983 International Motorcycle Show at the NEC in Birmingham. Looking at the Triumph stand, it appeared chock-full of new bikes. As well as the new TSS and TSX, there was, high up on a plinth and not available for close inspection, a wooden mock-up of the liquid-cooled T2000, now renamed Phoenix. There were two new short-stroke 600s as well, intended to replace the 650 Thunderbird – a single-carb Thunderbird and twin-carb Daytona. It all looked impressive, and was intended to attract funding for Meriden, now virtually mothballed. "They didn't have any money," said Bill Crosby, "'but the NEC let them have the stand for free. I think BMW donated the wood for the plinth; another company gave the carpet. At the factory, 28 people came in specially to build the show bikes, which were just mock-ups without cranks or gearbox internals."

As for the Bonneville, changes for '83 were limited to a stronger intermediate gear for the electric start (from engine DEA.33133), and a change of thread on the gearbox mainshaft. More pressing matters were in hand, and, even as full production ended in late 1982, there was still a glimmer of hope. In November it was announced that West Midlands County Council was to give the co-op a £465,000 grant to buy new machinery and fund exports. The exchange rate was more favourable now, so there was a greater possibility of selling bikes in the USA at a competitive price. The Council's Enterprise Board was even considering taking a £1million stake in the co-op, after consultants had checked the viability of the five-year plan. Their stipulation to this was match funding from a private investor. And a new home was in prospect as well, the ex-Triumph car plant at Foleshill Road in Coventry – the sale hadn't yet gone through, but was far enough down the road for a few laid off Meriden workers to go in voluntarily at a weekend and begin cleaning it up. A floorplan was drawn up for how this smaller factory could accommodate production of the Bonneville. And crucially, Tarmac Homes offered to buy the Meriden site for £1million.

Sadly, none of this ever happened. In the gloomy economic circumstances of 1983, no private investors came forward to match the Council's £1million stake. The Hesketh venture had just gone bust, which lost the private sector £2million, so it probably wasn't the right time to beg funding for another British motorcycle revival. The deal on the new factory fell through in May 1983 when Triumph was outbid. And although Tarmac's offer was still on the table, that money would be swallowed up by an overdraft. In any case, Triumph had nowhere to go.

So in July, months after Bonneville production effectively ended, a mass meeting of the co-op's membership approved a proposal to wind it all up. Meriden was liquidated the following month with debts of £3.8million, and everything was sold off, even down to the famous factory gates with their Triumph logo. And that

1979-83: On the slide

Above, left: AV frame, electric start and police equipment – a bid to win back some lucrative police contracts.

Above: For 1983, the standard TSX became the TSX4.

Left: Standard T140ES Bonneville looked much like the '82 TSS.

The Triumph Bonneville Bible

Above: US Bonneville followed the lead of the TSX.

Right: Short-stroke 600cc Daytona was a stillborn for 1983.

The last Meriden Bonneville of all? Owned by the London Motorcycle Museum.

was the end of the Meriden story.

But it wasn't the end of the Bonneville. Midlands businessman John Bloor (who would launch his all-new Triumph range in 1991) had outbid several rivals – one of whom was Triumph parts manufacturer Racing Spares – for the name and manufacturing rights. It wasn't, after all, Meriden that would make the final Bonneville, but Racing Spares' owner, Les Harris.

7

1985-88: Final fling

1985-88

Models:	Bonneville UK/Bonneville US
UK price:	£2760
Tank colour (all):	Black/Candy Apple Red, Black/gold lining
From engine number:	00003

If Les Harris had had his way, he would have bought the manufacturing rights to the Triumph name and to the Bonneville outright. As it was, he settled for the next best thing: a licence from John Bloor to build the Bonnie for five years, with an option to renew.

Harris was 44; a south Devon businessman who had built up the highly successful Racing Spares, making pattern parts for Triumphs, BSAs and Nortons. His three plants in Plymouth, Newton Abbot and Leighton Buzzard employed 80 people, and turned over £5million a year. His business empire wasn't on the scale of John Bloor's, but it was substantial, and familiar with the world of Triumph twins.

Harris was happy to talk to the press (hungry as ever for news of the 'rebirth' of Britain's motorcycle industry), and referred to the potential for large orders from the Third World, and even an assembly plant in Pakistan. His aim was to assemble an initial 20 bikes per week, eventually rising to as many as 300, with a price tag of under £2000, making his new Bonnie cheaper than the last one from Meriden. Production would start in the summer of 1984; only a matter of months after he had signed the licence.

Much of this early promise didn't come to fruition, however: the Harris Bonneville wasn't

Les Harris succeeded in bringing back the Bonneville, but sales didn't match expectations.

The Triumph Bonneville Bible

The Harris Bonneville came in US- or UK-spec.

Three years after the Harris Bonneville died, the new Triumph factory was in business, though it was a decade and a half before the Hinckley Bonneville appeared.

launched until summer 1985, average production rate was about nine bikes a week, and the launch price was £2760.

There were several reasons for this. The Triumph is a simple machine by modern standards, but still comprised of around 1500 parts, and although Racing Spares made some of these, many had to come from some 200 outside suppliers. (On the other hand, as Les Harris pointed out, many of these people, as the 1980s recession ground on, were only too glad of the work, despite the small quantities involved.) Some of the old dies were worn out (including that for the crankshaft) and had to be replaced, meaning more delay – not to mention great expense (Les Harris invested £1.5million in bringing the Bonneville back to life). And there were other complications. The crank, for example, was forged in Britain, but had to be shipped to Italy for machining as no company in the UK could take on the job.

Ironically, a major delay stemmed from John Bloor. Part of the Harris plan was to, sensibly, give the new Bonnie the stronger bottom end from the TSS, and a cooler running alloy barrel. By the summer of 1984, two prototypes had been built and had covered 80,000 miles each when John Bloor invoked the small print of the licence agreement: that the Harris bikes be to

The Royal Signals White Helmets Display Team remained loyal to Triumph, buying bikes from Les Harris after Meriden closed.

standard Meriden Bonneville-spec. More delays; more expense.

Eventually, on 25 June 1985, the Harris Bonneville was launched. It came in kickstart-only form, as the basic T140E in US- or UK-style. Reflecting the fact that some British suppliers had gone to the wall or given up on the motorcycle industry, several parts were bought from overseas, though the frames were built in Birmingham. Italy got the lion's share: front forks and rear shocks from Paioli; brakes from Brembo, and silencers from Lafranconi (the latter specially developed for the bike to comply with noise legislation and increasing ground clearance). Magura of Germany provided the switchgear, and – as before – the speedo and rev counter came from Veglia. The tyres were still Avon Roadrunners, though. As per spec, and in compliance with the licence small print, there were only tiny detail changes from the final Meriden Bonnies, although Amal carburettors made a comeback in place of the Bings. These were hybrids – Mk1 Concentrics with the Mk2's cold start slides, made in Spain.

Despite the disappointment to patriots of all this foreign content – not to mention the £2760 price tag – the Harris Bonneville was welcomed by the press. In *Classic Bike*, Mike Nicks thought the engine felt more tightly assembled than the Meriden version, a fact borne out by an oil consumption of only 200mpp (good by Bonneville standards). In the same magazine, Richard Simpson thought the rubber-mounted bars and footrests did a good job of quelling vibration; that the Bonneville handled well (though even this Triumph strong point had since been overtaken by more modern machinery); that it had good brakes but that the sit-up, feet-forward riding position was hard work at speed.

There were a few comments about quality niggles, and as time went on more serious complaints began to emerge. In 1989, Jim Grant wrote in *Classic Bike*: "... reliability and finish can be desperately poor ... dealers talk of wholesale warranty replacement of front and rear suspensions."

Against all the odds, Les Harris had succeeded in resuscitating the Bonneville, building 1260 new bikes until production finally ended in March 1988: the most obvious reason because the dies for the crankcases and cylinder head needed replacing, which Harris said would cost £400,000, but, beyond that, sales simply hadn't met expectations, partly because those Third World orders had never materialised; partly because the new Bonnie could not be sold in the USA (product liability insurance would have cost an eye watering £7million), and partly because not enough UK and European buyers came forward, despite all the regret that had been expressed when Meriden closed. "If everybody who said they were sad to see the end of the Bonnie had bought one," said Les Harris at the end, "I'd still be making them. They were not easy to sell."

The final Triumph Bonneville – engine number 001258 – was built on 9 March 1988, 29 years and over 300,000 bikes after Edward Turner had leant on the prototype and informed the meeting that it would send them all to Carey Street, home of the famous bankruptcy court. In the end it did, but that wasn't the Bonneville's fault ...

8

Living with a Bonneville

Choosing • Buying • Owning • Restoring

If you don't already own a Bonneville, you might have been inspired by this book to buy one, and the good news is that there's a lot of choice. As mentioned in the Introduction, Meriden built over 300,000 Bonnies, which makes this the most popular British twin of all; far more so than the Norton Commando or any variant of the BSA twin. Of course, many of these bikes have long since died a death – cannibalised to build a Triton, written off in an accident or just left mouldering in the back of a shed until sold off as an unrestorable box of bits.

But many others have survived, and paradoxically, despite being the most common postwar British bike, the Bonneville is probably the most sought-after as well. This means they aren't cheap (though T140s are more affordable), but, on the other hand, shouldn't be difficult to sell if you decide after all that the Bonneville is not the bike for you. Because there are lots of Bonnies about, and interest in them is strong, there's a good supply of spare parts, the price of which is reasonable.

Finally, although all Bonnevilles were based around the same air-cooled vertical twin, they did change in character quite a bit over the years. A 1960 pre-unit T120, for example, is a very different animal to a '79 T140E.

In short, whether you want a rorty sportster for some weekend fun or a more relaxed tourer, there should be something to suit you. And although they're aren't strictly Bonnevilles, the 650/750cc single-carburettor Triumphs are well worth considering, too: they're almost as fast, but with more tractable low-speed running.

Is it for me?

If you're thinking of buying a Bonnie as your first classic bike, think hard. Like any classic, the Triumph twin needs a lot of care and attention, and it's not really the right bike for 21st century commuting. While leather-clad young bloods of the '60s cheerfully rode their Bonnies every day, all year round, they were keen enough to take on the intensive maintenance that went with it, or willing to live with the oil leaks and unreliability that resulted from neglect.

In an age where bikes need only an oil check and chain adjustment between major services, the Bonneville demands a lot more looking after. We live in an age where consumer products keep working without much attention, but old bikes aren't like that.

Having said that, the later the model, the easier it is to live with, generally. Take a later T140 with electronic ignition, high-output alternator and halogen headlight. Some folk do use these bikes as everyday transport, and in fact a disc-braked T140 with all of those parts is the most practical proposition of any classic British bike. But for many, a Bonnie – of whatever age – is a second or third bike, brought out of the garage on sunny days.

Even then, it demands a different mindset

Living with a Bonneville

to that required for riding a modern bike. The relationship is based on a constant awareness of how the bike is running: has that nut vibrated loose? Is that the beginnings of a leak from the rocker box? If an indicator ceases to function, is it the bulb or just a loose connection? Keeping track of all these little 'events' are a part of Bonneville ownership, and many owners would say that they are integral to what makes owning one (or indeed any classic bike) more satisfying than a modern machine. You develop a relationship with a classic that is quite different to that you have with a bike that always starts on the button and never goes wrong.

A few other caveats apply to riding the Bonneville. If you've only ever ridden modern bikes, the Bonnie will seem quite crude. Again, this applies to an increasing extent the older the bike is. They do vibrate, but far less than you might expect, especially if revs are kept below 5000rpm. Use all of the performance, though, and the vibes will get through to both you and the bike.

By the standards of its day, the Bonnie had good brakes, once the twin leading shoe front drum was introduced in 1968. But earlier brakes aren't up to modern standards, and all Bonnies are still fast enough to get you into trouble. The same goes for pre-1966, six-volt electrics, with a headlight that's dimmer and less certain charging than any modern biker is used to. Also, don't forget that, up until 1975, the Bonneville had a right-footed gearchange and left-footed brake, something to bear in mind if you're used to things being the other way around.

Buy a Bonneville and – unless you can find one of the last ones with electric start – you will have to kickstart it. Again, this can be a culture shock for anyone brought up on modern machines, though it doesn't really need bulging thigh muscles – it's more about technique than strength: remembering to flood the carbs with fuel on a cold start. Electronic ignition, standard from 1979 and a popular aftermarket fitment, makes first- or second-kick starting much more likely. Actually, kicking a Bonnie into life can become one of the pleasures of owning one; another thing that builds the relationship: more so than simply thumbing a button does.

Upsides

Having got the dull but necessary warnings out of the way, we can get on to the upsides of owning a Bonneville, and there are plenty of them.

First, performance. Throughout the 1960s, the Bonnie was one of the fastest things on the road: a two-wheeled E-type that offered affordable high performance, just like the Jaguar. And although it was overtaken by the new breed of superbikes in the '70s, it's still a fast bike today, capable of delivering an exciting riding experience.

This all relates to acceleration rather than very high speeds, which, in any case, are becoming increasingly unacceptable on our crowded roads. The Bonneville isn't really a motorway machine. It will sit at a steady 70mph without becoming stressed (especially the higher-geared T140), but this really isn't its natural element, and any attempt to maintain higher speeds for long will be uncomfortable for the rider and stressful for the machine. In addition, the riding position of the T140 isn't comfortable at higher speeds, as the footrests are too far forward (an issue that Meriden never sorted out) combined with the US-spec high-rise bars that can make holding on to speeds of 70 and above quite hard

A Bonneville can be a rewarding bike to own, though does demand some commitment.

Happiness is (or can be) your own Bonnie: this is Curly and his tastefully personalised T120.

123

The Triumph Bonneville Bible

work. T120s had a slightly more lean-forward position, better suited to fast riding.

The Bonnie is most at home on single carriageway A or B roads, where it becomes a joy to ride, thanks to its strong mid-range power. Later bikes – leaner-running with more restrictive silencers – have less of that instant urge that so many riders love about the Bonneville, though they're still great fun to ride.

Good power is nothing without good handling, and this became another of the Triumph's strong points. It wasn't perfect in the early years as some early 1960s bikes were prone to high-speed weave, and/or a light front end, and the T140 had a distinct lack of ground clearance. The early '60s problems weren't fully resolved until Doug Hele's work in the middle of that decade, which gave 1966-on Bonnies handling as good as any other bike on the road, and better than most. This tradition carried on with the new frame in 1971, which, apart from its many flaws, was at least fun around corners. That isn't to say that a Bonneville will out-handle a FireBlade – its narrower tyres and less extreme geometry means it won't have the ultimate ability of a modern sports bike – but on a twisty A or B road, a Bonnie will always be tremendous, dependable fun.

Size has a lot to do with this. In an age where the biggest bikes have got heavier, wider and taller by the year, the Triumph twin is physically small and light, little bigger than a modern 250, and at around 400lb, weighs about the same. So despite the high performance image, it's not intimidating to sit on for the first time, and is light enough to push around easily. The only exception are the 1971/72 Bonnies, with their very high seats, though the comments about weight and overall size still apply.

Although many Bonnevilles are used purely for shorter weekend rides, they're also capable of longer trips, two-up, although this applies more to the T140, whose softer engine characteristics are better suited to touring. Unless you can find one of the rare Executives, Bonnies don't come with luggage.

There's another attraction of the Bonneville which we haven't mentioned yet, but it's the most obvious one of the lot. Beauty is in the eye of the beholder, of course, but you're unlikely to find anyone describing the Bonnie as an ugly bike. It really is a thing of beauty, thanks in large part to Edward Turner's inspired sense of style, with a family resemblance going back to the original pre-war Speed Twin. There's an elegance and simplicity to its lines which are almost symmetrical. The shape of the fuel tank has much to do with it: the slim rear end flaring out to present the 'Triumph' badges, usually accentuated by two-tone paintwork.

Of course, they're not all like that. The post-1971 UK spec bike's 'breadbin' tank could never be described as elegant, though it has a certain beefy appeal, and the 1981/82 Bonneville's Italian-made tanks seemed to lack any shape at all! Even so, the Bonnie remains one of the best-looking British twins. Buy one, and you will rarely tire of gazing at it.

Practicalities

Bonnevilles can be surprisingly cheap to run, given their high performance and semi-exotic status. Fuel consumption is 45-55mpg – less than that of an equivalent Japanese classic – though the single-carb Trophy and Tiger are slightly better. Some do suffer from being oil-thirsty, but this only really becomes an issue if you are covering a lot of miles.

One of the Bonnie's strongest points in terms of practical ownership is that spares back-up is very good, partly because there are lots of bikes around still and demand remains strong, and partly because the model didn't actually change that much, with many parts staying the same for years. The 1971 frame, for example, the cause of so many problems when it was launched, remained part of the Bonneville (in slightly modified form) right up until the last LF Harris machine was built in 1988. Typical 2012 prices were £80 for a pair of T140 pistons, £110 for a pair of exhaust downpipes (with balance pipe), and £16 for a front brake cable.

To support this, there's a huge fund of knowledge about the Bonneville out there, with many specialists who have been in the business for years, and know the bike inside out. Some, such as Norman Hyde, are ex-Meriden workers. Beyond the specialists, there's the Triumph Owner's Club, and the general community of thousands of experienced owners. Whatever your question about the Bonneville, somebody, somewhere should be able to answer it.

The bike isn't particularly hard on consumables, either – tyres, brakes, chains and sprockets – given its performance, but if a previous owner has skimped with a cheap chain and sprocket kit for example, then these won't last as long. With the best will in the world, the Triumph twin engine isn't as long-lived as the equivalent Honda. Component life depends on a whole raft of factors, including who last built

Living with a Bonneville

A bike like this, though far from concours, can still make a reliable ride.

the engine and the mechanical sympathy of its owner, but the cylinder head will probably need rebuilding every 20,000 miles or so, with new pistons (certainly rings) at 20-40,000 miles. Valves, guides, oversize pistons – all are readily available as new spares.

We mentioned earlier that the Bonneville needs careful maintenance, and it does, though the tasks (with the possible exception of the twin cb points ignition) aren't complicated or tricky to do. Setting the tappets, for example, is simpler than adjusting top end clearances on most overhead cam engines and, unlike the equivalent Japanese four-cylinder bike, there are two carburettors to balance rather than four. The single-carb Trophy and Tiger make this job simpler still.

The oil should be changed at least every 1500 miles – and preferably every 1000 – because the filtration system is coarse and can let impurities through over time. The price of oil may be going up, but, as the old saying goes, it's still a lot cheaper than bearings. Some owners fit an aftermarket oil filter kit, which uses a modern cartridge filter. A standard 20W50 low detergent mineral oil is fine for the T140. Tappets should also be checked every 1000/1500 miles, with the engine cold: a job which becomes more vital if the bike doesn't have hardened valve seats. It will run on unleaded fuel, but this can lead to valve seat recession, which will eventually close the tappet gap with resultant risk of burning out the valve. Hardened seats, a leaded fuel additive at every fill-up, or regular attention to the tappets are the alternatives.

Bonnevilles qualify for classic bike insurance, and if you can limit your mileage to an agreed figure, some insurance companies will offer a good deal. In the UK, Carole Nash and Footman James are just two insurance providers that offer this.

Investment potential is something else to think about. Even if you're buying a Bonnie simply with a view to enjoying riding it, it's nice to think that if you ever sell, you should get your money back. This has long been the case with the T120, especially the rarer 1959-62 pre-unit, and late '60s Bonnevilles in particular are highly sought-after. It used to be the case that the 1971-on oil-in-frame Bonnies were the poor relations, especially the T140s, with values languishing, thanks to reduced desirability. However, prices are again starting to rise, and while the models are still considerably cheaper than a T120, later Bonnevilles should hold their value. Some T140s, such as the TSS or Executive, should eventually be worth more than the standard bikes, thanks to their rarity. From an investment point of view,

The Triumph Bonneville Bible

'60s rarities such as the Thruxton Bonneville and the TT Special will always be the best bets.

Where to find your Bonnie

Finding a Bonneville is not difficult, as there are lots of them around, at least in the UK and USA, and there will always be a selection for sale, whatever time of year.

In the UK, keep an eye on the classified ads of *Nacelle*, the Triumph Owner's Club magazine – you'll need to join, but this is a good idea anyway, as it allows access to the helpful community of active Bonneville owners. A few ads – accessible to all – also appear on the club's website. There's also the *VMCC Journal, Old Bike Mart,* and on the newsagent shelves, *Classic Bike* and *The Classic Motorcycle*, which carry adverts from dealers as well as private sellers. Dealer stocks turn over regularly, especially in the spring and early summer, so it's well worth keeping an eye on the dealer websites which are (or should be) updated as soon as new bikes come in.

While on-line, there's always eBay, where there's usually a selection of Bonnevilles on offer, though these days far outnumbered by the many Hinckley Bonnies for sale. Here, though, even more so than with buying a bike through more traditional methods, it's a case of caveat emptor. Some buyers will happily bid for a bike without viewing it, but it's still worth a journey to assess the bike properly before bidding. You will have to be quick, though, as the eBay world moves fast. Make use of the 'seller's history' section to check how the seller has treated previous customers, and be aware that many dealers make use of eBay. It's also not unknown for bikes advertised for sale to be 'ghost' machines which don't really exist, or not in the form they are advertised. You could still pick up a bargain through eBay, but pre-bid viewing is strongly recommended.

Finally – though less popular now, thanks to the convenience of on-line buying – there are auctions. Specialist motorcycle auctions are still held up and down the UK, with prior notice given in the classic bike magazines. Although you'll need to make a special journey to attend one, and may come home empty-handed, prices are usually lower than those asked by a dealer or private seller. On the other hand, there's only a limited opportunity to inspect the bike, and you won't be able to test ride it. The golden rule, as with any other auction, is to decide in advance what your maximum bid will be and stick to it – it's all too easy to get carried away on the day, and end up paying over the odds. If your bid is successful, the bike becomes your responsibility straight away, so you'll either have to insure it and ride it home or have a bike trailer on hand.

Auctioneers

Bonhams www.bonhams.com/ Cheffins www.cheffins.co.uk/eBay www.ebay.com/H&H www.classic-auctions.co.uk/.

Shiny late T140V, but what lies below the glitter …?

Autojumbles will often have a few Bonnevilles for sale, such as this '71 T120.

Living with a Bonneville

Ready-to-ride or restore?

Buying a Bonneville offers the complete range of motorcycle purchase experience: everything from the familiar autojumble basket case (a collection of well-worn and rusty parts that may or may not add up to one complete bike) to a concours machine, built to better-than-new standard.

Which one suits you best depends on a great many things; not just your budget but also your time, inclination and skills with regard to undertaking a complete restoration. There's an undeniable romance about restoration projects, bringing a sick bike back to blooming health, and it's tempting to buy something that 'just needs a few small jobs' to bring it up to scratch. But there are two things to think about, here: once you've got the bike home and start taking it apart, those few small jobs could turn into big ones; restoration takes time, which is a precious thing in itself. Be honest with yourself – will you get as much pleasure from working on the bike as you will from riding it?

If you don't want to restore the bike yourself, then the obvious alternative is to hand over the whole thing to a professional. But, be warned: the cost will only be covered by the increased value of the bike if you've been lucky enough to find something rare, but unrestored, such as a Thruxton, which is highly unlikely, because the rarest Bonnies have already been hoovered up by collectors. As for more common-or-garden Bonnevilles, professionally restored bikes are, of course, worth a lot more than tatty ones, but rarely enough to cover the astronomical cost of a professional job.

You may still decide to go this route if you have the budget and don't have the time to do the job yourself. If so, there are several issues to bear in mind. First of all, when talking to the restorer, be absolutely clear what you want done. Do you want the bike to be simply roadworthy and usable, or 100 per cent original, or better than new? There's a whole debate surrounding the merits of 'ultimate restorations' that leave a Bonneville far shinier and built to a better standard than it ever was at Meriden. This approach will win show awards and (hopefully) involve superb workmanship. On the other hand, having spent that much on the bike, you might be reluctant to take it out on the road!

Whatever level of restoration you want, get a detailed estimate that is more or less binding. Restorers will understandably only want to give such an exact figure once they've dismantled the bike and worked out exactly what needs doing, but they should also accept what your budget ceiling is, and stop to consult if it looks in danger of being breached. Also check that the company you're dealing with has a good reputation – the owner's club, or one of the reputable parts suppliers – should be able to make a few recommendations. If their name is good, expect to go on a waiting list – a good restorer will have a steady flow of work that cannot be rushed.

If you do decide to do most or all of the work yourself, have a think about what skills you have, or would like to acquire. Can you weld, or paint? Are you confident with electrics, or major engine work? If the bike needs a complete rebuild, you might prefer to handle the chassis yourself, but hand over the engine/gearbox to a specialist.

An elderly Thunderbird needing complete restoration – but it's all there.

Some US export Bonnies subsequently came home, though not always complete!

Although the engine is relatively simple, it still takes skill to put together properly: that is, the difference between an engine that runs well and doesn't leak oil, and one that just runs, and leaks! Of course, it does help if you have a warm, well-lit garage with a solid workbench and a good selection of tools. The Haynes manual is still available new (though it doesn't cover the TSS), while copies of the original Triumph workshop manual, parts book and instruction manual all come up at autojumbles.

If you do any dismantling, take note of the order in which the various spacers, seals and washers fit, so that they slip straight back in in the right order. This applies to details like wheel bearings as well as the engine/gearbox unit. The frame shouldn't need any repair work apart from blasting and repainting. On a well-worn bike, don't forget the stands – the centre stand in particular may well be sloppy and need work.

Finally, Bonneville electrics don't have the best reputation, and these have to be reliable. New wiring looms are available, and well worth fitting to any bike that has been standing for some time, or has generally unreliable electrics. All connections, especially earths to the frame, must be clean and tight. Electronic ignition, if the bike doesn't already have it, is another big improvement, taking out the contact breaker points and making for better starting and cleaner running. This change is also invisible from the outside, so doesn't upset the original appearance.

All of this work, other commitments permitting, should be easily achievable over a winter rebuild. But if you've bought your restoration project in the spring, it can be frustrating to see the summer pass before you even get a chance to ride it.

A rolling restoration is one answer. Ultimately, it will take longer than doing everything in one go, but it means you get to ride the bike in the meantime, as well as spreading the cost over a longer period. That's not the way to achieve a concours finish, which can only really come after a complete nut-and-bolt rebuild, without the bike getting wet and gritty in the meantime. As ever, it all depends on what sort of experience you're looking for: riding, the rebuild experience itself, or a show winner?

Alternatively, you could forget all of the foregoing and just a buy a bike that's ready to ride but a bit tatty around the edges. Even though it's not concours, you should get a lot of fun out of it straightaway. And if after a few months you find that the Bonneville experience is worth pursuing, that's the time to take the bike off the road for a while and attend to the cosmetics.

Which model?

As already mentioned, although the Bonneville was in production for nearly 27 years based on the same format, it changed a great deal in character over that time. These changes occurred gradually, so it should be possible to choose the bike that suits you best, though which that might be depends not just on your budget, but what sort of riding you're planning to do.

Taking budget out of the equation for a moment (always a nice thing to do) the earliest pre-unit Bonnies give the most exciting riding experience; a late '60s T120 has the best handling, and a late '70s T140 will be the easiest to live with and most suitable for touring. T140s are also the cheapest Bonneville and probably the most numerous, so they could make a good first choice of classic bike. On the other hand, many prefer the classic proportions of the 1960s Bonnie compared to the squared-off UK spec T140.

Later Bonnevilles were available in US or UK spec on both sides of the Atlantic, and as many American-registered Triumphs have since been re-imported back to England, the difference is less important than it once was. US spec bikes have high-rise bars and slimmer 2.1- or 2.5-gallon (that's 2.5 or 3 US gallon) fuel tanks, but the difference isn't just aesthetic. The US riding position is harder work at high speed, allowing the wind to hit you square in the chest, and the smaller tank gives a shorter fuel range. Balance that against the better (but still not ideal) high-speed riding position and longer range of the UK bikes, although there's no denying they're not as pretty.

One other thing. The Bonneville always had a single carburettor equivalent, and these are almost as fast, easier to start and better on fuel. There's also no second carburettor to go out of synch with the first one. The Trophy TR6, Tiger 650 and Tiger 750 lack a little of the Bonneville's glamour, but are easier to live with. They used to be slightly cheaper as well, but buyers have caught on and at the time of writing there is virtually no difference in price.

The following is not a directive about which Bonneville you should buy, but rather a look at the strengths and weaknesses of each model so that you can decide for yourself. Prices vary, so rather than quoting actual figures, a percentage is given, indicating how model values relate to

Living with a Bonneville

each other. The 1963-70 T120 is taken as the baseline 100 per cent; the 1975-78 T140 is the cheapest variant, averaging 52 per cent of the baseline, and the pre-unit 1959-62 is the most expensive, at 149 per cent.

1959-62 T120

If you've set your heart on one of the pre-unit Bonnevilles, then you'd better get looking, because there are far fewer of these around than the unit T120s, especially the 1959 bike with its headlamp nacelle. Because they are rare, they're also expensive, and you're unlikely to find a pre-unit Bonnie 'ripe for restoration' as most will be pristine by now.

What you get is a genuinely exciting ride, with (from 1960) flat bars and a sporting position. The pre-unit 649cc twin delivers good power from 2000rpm upwards (though it won't like accelerating hard in top gear from there), and is free-revving. But it's also harsh, delivering serious vibration at high revs, especially with the 1960 duplex frame. The new frame was intended to improve handling, and although they did get better, the pre-unit T120s were still troubled by a high-speed weave.

A more serious problem (partially improved in 1961) was a lack of braking, in view of the bike's performance, and something that comes as a culture shock to 21st century riders used to ABS-equipped disc brakes. The dynamo electrics can overcharge, blowing bulbs and boiling batteries.

The pre-unit Bonneville is a good choice if you really are looking for an exciting weekend ride only, and are willing to pay more for its rarity.
Single-carb equivalent: Thunderbird or T110.
Strengths: The original, raw Bonneville experience. Rarity value.
Weaknesses: Weak brakes and tricky to set up carbs (pre-1961). 6-volt electrics not as reliable as later 12-volt system. Expensive.
Price level: 149 per cent.

1963-70 T120

To many, the unit-construction T120 is the ultimate Bonneville – it's slightly less uncompromising than the pre-unit, but has more of the classic Triumph style than does the T140. Although the '60s Bonneville was arguably over-tuned and over-stressed, it did incorporate some very useful improvements as the decade wore on, which is why many consider the '69/'70 to be the best Bonnie of all.

The riding position is a good compromise between sporting endeavour and touring

Pre-unit Bonnie gives the raw riding experience.

comfort, but the unit construction Bonnie is still a fast and exciting bike to ride, and now backed up by better handling and brakes. The real leap forward came in 1966 – the year of 12-volt electrics aided by a zener diode – with changes to the geometry to improve high-speed handling, and plenty of other details. The forks had better damping from '68, and throughout there were **several attempts** (not always successful) to mitigate oil leaks and vibration.

There aren't many variants to choose from, apart from the T120C competition-biased bike, plus the TT Special and Thruxton Bonneville. The latter two are a lot more expensive to buy, thanks to their rarity (the percentage value figure below refers to standard T120s only) – beware of fakes.

Some think a late '60s T120 is the best of all.

The Triumph Bonneville Bible

Still one of the cheaper routes to Bonneville ownership: an early '70s T120.

Single-carb equivalent: TR6 Trophy.
Strengths: Slightly more refined than the pre-units. Better brakes, 12-volt electrics and handling from 1966. Improved forks from '68.
Weaknesses: Over-tuning increases vibration and component failure.
Price level: 100 per cent.

1971-74 T120

Once the ugly duckling of the Bonneville family, purists didn't like the lumpy styling of UK spec bikes or the well-known problems of the new frame, and anyway, who needed indicators? Even in US guise, the last T120s do lack the grace of the pre-71 bikes; the seat height remains a problem for 1971/2 bikes, and the conical hub front brake is less powerful than the twin-leading shoe drum it replaced.

But if you can live with some of the downsides of the oil-in-frame T120 (as it is often known), there is something to be said for buying one. The new frame, for all its faults, does handle very well, and mechanically the bike is very similar to the 1970 Bonneville, with similarly rip-roaring performance. One of the final five-speed T120Vs would be a rare find indeed.

Cheapest Bonnie of all: the T140V.

Also, coming out of such a turbulent time, and so different in style to the '60s Bonnevilles, these bikes are period pieces, and not just another 1960s T120.

Because the oil-in-frame T120 has long been considered less desirable than its predecessor, it has been worth less as well, so is cheaper to buy, though prices are now starting to rise.
Single-carb equivalent: Tiger 650.
Strengths: Oil-in-frame gives good handling. Five-speed gearbox on the rare T120V.
Weaknesses: Very high seat in 1971/72; questionable front brake; lacks classic style.
Price level: 62 per cent.

1973-78 T140

There is a clear character difference between the 649cc T120 and 747cc T140. All of the T120s were sports bikes of their time, but by the time the T140 came along, it was clear that the Bonneville couldn't hope to keep up with the new generation of superbikes. Also, the factory knew that the Triumph twin could only hold together as a 750 if it came in a lower state of tune, so the cams were milder and the compression ratio lower. The engine was considerably strengthened as well, with a 10-stud cylinder head, triplex primary drive chain, and beefed-up bottom end.

The result of all this is a more torquey, more relaxed Bonneville than the 650; certainly no faster, but less stressed. Some think it actually vibrates more than the 650, but there is less need to use revs in the first place. It's a quite different machine.

Produced at a time of trouble for Meriden – just before and just after the blockade – T140s of this period did suffer from variable build quality, but 40-odd years later, most of that should have been sorted. Early T140s remain one of the most affordable routes to Bonneville ownership, with a good supply of reasonably priced spares and potential upgrades.
Single-carb equivalent: TR7 Tiger 750.
Strengths: Lowest prices. Stronger 750cc engine is less stressed and delivers more torque. Left-foot gearchange from 1976, decent Lockheed disc brake/s.
Weaknesses: More of a touring character than the sporting T120. Vibration still a problem. Quality variable.
Price level: 52 per cent.

1979-83 T140

The last Meriden Bonnevilles were arguably the best developed of all. The T140E might have

Living with a Bonneville

been stifled by legislation, but it also brought electronic ignition, a three-phase alternator, halogen headlight and timing side roller-bearing, adding to the increasing practicality of the early T140. Toward the end, the Bonneville had brakes, lights and electrics to contemporary standards, adding a four-valve oil pump in 1980.

There's even the option of electric start from that year, though this adds weight, and some riders still don't trust it after early teething troubles. Most agree it works better than Norton's 'electric assister' of a few years earlier...

There are a lot more variants to choose from in this era, with more options, special editions like the T140D and Royal Wedding, and, of course, the final TSS and TSX. The TSS in particular is destined to become a collector's item, because of its rarity, and because it was the last major development for the Bonneville.

Single-carb equivalent: TR7 Tiger 750.
Strengths: Steady development brings electronic ignition, a three-phase alternator, electric start – can be a practical day-to-day bike. Improved quality. TSS is rare and fast.
Weaknesses: Electric start needs care. TSS can be made reliable, but that's expensive.
Price level: 64 per cent.

1985-88 Harris Bonneville

The very last Bonnevilles of all offer no real advantage over the final Meriden-built bikes, as Les Harris was prevented from making any substantial improvements. The use of many Italian (and a few French and German) parts makes this less of a British bike, if that's what you're looking for. And there is evidence that the Harris Bonnevilles suffered from some of their bought-in components, though as with other quality issues, most of this will have been dealt with by owners over the years. Others say some Harris bikes were better quality than those of Meriden.

Single-carb equivalent: none.
Strengths: Similar riding experience to that of the Meriden T140s; cache for owning one of the last Bonnevilles.
Weaknesses: Non-British content of some components (if that bothers you).
Price level: 60 per cent.

Points to look for

You've decided that you really *do* want a Bonneville, which model will suit you best, and after not too much searching, hopefully, found one that sounds like the sort of thing you're looking for. So, confronted with the actual bike, what points should you look for?

Triumph twins are relatively simple, uncomplicated bikes, but it still pays to give any potential purchase a thorough examination before parting with your cash. A lot of the advice that follows would apply to buying any secondhand bike, though some of it is specific to the Bonneville. However confident you feel about buying/selling, it doesn't do any harm to take a friend along for a second opinion when looking at the bike. And if you're not, then having someone knowledgeable with you is a real help.

All the usual advice about buying a bike applies. When phoning in advance of viewing the bike, try to ascertain whether the person on the other end is a private or trade seller. Arrange to meet at their premises/home, not in a lay by or motorway services halfway between the two of you.

Engine/frame numbers

A golden rule of buying a secondhand Bonneville is to check that the engine and frame numbers are the same. If they match, this confirms that engine and frame were bolted together on the Meriden production line, and have stayed together ever since. Matching engine/frame numbers is a good selling point, which is why some of the classified ads mention it.

If they don't match, you may still have a perfectly good motorcycle, or there may be a valid reason for the mismatch, such as

Promising project: a rare Royal Wedding Bonnie missing a few parts.

The Triumph Bonneville Bible

Top: Check engine number matches that of the frame.

Above: Frame number can be hard to read.

The aesthetics of any Bonneville – the fuel tank.

This isn't just cosmetic – silencers can rust from the inside.

a replacement frame. But the bike won't be original, and the engine and frame could be from different years, which should be reflected in the price (and will make the bike more difficult to sell later on).

The engine number is located on the left-hand side, just below the cylinder barrel. The frame number is also on the left, at the top of the downtube by the steering head – it can be quite difficult to decipher, especially if the frame has been repainted. 'T120' in the engine/frame number denotes (as you would expect) a T120 650 and 'T140' a T140 750. Anything else is not a genuine Bonnie. Additional letters after the T120/140 denote a particular model: eg T120C. Later bikes had the engine number stamped with the Triumph logo to make tampering more difficult.

The engine number is on the left-hand crankcase, so it's possible the bike has a non-original right-hand case. This can be checked by looking for a number on one of the bolt bosses at the base of the crankcases. If the same number is marked on both crankcase halves, then they left the factory together. For an explanation of which engine/frame numbers relate to which year, see Appendix 2.

Paint/chrome

Bonnevilles have always been good-looking bikes, and the paintwork makes a big contribution to this. Look for evidence of quick and cheap resprays, with pinstriping, for instance, which doesn't line up with the tank badges. Faded paintwork isn't necessarily a bad thing, especially if it's original and gives the bike an overall patina: there are plenty of shiny, restored Bonnies around, so one in its original, if faded, Meriden finish is well worth keeping as it is.

Chrome plating is another important feature, used on the silencers, headlight shell, handlebars, parcel grid (if fitted), some mirrors and mudguards, tank badges and other parts. The quality of Meriden's plating is generally pretty good, though even the youngest will now be over 30 years old, so don't expect it to be perfect. The Silver Jubilee had chrome-plated primary drive, timing gear and gearbox covers – the chrome didn't always take well to the alloy casing, and doesn't weather well either. The Harris Bonneville chrome (1985-88) is thought to be of lesser quality as well.

Whichever Bonnie you're looking at, check the chrome for rust, pitting and general dullness. Minor blemishes can be polished away, but otherwise it's a case of rechroming, though as with the paintwork, there's something to be said for keeping something slightly tarnished, if it's the original finish.

Tinwork

There's not much tinwork to worry about on the Bonneville, just tank, mudguards and sidepanels. 1959 bikes also featured Triumph's famous headlight nacelle, and if it's still there (many were ditched) check that it's free of dents and rust.

Mudguards should be straight, free of rust around the rims, and secure. The front mudguard stays varied in detail over the years – substantial twin stays through the '60s, spindly rubber-mounted items in 1971/72, and a stronger type from '73. Harris front mudguards were bolted to the fork legs only.

Sidepanels were rounded and black up to 1970, the right-hand one acting as an oil tank, and the left-hand housing the toolkit. Check that the tank isn't leaking through the seams, as repair entails removal and flushing out. From 1971, the sidepanels were flat, in two pieces (which may not necessarily line up!) until '78.

Check the fuel tank for leaks around the tap and along the seams, as well as for dents

Living with a Bonneville

and rust. If the leak is from the tap itself (not uncommon) that's much easier to fix – actual tank leaks necessitate flushing the tank out thoroughly before firing up the welding torch: a job best left to the experts. Pinhole leaks can often be cured by Petseal, but anything more serious needs a welded repair.

Badges/trim

Tank badges come in various styles, according to era: the grille-type badge up to 1965; the 'eyebrow' of 1966-68; a simpler 'picture frame' badge from '69.

T140s either had the picture frame (US models) or a simple 'Triumph' script (all UK tanks, and some US). Whatever the badge, it should be fixed firmly in place, with decent chrome. They're sometimes missing on derelict bikes, but all badges are available new.

T120 sidepanels had transfers, and the T140 (and final T120s) screw-on badges: all are available, though rarer items specific to the T140D Special, Silver Jubilee, Royal Wedding and TSS may be harder to find.

T120s had a chrome strip along the top of the fuel tank to hide the centre seam, and the parcel grid, which Triumph stopped fitting in 1969 after an American rider was seriously injured during a collision. If the grid is fitted, it should be securely mounted, with chrome in good condition.

Seat

All Bonnevilles had a dual seat, which came in a wide variety of styles. The earliest pre-unit T120s had a thin black seat, while the move to unit construction in 1963 brought a two-tone seat with grey top and black sides. A ribbed, all-black seat was fitted for 1968, and thinned down for 1972 as part of the attempt to reduce the bike's seat height.

Special editions such as the Silver Jubilee and T140D had their own versions, though the later TSS and TSX reverted to a plain ribbed finish.

A pillion grabstrap was optional on some T120s, and a proper grabrail was fitted from 1969.

On all seats the metal pan can rust, which will eventually give way, though this is easy to check with the seat hinged up. Covers can split, which means, of course, that rain can get in; once the foam padding has become soaked it never dries out.

Complete new seats or just covers in various styles are available, though re-covering is a specialist job.

Seats can be re-covered.

Rubbers

Worn footrest rubbers are a reliable sign of high mileage, though not an infallible one as they're easy to replace. They should be secure on the footrest and free of splits. If the footrest itself is bent upward, this is a sure sign that the bike has been down the road at some point (Bonnevilles had non-folding rests) and if that's the case look for other telltale signs on that side of the bike.

On kickstart bikes, beware of worn smooth rubber on the kickstart – your foot's liable to slip off while kicking over the bike, with painful results. It should also be firm on the lever and not drop off after half a dozen kicks. If the engine needs that many kicks to fire it up, something's wrong there anyway.

Frame

There were four basic types of Bonneville frame. The 1959 single downtube frame lasted only a year, superseded by a duplex type, which improved handling, though early versions were liable to crack.

The unit construction Bonnie from 1963 saw a return to a single downtube frame, with altered geometry from '66 which brought handling to a fine pitch.

Finally, all-new for 1971 was the oil-in-frame design, early examples of which had problems with oil leaks and fractures. All '71-on Bonnies used this frame.

The most important job is to check whether the frame is straight and true. Crash damage may have bent it, putting the wheels out of line, and the surest way to check this is on the test ride – any serious misalignment should show up in a tendency for the bike to pull to one side.

A frame that is really shabby will necessitate a stripdown and repaint, though – as with the other paintwork – if it's original and fits with the patina of the bike, there's a good case for leaving

The Triumph Bonneville Bible

it as is. Bent or cracked brackets can be repaired – check those for the downpipes and horn in particular – but are a good bargaining point.

Stands

All Bonnies were fitted with both side and centre stands, though some owners removed the centre stand to improve ground clearance, something that was lacking on the T140.

The sidestand mounting clamp on 1963-67 bikes is a weak point as it doesn't reach right around the frame tube. When on the centre stand, the bike shouldn't wobble or lean, and the side stand shouldn't be floppy.

Brackets

Vibration can fracture brackets, so check those for the number plate, the chainguard and mudguard stays, also the fuel tank strap on T140s. It goes without saying that engine/gearbox mountings should be tight and not missing any nuts/bolts.

Lights

Check the headlight for a tarnished or rusted reflector, which is an MoT failure in the UK (new reflectors are available). There were three main styles of rear light: 1959-70, 1971-72, and the big, squared-off item from '73 on. All are available as pattern parts. One handy modification that doesn't affect outward appearance is an LED rear/brake light bulb: this is a straight swap, and will not blow.

Electrics/wiring

Triumph electrics improved dramatically over the years. The dynamo was replaced by an alternator in 1960, while '63 saw the magneto ignition ditched in favour of contact breaker points. There were 12-volt electrics with zener diode in 1966; improved cb points in '68, and a negative earth system with higher output alternator plus electronic ignition in 1979. The T140ES electric start Bonnie of '81 had a further boost in alternator output, and a bigger battery. On T140s, check that the alternator is doing its job by switching on lights, brake light and indicators with the engine idling – the indicators will probably slow, but should keep going.

Triumph (or Lucas) electrics don't have the best reputation, but owner attitude comes into it as well. Is the wiring neat and tidy, or flopping around? The many bullet connectors need to be clean and tight, and many odd electrical problems are simply down to bad connections or a poor earth.

Up to 1970, Bonnevilles came with an ammeter, which gives an indication of what's going on, but tends to go haywire at high revs. The T120 ignition warning light is there simply to tell you that the ignition is on; not whether or not the alternator is doing its job.

Finally, check that everything electrical works: lights, horn, indicators (if fitted) and brake light (T140s have a front brake light switch as well as a rear). The Lucas alloy switches (especially 1971-73) have a tendency to let in water – any malfunctioning switchgear is a bargaining lever.

Wheels/tyres

Most Bonnevilles have wire-spoked wheels, but the T140D, Royal Wedding and TSX (plus a few other '81/'82 bikes) had seven-spoke alloys. On steel-rimmed wire wheels, check the chrome on the rims, and on all wire-spoked wheels, check for loose spokes by gently tapping each one with a screwdriver – any that are off-key need tightening. Snapped spokes are a sign of

Below, right: New tyres are easy to source.

Wiring condition gives a good indication of owner care.

Living with a Bonneville

serious neglect. Alloy wheels should be checked for dents and cracks.

Tyres should have at least the UK legal minimum of 1mm tread depth across at least three-quarters of the width of the tyre. Beware of bikes that have been left standing for a long time (especially on the side stand) which allows the tyres to crack and deteriorate. New tyres of the right size are easy to find.

While you're looking at the wheels, on T140s check the brake discs for thickness and scoring. If the discs are chromed, check that this isn't flaking off, which will destroy the pads. Finally, check for fluid leaks at the hose junctions with the calliper and master cylinder.

Wheel/steering/swingarm bearings

With the bike on its centre stand, check the rear wheel bearings by grasping the wheel and trying to rock it from side to side. To test the front bearings, put the bike on full lock and trying rocking the wheel in a vertical plane. Any play at all means it's time for new bearings.

Now check the steering head bearings by swinging the handlebars lock-to-lock: they should move freely without any hint of roughness

Check forks and shocks for leaks.

Oil-in-frame (1971 on) engine oil is checked here.

The Triumph Bonneville Bible

or stiffness. Then check for play by applying full lock and trying to rock the wheel back and forth. The swingarm bearings are essential for good handling, but they will wear or even seize if they haven't been greased regularly. Check for wear by grasping the rear end of the swingarm and trying to rock it from side-to-side. There should be no perceptible movement.

Suspension

All Bonnevilles used the same basic suspension setup – non-adjustable front telescopic forks and twin rear dampers, which were adjustable for pre-load. Check both fork and shocks for oil leaks. The fork stanchion's chrome surface eventually pits, especially when exposed to the elements: gaiters do a good job of protecting the stanchion, so check that these aren't split. Check for play by grabbing the bottom of the forks and trying to rock them back and forth – play here indicates worn bushes, though it can be confused with play in the steering head bearings. While at the bottom of the forks, check that the end caps are not cracked.

The fork action should be smooth and free of clonks and rattles – check this on the test ride, and also that the shocks are damping effectively, not allowing the bike to 'pogo' after bumps.

Instruments

There were various styles of instruments on the Bonnie, and all but the very early machines had a matching speedo and tachometer, with an ammeter fitted until 1970. The grey-faced Smiths instruments were replaced by restyled black-faced ones in 1971, with anti-vibration rubber binnacles added later.

Later T140s also used similar-looking Veglia clocks in place of the Smiths. If either instrument isn't working, the cable is the most likely culprit, but if the mileometer's still working and the speedometer isn't then something more serious is amiss. Instrument repair is best left to a specialist, and there are plenty around who will do a good job.

Engine

You can tell a lot about the likely condition of a Triumph twin without hearing it run. These engines are easy to work on, encouraging owners without experience or the proper tools to have a go. Look for rounded-off bolts, chewed screws and damage to the casings around them.

As long as the engine is in good condition and has been put together properly, it should be reasonably oil-tight. Some oil misting or very minor leaks are nothing to worry about, but if the bike has a patch of oil underneath it, and the engine/gearbox has a serious leak, walk away, unless, of course, the price reflects the condition.

The condition of the engine oil is a good indication of owner care. Check it via the oil tank (up to 1970) or the filler cap under the nose of the seat (1971 on). Does it look reasonably fresh, or is it black (and, worse still, with particles floating in it)? Same thing with the gearbox – remove the filler cap and stick a finger inside to check whether the oil has been changed recently – is it nice, clean EP90 or a frothy sludge?

Right: Triumph twins don't have to leak oil.

Right: Check for damaged fasteners and general neglect.

Living with a Bonneville

Have a look at the carburettors. Is fuel leaking from anywhere, or from the tap?

Now start the engine. If kickstarted, it should fire up within two or three kicks, especially if the owner does this for you. The most likely cause of poor starting (not on bikes with electronic ignition) is nothing more serious than badly adjusted cb points and ignition timing. A more serious cause is lack of compression, due to general top end wear. If you have a compression tester, screw it into each sparkplug hole in turn, then, with the ignition off and the throttle held wide open, give the kickstart five or six kicks. With the engine hot, compression should be around 150psi; slightly higher if it's cold.
BB263

Electric start Bonnies do have their weaknesses, and the starter should engage cleanly without excessive noise – there shouldn't be any clunks.

Once started, the engine should idle evenly on both cylinders – if it sounds uneven, out of balance carbs or maladjusted cb points are the most likely cause, though a knowledgeable owner should already have these spot on. Air leaks in the inlet hoses between the carbs and air filters are another cause of uneven idling. Check that the oil is returning by removing the filler cap on the oil tank (up to 1970) or under the seat nose (1971 on) – a spurt or series of bloops of oil should be clearly visible. If not, switch off the engine immediately (or damage will ensue), make your excuses and leave.

T140s have a far more useful set of warning lights than the T120s, including those for low charge and oil pressure. Check that these light up when the ignition is switched on, and flicker out as soon as the engine starts.

If you're used to quiet and smooth water-cooled engines, don't be alarmed by the merry clattering emanating from the Triumph's rocker boxes, as they all do that. A real sign of trouble is knocking or rumbling from the bottom end, which will mean a complete engine rebuild. Beware of loud megaphone 'silencers' that can mask any of this, and don't buy a bike with a noisy bottom end, unless it's cheap. Engine parts to cure all these problems are widely available.

While the engine's running, look back at the silencers and blip the throttle. There's likely to be a small amount of blue smoke, as many Bonneville engines burn oil as a matter of course. A lot of smoke is a sign of general wear in the top end, but again, all of the parts needed – including oversize pistons for both 650 and 750 – are widely available. Out on the test ride, blue smoke under power indicates bore wear; that on the overrun is more likely to be valves and guides. Black smoke indicates rich running, which could be carburettor wear or even just a blocked air filter. Bikes without air filters should be avoided, as you don't know what impurities the engine has taken in – early Bonnies didn't have filters, but you can take originality too far.

Primary drive

While the engine's running, listen for clonks or rumbles inside the primary drive, which could be due to wear in the clutch and its shock absorber, the engine sprocket chattering on worn splines, or a loose alternator rotor. If there's a noise, it's a good bargaining point to get the price down. Pre-unit primary chains are prone to rapid wear but the unit chain should also be checked for tension – unscrew the filler cap and check the tension with a finger. While at the primary drive, on bikes with a breather pipe (1970 on) check that the elbow is secure; ditto the breather hose leading to the airbox or rear mudguard.

Chain/sprockets

With the engine switched off, have a good look at the final drive chain and sprockets – is the chain clean, well lubed and properly adjusted? Try pulling one link away from the back of the sprocket: if more than half a tooth is visible, the chain needs replacing. If the sprocket teeth are hooked, or any are damaged (or worse still, missing) that needs replacing, too.

Battery

Hinge up the seat and have a look at the battery. Acid splashes are a sign of overcharging, as is a low electrolyte level. The battery should be secure under its rubber strap (if fitted).

A small amount of blue smoke isn't a problem.

Exhaust

On all bikes, check that the downpipes are securely fixed to the cylinder head – a loose fit causes air leaks – and examine all joints for looseness and leaks. Check the silencers (especially underneath) for rust and splits and that they are solidly mounted.

Test ride

The test ride should be for at least 15 minutes. It's understandable that some sellers are reluctant to let a complete stranger loose on their pride and joy, but this goes with the territory when selling a bike. As long as you leave the vehicle you arrived on/in, a test ride is a reasonable request. Take your driving licence in case the seller wants to see it.

A Bonneville in good condition should have a good, beefy mid-range, and should pull cleanly without hesitation. If it does hesitate, or has flat spots, suspect the carburettors or ignition. Despite all the talk of vibration, the vibes should only be a background thrumming until over 4-5000rpm. If possible, cruise the bike at 70mph for five minutes, and check for oil leaks when you get back. All Bonnevilles will crack 100mph, but they weren't designed for the motorway age, and the vibes will become unpleasant over 5000rpm.

The clutch is heavier than on many modern bikes, but take-up should be smooth and progressive, with no dragging or slipping. The gearchange is slightly stiffer on T140s, but on all bikes the change should be positive, with no jumping out of gear. A clonk on engaging first gear is normal, but there shouldn't be any graunching, with the bike making a little hop forward. Neutral can be difficult to find at a standstill (later T140s do have a neutral light, though it's not infallible), and it's often easier to slip into neutral just before you roll to a stop.

Triumph's reputation for good-handling bikes, especially from the mid-60s on, was well deserved, though earlier Bonnies are not as sure-footed at high speeds. Bonnevilles are relatively light bikes with stiff suspension; very agile and easy to flick through corners. Any vagueness or weaving is usually down to worn forks, rear shocks or tyres. They should never feel soft or wallowy – if so, the damping in forks or shocks is the most likely cause. The bike should also run in a straight line without wandering to one side.

Front and rear brakes should both give progressive, smooth performance. Bear in mind that earlier drum brakes – those on the pre-unit T120 in particular – are not up to modern standards, and later twin-leading shoe front drums need to be correctly adjusted to work as they should. Cables should feel smooth and well lubed. The T140's disc brakes are better. Spongy hydraulic brakes are likely to have a fluid leak somewhere.

Back at base after the test ride, check that the engine settles back to an even idle before switching off. Have a final visual check for any new oil leaks – at the rocker boxes, pushrod tubes, cylinder barrel base, the gearbox sprocket, and under the crankcase.

Registration

The following specific information applies to UK legislation, but wherever you are, in order to be road-legal your Bonneville will need to be registered and pass a roadworthiness test. If the bike is already up and running with a current V5 document and MoT, then all well and good: you can put down the book and happily ride off along the nearest stretch of tarmac.

But life isn't always as simple. Back in the early 1980s, the old buff logbooks were replaced by the V5, and all vehicle registrations were transferred to the DVLA. In any case, the Triumph you've bought and/or restored may not have been on the road since that momentous change, either because it's been sat mouldering in someone's shed for the past quarter century, or was reduced to a box of bits long before the change came in. Or it may have had its identity legally changed – in other words, the registration number has been bought as a personalised plate to pump up another's self-esteem.

Whichever of these is the case, the bike will have to be re-registered. There was a time when the DVLC insisted that re-registered vehicles could only be issued with a 'Q' plate, which looked a little naff on a 1961 Bonneville, or for that matter anything old and classic. It has since relented and will provide an age-related plate that looks right on the bike. And if the bike's original registration can be traced (via the engine/frame number) and no one's nabbed it in the meantime, you can even use that.

However, you do need to prove that the bike exists, and really is the age you are claiming it to be. Fortunately, the Triumph Owners Motor Cycle Club (TOMCC) in the UK will provide a Certificate of Age that confirms when the bike was first registered. You'll need to send the club a whole sheaf of documentation to support your claim, including pictures of the bike, rubbings of the engine and frame numbers, the old logbook,

Living with a Bonneville

Top Ten Bonneville upgrades

Upgrade	Benefits
Electronic ignition	Easier starting, exact ignition timing
Morgo or 4-valve oil pump	More reliable oil supply
Three-phase alternator	High electrical output
Alloy cylinder barrel	Cooler running
Belt primary drive	Smoother transmission
Rearset footrests (T140)	Better high-speed riding position
Stainless steel brake hose	More positive braking feel
Valve guide oil seals	Reduced oil consumption
Regulator/rectifier	Replaces both rectifier and zener diode
Cartridge oil filter	Improved oil filtration

For suppliers, see list of specialists in Appendix 5

and any old MoT certificates and tax discs, plus any other evidence of the bike's age. Also include forms V55/5 and V765, duly completed. If all this tallies, and the TOMCC confirms the bike's true age from the factory despatch records, it will forward the whole lot to DVLC, which will check it and (hopefully) approve the granting of an age-related plate.

In the meantime, get the MoT and insurance sorted out, using the frame number to identify the bike. Contact your local Vehicle Registration Office, explaining what you're intending to do, and send it the complete V55/5, dating information from TOMCC, MoT and insurance documents, plus the fee. If the VRO is happy with all of this (and it should be, after all the trouble you've been to) then it will issue an age-related number. Job done!

MoT

To avoid wasting time and money on a failed MoT test, check over the bike yourself before booking the test. Vehicles registered before 1960 no longer need an MoT test in the UK, so 1959 Bonnevilles qualify for exemption. However, it's worth having the same checks done by an MoT test station – the piece of paper still confirms that the bike was legal and roadworthy when it was tested.

Before the test, check that all of the lights work and the reflector

Below, left: Electronic ignition is well worth having; denoted by finned cover.

Below: A cartridge oil filter does a better job than the standard gauze.

The Triumph Bonneville Bible

If a Meriden Bonneville isn't for you, the Hinckley version offers all mod cons.

is good and shiny. Check the forks, steering head bearings, and (if applicable) swingarm bearings for wear. Are the chain and sprockets in good condition? The handlebars should swing freely lock-to-lock without snagging or binding the cables.

It goes without saying that tyres will have more than the legal minimum tread, not perished and free of splits (check specifically for the latter on bikes that have been standing for a while). If there's any doubt about the brake linings or cables, fit new ones.

One other thing (though it doesn't really apply to the T140). Ask fellow classic bike owners where they get their machines MoTd. Why? Because some testers will rarely have come across a bike of the Bonneville's age, and compared to the modern machinery they're used to testing, the lights and brakes of, say, an early T120 will seem feeble by modern standards. A tester used to classics will understand that these components are as good as they can be, but certainly won't pass anything that isn't safe.

The 21st century Bonneville

It seems heresy to even mention the Hinckley Triumph Bonneville in a book devoted to the Meriden original, but here goes. A lot of people love the original, and put up with its quirks as part of the ownership experience. But for others, it's simply too much hassle, and for them, a Hinckley Bonneville could be the answer.

It might look vaguely similar to the T120 but the Hinckley Bonnie is a very different bike. It's heavier than the original, and less sporting; fatter and more comfortable, and there's a good reason why. Back in the 1960s, the average Bonneville buyer was in his/her early 20s; now they're 30 years older, which the bike reflects.

So, although it's not the same blood-and-thunder ride as the original, the Hinckley Bonnie is much easier to live with, starts on the button, and needs little maintenance between dealer services. The early Hinckleys now cost less than a Meriden T140: you pays your money and you takes your choice ...

APPENDIX I

Model profiles

We intend that this book be the definitive reference source for these classic motorcycles. To this end, if a reader can provide information currently missing from the following specifications, we should be very pleased to hear from them.

Fuel tank colours: For two-tone fuel tanks, first colour listed is the upper half of the tank, second colour is the lower half. For all other models, first colour listed is the base colour, second colour listed is either flashes, scallops or pinstriping. UK refers to UK and General Export Bonnevilles, US to US Bonnevilles.

Note: Some detailed specifications varied according to model and whether UK/US spec.

1959 T120

Bore x stroke	71 x 82mm
Capacity	649cc
Compression ratio	8.5:1
Carburettors	2 x Amal Monobloc
Power	46bhp @ 6500rpm
Primary drive:	
Type	Duplex chain
Engine sprocket	24T
Clutch sprocket	43T
Gear ratios:	
1st	11.2:1
2nd	7.8:1
3rd	5.5:1
4th	4.6:1
Final drive:	
Type	Chain
Gearbox sprocket	18T
Rear sprocket	46T
Engine speed (top gear @ 10mph)	594rpm
Electrics:	
System	6-volt, 60 watt dynamo
Ignition	Manual advance magneto
Headlight	30/24 watt
Tyres:	
Front	3.25-19
Rear	3.50-19
Brakes:	
Front	8in drum
Rear	7in drum
Frame type	Tubular steel, single downtube
Steering head angle	64.5 degrees
Fuel tank capacity (Imp galls):	
UK	4.0 gallons
US	3.5 gallons
Oil tank capacity	5 pints
Dimensions:	
Wheelbase	55.5in
Ground clearance	5in
Width (at handlebars)	28.5in
Seat height	30.5in
Weight	404lb (kerb weight)
Fuel consumption	na
Top speed	115mph
0-60mph	na
Standing quarter mile	na
Performance figures in gears @7000rpm	na
Tank colours (UK/US)	Pearl Grey/Tangerine (early); Pearl Grey/Azure Blue (late)

The Triumph Bonneville Bible

1964 T120

Bore x stroke	71 x 82mm
Capacity	649cc
Compression ratio	8.5:1
Carburettors	2 x Amal Monobloc
Power	46bhp @ 6500rpm
Primary drive:	
Type	Duplex chain
Engine sprocket	29T
Clutch sprocket	58T
Gear ratios:	
1st 11.81:1	2nd 8.17:1
3rd 5.76:1	4th 4.84:1
Final drive:	
Type	Chain
Gearbox sprocket	19T
Rear sprocket	46T
Engine speed	
(top gear @ 10mph)	na
Electrics:	
System	6-volt, alternator
Ignition	Contact breaker points
Headlight	30/24 watt
Tyres:	
Front	3.25-18
Rear	3.50-18
Brakes:	
Front	8in drum
Rear	7in drum
Frame type	Tubular steel, single downtube
Steering head angle	65 degrees
Fuel tank capacity (Imp galls):	
UK	4 gallons
US	3 gallons
Oil tank capacity	5 pints
Dimensions:	
Wheelbase	54.5in
Ground clearance	5in
Width (at handlebars)	28.5in
Seat height	30.5in
Weight	363lb (kerb weight)
Fuel consumption	56mpg
Top speed	115mph
0-60mph	6.5sec
Standing quarter mile	na
Performance figures in gears	
@7000rpm	na
Tank colours (UK/US)	Gold/Alaskan White

Specs/performance figures from Motorcycle Mechanics, May 1964

1967 T120

Bore x stroke	71 x 82mm
Capacity	649cc
Compression ratio	9.0:1
Carburettors	2 x Amal Concentric Mk1
Power	46bhp @ 6500rpm
Primary drive:	
Type	Duplex chain
Engine sprocket	29T
Clutch sprocket	58T
Gear ratios:	
1st 11.81:1	2nd 8.17:1
3rd 5.76:1	4th 4.84:1
Final drive	
Type	Chain
Gearbox sprocket	19T
Rear sprocket	46T
Engine speed	
(top gear @ 10mph)	na
Electrics:	
System	12-volt, alternator
Ignition	Contact breaker points
Headlight	50/40 watt
Tyres:	
Front	3.00-19
Rear	3.50-18
Brakes	
Front	8in drum
Rear	7in drum
Frame type	Tubular steel, single downtube
Steering head angle	62 degrees
Fuel tank capacity (Imp galls):	
UK	4 gallons
US	2.1 gallons
Oil tank capacity	5 pints
Dimensions:	
Wheelbase	54.5in
Ground clearance	5in
Width (at handlebars)	28.5in
Seat height	30.5in
Weight	365lb (kerb weight)
Fuel consumption	58mpg
Top speed	113mph
0-60mph	6.0sec
Standing quarter-mile	15.8sec/86mph
Performance figures in gears	
@7000rpm	na
Tank colours (UK/US)	Aubergine/Gold

Specs/performance figures from Motorcycle Mechanics, Dec 1966

Model profiles

1969 T120

Bore x stroke	71 x 82mm
Capacity	649cc
Compression ratio	9.0:1
Carburettors	2 x Amal Concentric Mk1
Power	47bhp @ 6700rpm
Primary drive:	
Type	Duplex chain
Engine sprocket	29T
Clutch sprocket	58T
Gear ratios:	
1st	11.81:1
2nd	8.17:1
3rd	5.76:1
4th	4.84:1
Final drive:	
Type	Chain
Gearbox sprocket	19T
Rear sprocket	46T
Engine speed (top gear @ 10mph)	649rpm
Electrics:	
System	12-volt, alternator
Ignition	Contact breaker points
Headlight	50/40 watt
Tyres:	
Front	3.00-19
Rear	3.50-18
Brakes:	
Front	8in tls drum
Rear	7in drum
Frame type	Tubular steel, single downtube
Steering head angle	62 degrees
Fuel tank capacity (Imp galls):	
UK	4 gallons
US	2.1 gallons
Oil tank capacity	5 pints
Dimensions:	
Wheelbase	55in
Ground clearance	5in
Width (at handlebars)	27in
Seat height	31.5in
Weight	390lb (kerb weight)
Fuel consumption	na
Top speed	na
0-60mph	na
Standing quarter-mile	na
Performance figures in gears @7000rpm	na
Tank colours (UK/US)	Olympic Flame/Silver

Specs/performance figures from Triumph brochure, 1969

1971 T120R

Bore x stroke	71 x 82mm
Capacity	649cc
Compression ratio	9.0:1
Carburettors	2 x Amal Concentric Mk1
Power	50bhp @ 7000rpm
Primary drive:	
Type	Duplex chain
Engine sprocket	29T
Clutch sprocket	58T
Gear ratios:	
1st	12.08:1
2nd	8.36:1
3rd	6.14:1
4th	4.95:1
Final drive:	
Type	Chain
Gearbox sprocket	19T
Rear sprocket	47T
Engine speed (top gear @ 10mph)	na
Electrics:	
System	12-volt, alternator
Ignition	Contact breaker points
Headlight	45/35 watt
Tyres:	
Front	3.25-19
Rear	4.00-18
Brakes:	
Front	8in tls alloy drum
Rear	7in alloy drum
Frame type	Tubular steel, duplex, oil-bearing spine
Steering head angle	na
Fuel tank capacity (Imp galls):	
UK	4 gallons
US	2.5 gallons
Oil tank capacity	4 pints
Dimensions:	
Wheelbase	56in
Ground clearance	6.5in
Width (at handlebars)	32in
Seat height	34.5in
Weight	399lb (kerb weight)
Fuel consumption	48mpg
Top speed	112mph
0-60mph	5.8sec
Standing quarter-mile	14.24sec/92.87mph
Performance figures in gears @7000rpm:	
1st	45mph
2nd	65mph
3rd	88mph
4th	110mph
Tank colours (UK/US)	Tiger Gold/Black

Specs/performance figures from Cycle World, May 1971/ Bonnie by J R Nelson

The Triumph Bonneville Bible

1973 T140V

Bore x stroke	76 x 82mm
Capacity	744cc
Compression ratio	8.25:1
Carburettors	2 x Amal Concentric Mk1
Power	n/a
Primary drive:	
Type	Triplex chain
Engine sprocket	29T
Clutch sprocket	58T
Gear ratios:	
1st	12.25:1
2nd	8.67:1
3rd	6.58:1
4th	5.59:1
5th	4.70:1
Final drive	
Type	Chain
Gearbox sprocket	20T
Rear sprocket	47T
Engine speed	
(top gear @ 10mph)	na
Electrics:	
System	12-volt, alternator
Ignition	Contact breaker points
Headlight	45/35 watt
Tyres:	
Front	3.25-18
Rear	3.50-18
Brakes:	
Front	10in disc
Rear	7in alloy drum
Frame type	Tubular steel, duplex, oil-bearing spine
Steering head angle	62 degrees
Fuel tank capacity (Imp galls):	
UK	4 gallons
US	2.1 gallons
Oil tank capacity	4 pints
Dimensions:	
Wheelbase	57.5in
Ground clearance	7.5in
Width (at handlebars)	31in
Seat height	31.5in
Weight	409lb (kerb weight)
Fuel consumption	42mpg
Top speed	107mph
0-60mph	5.1sec
Standing quarter-mile	13.65sec/93.94mph
Performance figures in gears @7000rpm:	
1st	44mph
2nd	62mph
3rd	82mph
4th	97mph
5th	111mph
Tank colours (UK/US)	Hi-Fi Vermillion/Gold

Specs/performance figures from Cycle World, May 1973

1974 T120V

Bore x stroke	71 x 82mm
Capacity	649cc
Compression ratio	9.0:1
Carburettors	2 x Amal Concentric Mk1
Power	46bhp @ 6500rpm
Primary drive:	
Type	Duplex chain
Engine sprocket	29T
Clutch sprocket	58T
Gear ratios:	
1st	12.78:1
2nd	9.07:1
3rd	6.92:1
4th	5.89:1
5th	4.95:1
Final drive:	
Type	Chain
Gearbox sprocket	20T
Rear sprocket	47T
Engine speed	
(top gear @ 10mph)	na
Electrics:	
System	12-volt, alternator
Ignition	Contact breaker points
Headlight	45/35 watt
Tyres:	
Front	3.25-18
Rear	3.50-18
Brakes:	
Front	10in disc
Rear	7in alloy drum
Frame type	Tubular steel, duplex, oil-bearing spine
Steering head angle	62 degrees
Fuel tank capacity (Imp galls):	
UK	4 gallons
US	3 gallons
Oil tank capacity	4 pints
Dimensions:	
Wheelbase	54.5in
Ground clearance	5in
Width (at handlebars)	28.5in
Seat height	31in
Weight	412lb (kerb weight)
Fuel consumption	45mpg
Top speed	112mph
0-60mph	na
Standing quarter-mile	14.2sec/92mph
Performance figures in gears @7000rpm	na
Tank colours (UK/US)	Purple/White

Specs/performance figures from Motor Cycle, 21 Sept 1974

Model profiles

1979 T140E

Bore x stroke	76 x 82mm
Capacity	744cc
Compression ratio	7.9:1
Carburettors	2 x Amal Concentric Mk1
Power	n/a
Primary drive:	
Type	Triplex chain
Engine sprocket	29T
Clutch sprocket	58T
Gear ratios:	
1st	12.15:1
2nd	8.63:1
3rd	6.58:1
4th	5.59:1
5th	4.70:1
Final drive:	
Type	Chain
Gearbox sprocket	20T
Rear sprocket	47T
Engine speed (top gear @ 10mph)	na
Electrics:	
System	12-volt, alternator
Ignition	Electronic
Headlight	45/40 watt
Tyres:	
Front	4.10-19
Rear	4.10-19
Brakes:	
Front	10in disc
Rear	10in disc
Frame type	Tubular steel duplex, oil-bearing spine
Steering head angle	62 degrees
Fuel tank capacity (Imp galls):	
UK	4 gallons
US	2.5 gallons
Oil tank capacity	4 pints
Dimensions:	
Wheelbase	54.5in
Ground clearance	5in
Width (at handlebars)	28.5in
Seat height	31.7in
Weight	425lb (kerb weight)
Fuel consumption	42mpg
Top speed	110mph
0-60mph	5.8sec
Standing quarter-mile	13.86sec/93.36mph
Performance figures in gears @7000rpm	na
Tank colours:	
UK	Beige/Gold, Black/Red
US	Dark Blue/Silver, Black/Silver, Candy Apple Red/Silver

Specs/performance figures from Cycle World, April 1978

1981 T140V Electro

Bore x stroke	71 x 82mm
Capacity	649cc
Compression ratio	7.9:1
Carburettors	2 x Bing CV 32mm
Power	55bhp @ 7000rpm
Primary drive:	
Type	Triplex chain
Engine sprocket	29T
Clutch sprocket	58T
Gear ratios:	
1st	12.14:1
2nd	8.63:1
3rd	6.58:1
4th	5.59:1
5th	4.70:1
Final drive	na
Engine speed (top gear @ 10mph)	na
Electrics:	
System	12-volt, 176w alternator
Ignition	Electronic
Headlight	45/40 watt
Tyres:	
Front	4.10-19
Rear	4.25-18
Brakes:	
Front	10in disc
Rear	10in disc
Frame type	Tubular steel duplex, oil-bearing spine
Steering head angle	62 degrees
Fuel tank capacity (Imp galls):	
UK	4 gallons
US	2.5 gallons
Oil tank capacity	4 pints
Dimensions:	
Wheelbase	54.4in
Ground clearance	5in
Width at handlebars	28.5in
Seat height	31.2in
Weight	444lb (kerb weight)
Fuel consumption	52mpg
Top speed	112mph
0-60mph	6.5sec
Standing quarter-mile	14.96sec/87.3mph
Performance figures in gears @ 7000rpm	na
Tank colours (UK/US)	Black/Candy Apple Red, Steel Grey/Candy Apple Red, Silver Blue/Black, Black/Gold, Smokey Flame/Gold, Smokey Blue/Gold

Specs/performance figures from Cycle World, Nov 1981

The Triumph Bonneville Bible

1982 T140W TSS

Bore x stroke	76 x 82mm
Capacity	744cc
Compression ratio	9.5:1
Carburettors	2 x Amal Mk2 34mm
Power	57bhp @ 6500rpm
Primary drive	Triplex chain

Gear ratios:
- 1st . . . . 12.25:1   2nd 8.63:1
- 3rd . . . . 6.58:1   4th 5.59:1
- 5th 4.7:1

Final drive	Chain
Engine speed (top gear @ 10mph)	na

Electrics:
System	12-volt, 200w alternator
Ignition	Electronic
Headlight	60/45 watt

Tyres:
Front	4.10-19
Rear	4.10-18

Brakes:
Front	2 x Lockheed discs
Rear	Single Lockheed disc
Frame type	Tubular steel, duplex, oil-bearing spine
Steering head angle	62 degrees

Fuel tank capacity (Imp galls):
UK	4 gallons
US	2.5 gallons
Oil tank capacity	4 pints

Dimensions:
Wheelbase	56in
Ground clearance	7in
Width (at handlebars)	27in
Seat height	30.5in
Weight	410lb (kerb weight)
Fuel consumption	43mpg
Top speed	122.24mph
Standing quarter-mile	14.28sec/95.34mph

Performance: (speeds in gears @ 7000rpm)
- 1st. . . . . .45mph   2nd 59mph
- 3rd . . . . .77mph   4th 90mph
- 5th 108mph

Tank colours:
UK	Blakc, Smokey Flame/Gold, Smokey Blue/Gold
US	Smokey Flame/Ivory, Smokey Blue/Silver, Silver Blue/Black, Black/Candy Apple Red
TSS	Black/Gold
Royal Wedding (UK)	Chrome/Black
Royal Wedding (US)	Chrome/Silver Blue
Executive	Smokey Flame, Black/Gold

Specs/performance figures from Bike, Aug 1982

1986 Harris T140V

Bore x stroke	76 x 82mm
Capacity	744cc
Compression ratio	7.9:1
Carburettors	2 x Amal Mk 1.5
Power	50bhp @ 6500rpm

Primary drive:
Type	Triplex chain
Engine sprocket	29T
Clutch sprocket	58T

Gear ratios:
Top	4.74:1

Final drive:
Type	Chain
Gearbox sprocket	19/20T
Rear sprocket	47T
Engine speed (top gear @ 10mph)	636rpm

Electrics:
System	12-volt, 200w alternator
Ignition	Electronic
Headlight	55/50 watt

Tyres:
Front	100/90 H19
Rear	110/90 H18

Brakes:
Front	2x 260mm discs
Rear	Single disc
Frame type	Tubular steel, duplex, oil-bearing spine
Steering head angle	62 degrees

Fuel tank capacity (Imp galls):
UK	4 gallons
US	2.8 gallons
Oil tank capacity	4 pints

Dimensions:
Wheelbase	56in
Ground clearance	na
Width (at handlebars)	na
Seat height	31in
Weight	410lb
Top speed	115mph
0-60mph	5.5sec
Fuel consumption	50mpg
Standing quarter mile	na
Performance figures in gears @7000rpm	na
Tank colours (UK/US)	Black/Candy Apple Red, Black/Gold

Specs/performance figures from Classic Bike, May 1986

APPENDIX 2

Engine and frame numbers

Engine and frame numbers on the Bonnevilles were the same, and were preceded by the model code. The pre-unit 650s with the duplex frame used a D prefix, and unit 650s used a DU prefix. Additional suffixes were used to designate model type or condition: eg TT (model type); C (high compression), or P (police). Some of these appeared in certain markets only.

Year	Numbers
1959	020076-029363
1960	029364-030424, then D101-D7726
1961	D7727-D15788
1962	D15789 on
1963	DU101-DU5824
1964	DU5825-DU13374
1965	DU13375-DU24874
1966	DU24875-DU44393
1967	DU44394-DU66245
1968	DU66246-DU85903
1969	DU85904-DU90282

New engine/frame number from later in 1969, with a two-letter prefix for month and model year, followed by model type and serial number. From July 1980 a third letter, A, was added.

Year	Numbers
Later 1969	NC00100-HC24346
1970	JD24848-ND60540
1971	NE01436-HE30869
1972	HG30870-JGXXXXX
1973	JH15101-GH36466
1974	GJ55101-NJ60061
1975	DK61000-GK62248
1976	HN62501-GN72283
1977	GP73000-JP84931
1978	HX00100-HX10747
1979	HA11001-KA24999
Later 1979	XB24609*-XB24790*
1980	PB25001-KB27500

The Triumph Bonneville Bible

1981	KDA28001-DDA29427
1982	EDA30001-BDA31693
1983	BEA33001-AEA34389
1985	FN000002 - FN000191
1986	GN000192-GN000788
1987	HN000789-HN001176
1988	JN001177-JN001258

182 1979 bikes marked in error with B letter

Model prefixes

T120	Standard T120 four-speed
T120R	USA export version
TR7/A	1960 Road Sports, USA only (not stamped on engine/frame numbers)
TR7/B	1960 Street Scrambler, USA only (not stamped on engine/frame numbers)
T120C	T120 Competition (and TT Special 1964-65)
T120TT	TT Special (1966-67)
T120V	T120 five-speed
T140V	Standard T140 five-speed
T140RV	USA export version
T140J	Silver Jubilee limited edition
T140E	1978 1/2 on; 'E' denotes EPA emissions compliance
T140D	1979 Bonneville Special
T140EX	Executive
T140ES	Electro
T140AV	Anti-Vibration engine mountings.
T140LE	Royal Wedding limited edition.
T140W TSS	Eight-valve TSS
T140TSX	TSX custom

APPENDIX 3

Major changes, year-by-year

Years refer to model years, which usually began in August – eg: 1967 model year ran from August 1966 to July 1967. Some changes were made partway through the model year rather than at the beginning.

1959
Bonneville T120 introduced. Twin carburettor; high compression version of T110. Headlight nacelle and valanced mudguards.

1960
Separate chrome headlight and slimmer mudguards. New duplex frame without lower bracing rail (reintroduced this year); steeper steering head angle and shorter wheelbase. New forks similar to those of 350/500 twins. Amal Monoblocs with integral float chambers. Alternator replaces dynamo. Matching speedo and tachometer on US-spec T120R only.

1961
Crankshaft balance factor increased to 71 per cent; later 85 per cent. Wider flywheel. Lucas RM19 alternator, 22T gearbox sprocket (up from 21T).

1962
Steeper steering head angle; 140mph speedometer; fully floating brakes. TR7/A renamed T120R, and TR7/B now T120C, the latter with high pipes, competition magneto, bashplate and Trials Universal tyres.

1963
Unit-construction engine with 9-stud cylinder head and duplex chain primary drive. Twin contact breaker points with twin ignition coils replace magneto. Six-plate clutch. Air filter standard in USA; optional in UK. New single downtube frame; engine carried by duplex cradle. TT Special launched for USA: competition only with no lights or passenger footpegs, plus high-level pipes, larger $1\frac{3}{16}$in Amal and 11.2:1 compression ratio.

1964
Larger valves and carburettors; magnetic Smiths speedo and tachometer. Redesigned forks; Dunlop Gold Seal K70 tyres; air filter now standard.

1965
Threaded hole in top of crankcase to locate TDC; oil pressure indicator button on relief valve deleted. Aluminium exhaust downpipes screw-in stubs (changed back to steel later in year). Forks have longer travel; shallower angle for propstand. Downswept exhaust for TT Special. Thruxton Bonneville introduced, with blue-printed engine, single float chamber, extra valve lift/duration; also steeper steering head angle, 19in wheels and air scoop on front brake.

1966
Increased power from 9:1 compression; R type tappets; sports cams and bigger carburettors; lighter flywheel; roller-bearing on timing side; oil supply to exhaust camshaft. Speedo drive from rear wheel. Frame geometry changes (steeper steering head angle and increased trail) to improve high-speed handling. 12-volt electrics (initially with two 6-volt batteries) with zener diode. 'Eyebrow' tank badge.

1967
Oilways in tappet block; E3134 inlet camshaft; thicker con-rods; oil pump with increased scavenge capacity. Amal Concentric carburettors replace Monoblocs. Headlight switch in headlight shell; 150mph speedo; spongy handlebar grips. Final year for TT Special.

1968
Lucas 6CA cb points with external condensers mounted under fuel tank; strobe facility for setting ignition timing. Finned zener diode now under headlight and ignition switch moves to left-hand fork upper cover. New twin-leading shoe front drum brake; forks with improved damping and a stronger swingarm. 12-point cylinder barrel nuts.

1969
Mid-year change to engine/frame numbering system. Reversion to pre-1966 heavier flywheel. RR56 aluminium alloy con-rods; Hepolite pistons with dome crowns. Exhaust camshaft nitrided and oil pump has larger feed plunger. New pushrod oil sealing arrangement and second oil seal added behind cb points chamber. Oil pressure switch and warning light; front brake light switch. Balance pipe between exhaust downpipes. New 'picture frame' tank badges. Parcel grid dropped.

1970
New crankcase breather system into chaincase, with breather pipe exiting under rear mudguard. Leaf spring gear selector. Forks with hard-chrome-plated stanchions. Speedo/tachometer with black facings from mid-year.

1971
Major relaunch. New frame with main spine containing engine oil. Ceriani-style forks and new conical hub drum brakes front and rear. New styling with flat sidepanels and slab-sided 4-gallon tank for UK-spec Bonnevilles. Shorter mudguards. Indicators standard with Lucas switchgear; new instruments; many detail changes.

1972
Frame modified to lower seat height (from April 1972). 2.5-gallon US fuel tank reintroduced. New cylinder head with larger rocker inspection caps. Exhaust pipes direct press-fit into head. Three-ball clutch lever. Five-speed gearbox optional.

1973
T140V Bonneville 750, based on T120, bored out initially to 724cc, then 747cc. Stronger conrods and timing side main bearing; larger capacity oil pump; triplex primary drive; ten-stud cylinder head; stronger clutch springs. New high gear and layshaft in gearbox. Front disc brake (10in Lockheed) standard. Fork gaiters and chrome mudguards on UK Bonneville.

Major changes, year-by-year

1974
Few changes due to factory blockade, but work progresses on left-foot gearchange. Extra attachment points and new gaskets for rocker inspection covers. New oil seal O-ring for gearbox sprocket, plus other minor changes.

1975
Few changes due to factory blockade.

1976
Left-foot gearchange, rear disc brake, re-angled pillion footrests. Changes to silencer internals and airbox to reduce noise. Front mudguard loses numberplate mounting holes. Lucas switchgear (left-hand cluster) improved. New instruments. T120 dropped.

1977
Revised front mudguard mounting; metal sparkplug caps. Silver Jubilee special edition in silver, red, white and blue; 4.10 Dunlop K81 tyres; special badges; 'upside down' Girling rear shocks.

1978
T140E Bonneville launched in USA January 1978 to comply with EPA emissions legislation. Amal Mk2 carburettors; revised breather system, and timing side main bearing is roller bearing. Lucas Rita electronic ignition. Negative earth electrics with higher output three-phase alternator. Improved Lucas switchgear; neutral light; underseat helmet locks; fork gaiters. Allen bolts replace crosshead screws in engine/gearbox covers. 7.9:1 compression standard on all bikes; metal/composite cylinder head gasket; improved fork oil seals; sealed wheel bearings; gas-filled Girling shocks. Veglia instruments replace Smiths.

1979
T140D Special launched with black and gold colour scheme; high bars, stepped seat; two-into-one exhaust and alloy wheels. T140E launched in UK.

1980
T140ES Bonneville Electro launched with Lucas M3 starter motor driving through timing gears; higher output RM24 alternator and bigger battery. T140EX Executive launched with nose fairing; panniers and topbox, all in matching Smoke Red; circular mirrors. On all models, larger capacity, four-valve oil pump; easier primary chain adjustment; high-mounted rear brake calliper; thicker swingarm and higher footrests; rubber-mounted indicators. Avon Roadrunners replace Dunlop TT100s.

1981
Oil seals fitted to inlet valve guides; softer clutch springs; nylon-lined clutch cable; 60/45 watt sealed beam headlight, Bing CV carburettors, sintered metal Dunlop brake pads. Twin front disc brakes optional; Monza-style fuel filler caps. Limited number of AV (anti-vibration) Bonnevilles delivered to the police.

1982
T140LE Bonneville Royal limited edition launched: chrome/black tank and matt black engine for UK; Smokey Blue tank and polished engine for US. TSS launched, with eight-valve head, strengthened bottom end and claimed 20 per cent more power; 120mph+ top speed and 14.28sec standing quarter-mile. TSX launched: factory custom with alloy wheels, high bars, stepped seat and fat rear tyre on 16in wheel. On standard Bonneville, longer sidepanels, stainless steel mudguards and dogleg clutch/brake levers.

1983
Stronger intermediate gear for electric start.

APPENDIX 4

Road tests

This road test list is by no means exhaustive: there will have been plenty of others, but those listed here are from British and American mainstream magazines that are relatively easy to find. Only contemporary road tests are listed, and, whether or not you agree with their findings, these articles are often a good indication of the correct specification for each year. And they do make interesting reading ...

T120 UK	..*Motor Cycle*, December 1 1960
T120 UK	..*Motorcycling*, June 1 1961
T120 UK	..Motorcycling, August 24 1961
T120 US	..*Cycle World*, January 1962
T120R US	..*Hot Rod*, June 1963
T120 UK	..*Motor Cycle*, November 1 1962
T120C TT Special	..*Cycle World*, May 1963
T120 UK	..*Motor Cycle*, May 21 1964
T120 UK	..*Motorcycle Mechanics*, May 1964
T120 UK	..*Motorcycle Mechanics*, October 1964 (with Monza sidecar)
T120R US	..*Motorcyclist*, April 1965
T120 UK	..*Motor Cycle*, May 27, 1965
T120R US	..*Cycle World*, January 1966
T120 UK	..*Motorcycle Illustrated*, Feburary 1966
T120R US	..*Cycle*, September 1966
T120R US	..*Modern Cycle*, December 1966
T120 UK	..*Motorcycle Mechanics*, December 1966
T120UK	..*Motorcycle Illustrated*, April 1967
T120R US	..*Cycle Guide*, August 1967
T120R US	..*Motorcycle World*, September 1967
T120 UK	..*Motor Cycle*, February 2 1967
T120R US	..*Triumph Sport Cycle*, summer issue
T120 UK	..*Motorcycle Mechanics*, May 1968
T120 UK	..*Motorcycle Mechanics*, January 1969
T120R US	..*Cycle*, March 1969
T120R US	..*Modern Cycle*, March 1969
T120R US	..*Cyclesport*, December 1969

Road tests

Model	Publication
T120R US	*Cycle Guide*, February 1970
T120R US	*Cycle World*, May 1971
T120 UK	*Motorcycle Sport*, August 1971
T120R UK	*Bike*, Autumn 1971
T120R US	*Cycle Guide*, January 1972
T120R US	*Popular Cycling*, March 1972
T120R US	*Cycle*, May 1972
T120RV US	*Cycle World*, June 1972
T120R US	*Supercycle*, June 1972
T140V UK	*Motorcycle Mechanics*, March 1973
T140V US	*Cycle World*, May 1973
T140V UK	*Bike*, November 1975
T140V US	*Cycle Illustrated*, March 1976
T140V UK	*Which Bike?*, July 1976
T140V US	*Cycle Guide*, September 1976
T140V UK	*The Biker*, January 1977 (vs Kawasaki Z650)
T140E UK	*Super Bike*, August 1977
T140J US	*Motorcycle World*, January 1978
T140V US	*Cycle World*, April 1978
T140E US	*Motorcyclist*, August 1978 (vs Harley-Davidson Sportster)
T140E UK	*Motorcycling Monthly*, October 1978
T140E UK	*Bike*, January 1979
T140D UK	*Motorcycle Mechanics*, January 1979
T140E UK	*Super Bike*, June 1979
T140D US	*Cycle Guide*, July 1979
T140D UK	*The Biker*, July 1979
T140D US	*Motorcyclist*, August 1979
T140E UK	*Motorcycling Monthly*, August 1979 (5000-mile test)
T140D UK	*Bike*, September 1979
T140E UK	*Super Bike*, June 1980
T140E UK	*The Biker*, July 1980
T140EX UK	*The Biker*, August 1980
T140ES UK	*Which Bike?*, September 1980
T140ES UK	*Motorcycle Enthusiast*, Vol1, issue 4
T140EX US	*Rider*, February 1981
T140ES UK	*Motorcycle Mechanics*, March 1981
T140E UK	*Bike*, May 1981
T140ES US	*Motorcyclist*, July 1981
T140ES UK	*Classic Bike*, April/May 1981
T140ES UK	*Motorcycling Monthly*, September 1981
T140ES US	*Cycle World*, November 1981
T140EX US	*Rider*, January 1982 (group test)
T140ES UK	*Bike*, January 1982
TSS UK	*Classic Bike*, July 1982
TSS UK	*Bike*, August 1982
TSS US	*Rider*, February 1983
Harris T140 US	*Classic Bike*, March 1986
Harris T140 UK	*Classic Bike*, May 1986

Appendix 5

Clubs, contacts and suppliers

Clubs

Bonneville Owners Club
www.bonnevilleowners.com

Triumph International Owners Club (USA)
www.tioc.org

Triumph Owners Club (Germany)
www.tmoc.de

Triumph Owners Club (UK)
www.tomcc.org

Triumph Owners Motorcycle Club (Australia)
www.tomcc.com.au

Triumph Owners Motorcycle Club (Denmark)
www.triumphmc.dk

Triumph Owners Motorcycle Club (New Zealand)
www.tomcc.co.nz

Triumph Owners Motorcycle Club (Norway)
www.tomcc-n.com

Triumph Owners Motorcycle Club (Sweden)
tomccsweden.org

Spares suppliers/restorers

This is not intended to be an exhaustive list. We've concentrated on UK and US businesses, and there are many other Triumph spares suppliers and restoration specialists. Some of them sell spares only, but they should be able to recommend other businesses for restoration and repair work. All of those listed here were active at the time of writing.

A Gagg & Sons (Nottingham, England)
Spares
Tel: 0115 978 6288
Web: www.gagg-and-sons.freeserve.co.uk

Autovalues Engineering (Yorkshire, England)
Morgo oil pumps, cylinder barrels
Tel: 01274 614424
Web: www.morgo.co.uk

Baxter Cycle (IA, USA)
Spares
Tel: (712) 781-2351
Web: www.baxtercycle.com

Big D Cycles (TX, USA)
Spares, restoration
Tel: (214) 339-2285
Web: bigdcycle.com

British Only (MI, USA)
Spares
Tel: 1(800) BRT-ONLY
Web: www.British-only.com

Britbits (Dorset, England)

Clubs, contacts & suppliers

Spares
Tel: 01202 483675
Web: www.motorcycle-uk.com/britbits

British Cycle Supply (Nova Scotia, Canada)
Spares
Tel: (902)542 7478
Web: www.britcycle.com

British Spares (Wellington, New Zealand)
Spares
Tel: 64 4 939 8819
Web: www.britishspares.com

Burton Bike Bits (Leicestershire, England)
Tel: 01530 564362
Web: www.burtonbikebits.net

Camelford Bike Bits (Cornwall, England)
Spares
Tel: 01840 213483

Carl Rosner Motorcycles (London)
Spares
Tel: 020 8657 0121
Web: www.carlrosner.co.uk

Collins Cycle (PA, USA)
Restoration
Tel: (412) 872-8475
Web: www.collinscycle.com

Deer Park Cycle (MD, USA)
Spares, restoration
Tel: (410) 833-7150
Web: www.deerparkcycle.com

Dick Smith (London)
Spares
Tel: 020 8405 4179
Web: www.baronspeedshop.com

Grin Triumph (Fife, Scotland)
Tel: 0776 555 3258
Web: www.grintriumph.com

Hermy's Cycle Shop (PA, USA)
Spares
Tel: (215) 562-7303
Web: www.hermys.com

Hughie Hancox (England)
Books, DVDs
Web: www.hughiehancoxrestorations.co.uk

Klempf's British Parts (MN, USA)
Spares
Tel: (507) 374-2222
Web: wwwklempfsbritishparts.com

M S Motorcycles (England)
Paint supplies
Tel: 07773 296826
Web: www.msmotorcyclesuk.com

Norman Hyde (Warwickshire, England)
Spares
Tel: 01926 497375
Web: www.normanhyde.co.uk

Reg Allen (London)
Spares
Tel: 020 8567 1974
Web: www.reg-allen-london.co.uk

Rockerbox Motorcycles (Surrey, England)
Spares
Tel: 01252 722973
Web: www.rockerbox-motorcycles.com

Roebuck Motorcycles (London)
Spares
Tel: 020 8868 1231

Skye Classic Motorcycles (Cornwall, England)
Tel: 01503 250846
Web: www.skye-classic-motorcycles.co.uk

SRM Engineering (Aberwystwyth, Wales)
Spares, upgrades
Tel: 01970 627771
Web: www.srmclassicbikes.com

Supreme Motorcycles (Leicestershire, England)
Spares
Tel: 01455 841133
Web: www.suprememotorcycles.co.uk

T8 Triumph Spares (Suffolk, England)
Spares
Tel: 01394 279929
Web: www.t8ts.co.uk

The Bike Shed (Hertfordshire, England)
Restoration, servicing
Tel: 01920 830931
Web: www.inventivestudios.co.uk/thebikeshed/

TMS (Nottinghamshire, England)
Spares

The Triumph Bonneville Bible

Tel: 0115 950 3447
Web: www.tms-motorcycles.co.uk

Tony Hayward (North Wales)
Belt drive kits
Tel: 01244 830776

Tri-Core (Herefordshire, England)
Spares
Tel: 01432 820752
Web: www.tri-corengland.com

Tri-Supply (Devon, England)
Spares 1946-70
Tel: 01404 47001
Web: www.trisupply.co.uk

Unity Equipe (Lancashire, England)
Spares

Tel: 01706 632237
Web: www.unityequipe.com

Wilemans Motors (Derbyshire, England)
Spares
Tel: 01332 342813

L P Williams (England)
Tel: 01524 770956
Web: www.triumph-spares.co.uk

Wolf Cycles (MD, USA)
Spares
Tel: (410) 247-7420
Web: www.wolfcycles.com

Bibliography

Books

Not all of these books are in print, but most should be available through on-line suppliers and secondhand bookshops.

Ayton, Cyril (ed), *Triumph Twins from 1937*, Bay View Books, 1990
Bacon, Roy, *Triumph Twins & Triples*, Osprey, 1981
Strategy Alternatives for the British Motorcycle Industry, The Boston Consulting Group Limited, 1975
Brooke, Lindsay & Gaylin, David, *Triumph Motorcycles in America*, Motorbooks International, 1993
Cycle World On Triumph 1967-1972, Brooklands Books
Cycle World On Triumph 1972-1987, Brooklands Books
DeFazio, Danny, *T140*, Sump Publishing, 2009
Hancox, Hughie, *Tales of Triumph Motorcycles and the Meriden Factory*, Veloce Publishing, 2000
Hancox, Hughie, *Triumph Production Testers' Tales*, Veloce Publishing, 2012
Henshaw, Peter, *Triumph Bonneville: Essential Buyers Guide*, Veloce Publishing, 2008
Nelson, J R, *Bonnie: The Development History of the Triumph Bonneville*, G T Foulis
Norton Villiers Triumph Limited, *Meriden: Historical Summary 1972-74*,
Rosamond, John, *Save the Triumph Bonneville*, Veloce Publishing, 2009
Wilson, Steve, *British Motorcycles Since 1950, (Vols 2, 5 and 6)*, Patrick Stephens Limited
Woolridge, Harry, The Triumph Speed Twin & Thunderbird Bible, Veloce Publishing, 2004
Woolridge, Harry, The Triumph Trophy Bible, Veloce Publishing, 2006

Magazines

Bike
British Bike Magazine
Classic Bike
Classic Motorcycle Mechanics
Cycle World
Motorcycle News
Motorcycle Sport & Leisure
Motorcycling
The Classic Motorcycle
The Motor Cycle

More terrific Triumph books from Veloce!

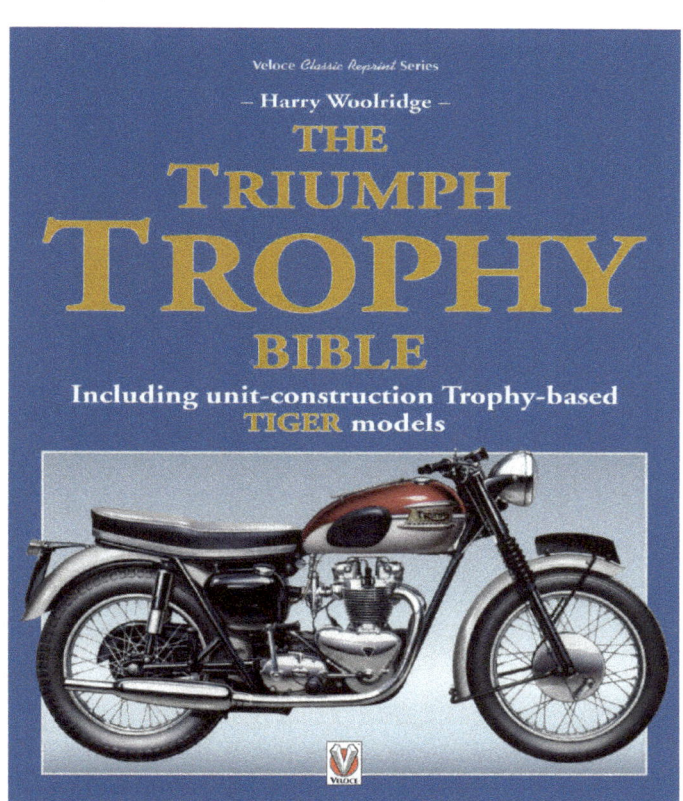

Complete year-by-year history of the Trophy (and unit construction Tiger twins) from 1949 to 1983. Includes original factory model photos, technical specifications, colour schemes, engine and frame numbers, model type identification, and details of Trophy and Tiger achievements. THE complete source book.

25x20.7cm • Hardback • 144 pages • 130+ col/b&w photos • ISBN: 9978-1-845849-74-0

Complete technical development history of the Triumph Speed Twin and Thunderbird motorcycles, and an invaluable reference source to identification, specification, exact year of manufacture and model type. a MUST for all Triumph fans.

25x20.7cm • Hardback • 144 pages • 55 col/95 b&w photos • ISBN: 978-1-845849-82-5

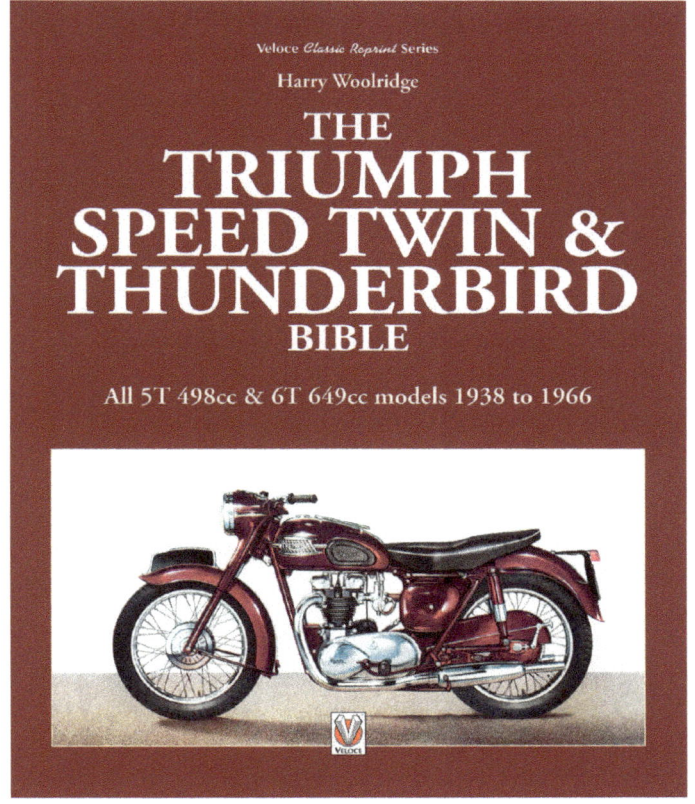

Prices subject to change; p&p extra: call 01305 260068/email info@veloe.co.uk
www.veloce.co.uk

The story of one worker's time on the Triumph Production Testing team from 1960 to 1962, packed with funny anecdotes about a tester's daily life. With guides to fixing problems on the 1960s models, this is an intimate and absorbing account of life in one of Britain's most famous factories.

25x20.7cm • Paperback • 160 pages • 183 col/b&w photos • ISBN: 978-1-845844-41-7

Hughies Hancox worked at Triumph from 1954 until its closure in 1974: this is the story of his life in the famous Meriden factory, and his many adventures with Triumph motorcycles and Triumph people.

25x20.7cm • Paperback • 144 pages • 91 b&w photos & illustrations • ISBN: 978-1-787115-49-1

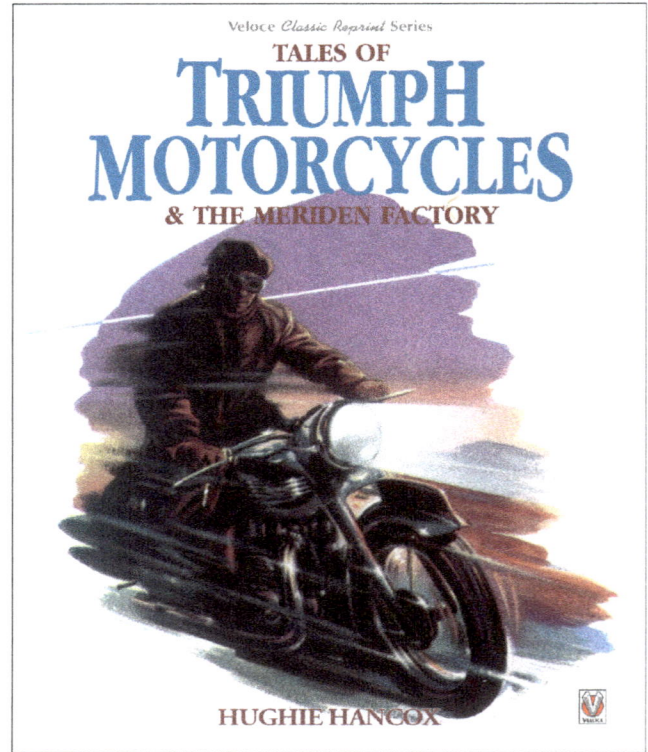

Index

Allen, Johnny 13, 16, 17
AMA 55
Ariel Three 58
Armstrong 102, 105
Auctions 126
AV frame 108

Barton, John 70
Bauer, Dr Stephan 62
Benn, Tony 77-80, 82, 85
Bonneville, year-by-year:
  1959 17-20
  1960 20-23
  1961 23, 24
  1962 24-26
  1963 28-32
  1964 32-35
  1965 35-39
  1966 39-42
  1967 42-46
  1968 46-49
  1969 49-52
  1970 52-56
  1971 60-66
  1972 66-69
  1973 69-74
  1974 74-79
  1975 80-83
  1976 83-86
  1977 86-92
  1978 92-97
  1979 98-102
  1980 102-105
  1981 105-110
  1982 110-115
  1983 115-118
  1985-88 119-121
Boston Consulting Group 82
BSA decline 58
BSA/Triumph
  co-operation 28, 29, 34
Buying secondhand:
  Badges/trim 133
  Brackets 134
  Electrics/wiring 134
  Engine 136, 137
  Engine/frame numbers 131, 132
  Exhaust 138
  Frame 133
  Instruments 136
  Lights 134
  Paint/chrome 132
  Pre-MoT checks 140
  Primary drive 137
  Rubbers 133
  Seat 133
  Stands 134
  Suspension 136
  Test ride 138
  Tinwork 132, 133
  Wheel/steering/swingarm bearings 135, 136
  Wheels/tyres 135

Choosing a Bonneville:
  1959-62 T120 129
  1963-70 T120 129, 130
  1971-74 T120 130
  1973-78 T140 130
  1979-83 T140 130, 131
  1985-88 Harris 131
Coates, Rod 55

Desert racing 12, 15, 20, 25
Dudek, Joe 25
Dunstall 52

East/West Coast
  differences 43
Electric start 102
Electronic ignition 94
Eustace, Brian 66
Export Credit Guarantee 79, 97, 107

Five-speed gearbox 69, 72

GEC 59, 92, 100

Harley-Davidson 10, 15, 25
Hele, Doug 30, 38, 41, 47, 58, 65, 72
Honda:
  CB450 35
  CB750 38, 49, 56, 80, 85
  Sales strategy 22, 32
Hinckley Bonneville 140
Hopwood, Bert 29, 30, 38, 58, 65-67, 69, 74, 82
Huckfield, Leslie 77

Insurance 125, 126
Investment potential 125
ISDT 15

Japanese motorcycle
  industry 22
Jofeh, Lionel 38, 58, 64, 65
Johnson, Bill 17, 22
Johnson, Denis 85
Johnson Motors 15, 22, 35, 42
Jones, Brian 92, 94

Kalinski, Felix 66
Kawasaki triples 56

Leppan, Bob 34, 42, 62
Lucas 21, 23, 41

Maintenance 126
Manganese Bronze
  Holdings 75
McCormack, Denis 15, 17, 66
Modular range 70, 74
Montlhéry 10, 17

Nelson, John 64, 92
Norton Commando 49, 62, 75, 79, 80

Owners' views (1965) 39
Owning a Bonneville 122, 126

Paintwork 33-34
Poore, Dennis 67, 74, 77, 79, 82
Price, Brenda 92

Production Racing 38, 39, 49

Quality control 23, 48, 50, 72, 85, 96, 108, 121

Robinson, Geoffrey 77, 79, 85, 100, 101, 105
Rosamond, John 64, 92-on

Seat height 65, 130, 133
Shawcross, Lord 66, 75
Shilton, Neale 31
Simon, Ted 93
Slickshift 14, 18
Speed records 13, 26, 42
Stokes, Lord 88
Sturgeon, Harry 38
SU carburettor 108
Suzuki 56, 105

Tait, Percy 16, 18, 41
Thornton, Peter 65
Triumph Corporation
  (USA) 15, 42
Triumph models:
  750cc (US only, 1970) 55
  750 T140 development 67, 70, 71
  Bandit 350 61, 64, 66
  Bonneville
    Executive 104, 105
  First prototype 16, 17
  Royal Wedding 107, 112
  Saint 44
  Speed Twin 8, 9
  Silver Jubilee 87-90
  T140D Special 98, 99
  T140E 94-97

T140ES 103, 104
Thruxton 38, 39, 41
TR7/A 20
TR7/B 20
TSS 113, 114
TSX 114, 115
TT Special 31, 32, 37, 38, 42, 46
T70 8
T85 9
T90 8
T100 9, 10
T110 11-12, 14, 18, 20
T2000 110, 116
Thunderbird 9-10
Thunderbird (1981/2) 107
Tiger Trail (1981/2) 107
TR5 13
TR6 12, 13, 18, 43, 44
Trident 38, 49, 53, 55, 60, 65, 69
Trident T180 86
Turner, Edward 8, 14, 16-18, 22, 23, 29, 30
Turner, Eric 65
Twin-leading shoe
  brake 47-48

Umberslade Hall 58, 66
Unit construction 28-30

Varley, Eric 82, 101

Webcor 55
Wickes, Jack 28
Wilson, Jack 63

www.ingramcontent.com/pod-product-compliance
Lightning Source LLC
Chambersburg PA
CBHW040739300426
44111CB00026B/2987